Breaking Time's Arrow

MATTHEW McDONALD

Breaking Time's Arrow

Experiment and Expression in the
Music of Charles Ives

INDIANA UNIVERSITY PRESS

Bloomington & Indianapolis

This book is a publication of

Indiana University Press
Office of Scholarly Publishing
Herman B Wells Library 350
1320 East 10th Street
Bloomington, Indiana 47405 USA

iupress.indiana.edu

Telephone   800-842-6796
Fax   812-855-7931

♻ The paper used in this publication meets the minimum
requirements of the American National Standard
for Information Sciences—Permanence of Paper for
Printed Library Materials, ANSI Z39.48–1992.

Manufactured in the United States of America

Library of Congress Cataloging-in-Publication Data

McDonald, Matthew (Matthew James), author.
    Breaking time's arrow : experiment and expression
in the music of Charles Ives / Matthew McDonald.
    pages cm — (Musical meaning and interpretation)
    Includes bibliographical references and index.
    ISBN 978-0-253-01273-9 (cloth : alkaline paper)
— ISBN 978-0-253-01276-0 (ebook) 1. Ives, Charles,
1874-1954—Criticism and interpretation. I. Title. II.
Series: Musical meaning and interpretation.
    ML410.I94M45 2014
    780.92—dc23

                                                    2014012350

Contents

Preface

In 2001, I began researching the music of Charles Ives. I spent countless hours at the piano that summer, familiarizing myself with every score I could get my hands on. I particularly remember accompanying myself through the entire set of *114 Songs*—quite a feat, as I'm a pianist but no singer. Originally, I had outlined a thorough consideration of time and temporality in Ives's music, but, ultimately, a small portion of this outline ballooned into the entire project. After completing my thesis and converting one chapter into an article, I had no plans or desire to develop the material further, but after a few years, rejuvenated, I returned to the research as the partial foundation for a new book project. By this time, however, I had grown dissatisfied with much of my previous work and discarded it in favor of completely new material. I envisioned that this would be a "definitive" statement of my ideas about Ives's music, a culmination of my work over the previous several years. It eventually became clear, however, that I would never be fully satisfied with the book and could tinker with it forever; the printed version, inevitably, would always feel unfinished. Its fixed form belies the reality of my research, which would be better represented by the endless pages of notes and drafts on my desk and hard drive, many discarded or forgotten, their potential contribution to the whole left unclear or undetermined.

Around 1910, Charles Ives began work on what he referred to as an overture or concerto inspired by Ralph Waldo Emerson. Originally, this was to be one in a set of several overtures devoted to great "Men of Literature," but ultimately Ives made significant progress on only two. While composing the *Emerson Overture*, Ives developed some of its cadenzas as studies for solo piano, one of which he completed. After suspending work on the overture, Ives had no evident plans to develop the material further, but he later returned to it as the foundation for a new piece, the first movement of the *Concord* Sonata. For the *Concord* movement, however, Ives discarded much of the music of the overture and added a significant amount of new material. The first movement of the *Concord,* many believe, is the "definitive" musical expression of Ives's ideas about Emerson, and in 1920 Ives presented it to the musical community as the culmination of his work as a composer. Ives stated on many occasions, however, that he would likely never be fully satisfied with the music and could tinker with it forever; the "Emerson" music, inevitably, would remain "unfinished." The fixed form of the *Concord* movement belies the reality of Ives's musical conception, which is better represented by the multiple versions and endless pages of sketches and emendations, many discarded or forgotten, their status unclear or undetermined.

At this point it may seem that I have been writing about Ives for so long that I can no longer separate my own creative process from his. But the parallels I have drawn are both genuine and unsurprising. Writing about music is in large part a creative act, and one that has much in common with writing music. Perhaps there are music scholars who produce essays like Mozart produced scores, but most of us, I suspect, follow the Beethovenian model. Academic writing, especially in the era of word processing, is largely a process of cutting and pasting, deletions and insertions. Like most pieces of music, the finished academic product presents itself confidently, with few traces of its convoluted genesis. But here is where the analogy with Ives's music ends. Ives's music is remarkable for the extent to which it bears the traces of its Frankensteinian construction. Pieces are often characterized by extreme fragmentation, stark juxtapositions of highly contrasting segments of music that are very often borrowed from other sources or from Ives's own body of work.

While studying Ives's compositional process, as when actually writing about it, I began to experience my scholarly work in parallel with Ives's compositional work. As I examined Ives's notoriously unruly manuscripts, the process of negotiating the photocopies (organized in folders within boxes), the manuscripts themselves (organized likewise), the printed scores, and the formidable catalogues of John Kirkpatrick and James Sinclair made me feel that I was being forced to channel Ives himself, to embody his peculiar sense of organization—or lack thereof—as I tried to keep these various documents, boxes, books, and other materials organized on the medium-sized desk assigned to me in the Yale music library and the growing number of trolleys at my side.

But channeling Ives is not an experience that holds much appeal. Ives is a fascinating and problematic figure. There is much to admire about his life and views, and much to be critical of as well. These topics require an even-handed approach, one that has too often been missing in studies of the composer and his music. Frank Rossiter drew attention to what he called the "Ives Legend," brilliantly explicating the mythology through an eight-point dissection of an article by the critic R. D. Darrell (Rossiter 1975: 248–49). More recently, Gayle Sherwood Magee has pointed to the persistence of this legend and "the advocacy role that shapes most scholarship and biography" (2008: 2). Ives's musical output is exceptionally eclectic, which has always been a big part of its attraction for me. But although I love much of it, I'll freely admit that there are more than a few pieces I don't care for. And as for his ideas, they run the gamut from inspiring to repugnant. Nonetheless, his music and ideas create unique and fertile imaginative spaces through which to listen to and think about music. This is what brought me back to Ives's music as a subject, and this is the aspect of my subject I hope to elucidate and enrich.

* * *

Some General Notes Regarding Dates and Nomenclature

Dating Ives's music is an immense challenge that has been taken on by many over the years. Ives himself provided the early data, with John Kirkpatrick doing the heavy lifting after Ives's death, his work culminating in the *Temporary Mimeographed Catalogue* (1960). More recently, Magee and James Sinclair have worked toward an updated, more reliable chronology. Throughout the book, I draw on the latter scholarship, as reported in Grove Music Online (Burkholder, Sherwood, and Sinclair 2012) and amplified in Sinclair's *A Descriptive Catalogue of The Music of Charles Ives* (1999). Readers interested in more detail should begin by consulting Sinclair's catalogue.

- All references to manuscripts from the Charles Ives Collection at Yale University follow James Sinclair's microfilm numbers; these are always designated with an "f" followed by a four-digit number ("f6678," for example).
- When relevant, pitches are identified using the scientific nomenclature that designates middle C as C4, the pitch one octave above as C5, the pitch one whole step below as B♭3, and so forth.
- Barlines appear only sporadically in the printed editions of many works, such as the *Concord* Sonata, "Majority," "Nov. 2, 1920," and "Grantchester." For these pieces, I will refer to specific passages by identifying the page, system, and (when applicable) measure. For example, in the original, 1922 edition of Ives's *114 Songs,* "p. 50/1/2" would refer to the second measure of the first system on p. 50 (from the opening of "Nov. 2, 1920"); "p. 51/1" would refer to the first system on p. 51, which is not subdivided into measures.

Acknowledgments

It is a pleasure to thank the individuals and organizations that have provided me essential assistance and support. Much of my work on this book was supported by a fellowship from the American Council of Learned Societies. A Provost Grant from Northeastern University funded my study of the Charles Ives Papers at Yale University. Most recently, a generous subvention grant from the Charles Ives Society assisted with production of the book.

The series editor, Robert Hatten, was enthusiastic from the beginning; his close reading of the manuscript and thoughtful suggestions made the book much better. Raina Polivka, the music, film, and humanities editor at Indiana University Press, and her assistant, Jenna Whittaker, are a dedicated editorial team, and their organization and attention to detail kept the project running smoothly. Nancy Lightfoot and Eric Schramm inspected the manuscript carefully at the copyediting stage.

Emily Ferrigno and Suzanne Eggleston Lovejoy at the Yale University Library were patient guides as I navigated the Charles Ives Papers. James Sinclair generously provided me access to David G. Porter's unpublished notes on his reconstruction of Ives's *Emerson Concerto*.

Isabel Meirelles designed the book's cover; she was a pleasure to work with and a marvel to watch in action. Marilyn Bliss kindly agreed to compose the index.

My interest in the topic of the book can be traced to two formative musical experiences: an undergraduate seminar on "Time in Contemporary Music" with Justin London at Carleton College and my performances of Ives's songs with Helen Pridmore and El Ron Maltan. Thanks to all three for sending me in this direction.

Many of my colleagues in the Music Department at Northeastern have encouraged me with their interest in my project, particularly Anthony DeRitis, Douglas Durant, Hubert Ho, Hilary Poriss, Ron Smith, and Judith Tick.

Gayle Sherwood Magee read the entire manuscript and provided extremely useful insights. Many others have read and offered valuable feedback on parts of the book, including David Clampitt, Michael Friedmann, David Goodrich, Sumanth Gopinath, James Hepokoski, Michael Klein, Lawrence Kramer, Robert P. Morgan, and David Nicholls. Others have assisted me in various ways, including Matt BaileyShea, Neely Bruce, David Greetham, Debra Mandel, Margaret McDonald, Arthur Rishi, and David Rothenberg.

I am especially grateful to my family. First and most important, Jessica Berson provided practical, emotional, and intellectual support on a daily basis, and took me out for a great dinner when I finished the manuscript. Most aspects of the book were shaped by our discussions and brain-storming sessions, and her highly communicative prose has been a great influence on my own. Thank you, Jess. Leo and Henry McDonald gave constant incentive to work efficiently. Finally, Mary Ann and Jim McDonald offered unwavering interest and encouragement, and exceeded any reasonable expectations in their willingness to read what I'd written. They also got me interested in music in the first place. This book is dedicated to them.

I would like to thank the following publishers and the Yale Music Library for their permission to reprint portions of the following:

Four Transcriptions from "Emerson"
By Charles Ives
Copyright © 2002 by Associated Music Publishers, Inc. (BMI)
Based upon material from Ives's "Concord Sonata," © 1947 by Associated
    Music Publishers, Inc.
Ink score, The Charles Ives Papers, Yale University Music Library
International Copyright Secured. All Rights Reserved.
Reprinted by Permission.

I Come to Thee
By Charles Ives
Copyright © 1983 by Associated Music Publishers, Inc. (BMI)
Pencil sketch, The Charles Ives Papers, Yale University Music Library
International Copyright Secured. All Rights Reserved.
Reprinted by Permission.

Orchestral Set no. 2
By Charles Ives
Copyright © 2002 by Peer International Corporation
Reprinted by Permission.

Sonata no. 1 for Piano
By Charles Ives
Copyright © 1990 by Peer International Corporation
Ink sketch, The Charles Ives Papers, Yale University Music Library
Reprinted by Permission.

The Unanswered Question
By Charles Ives
Copyright © 1985 by Peer International Corporation
Pencil sketch, The Charles Ives Papers, Yale University Music Library
Reprinted by Permission.

The Anti-Abolitionist Riots in the 1830's and 1840's (Study no. 9) for Piano
By Charles Ives
Copyright © 1949 by Theodore Presser Company
Reprinted by Permission.

Breaking Time's Arrow

Introduction: Ives and Time

Telling What Will Happen in the Past

In 1922, Ives self-published his *114 Songs,* an assemblage spanning his full compositional career and a compendium of the techniques and subject matter of his music. Two years earlier, he had published his *Concord* Sonata and the accompanying *Essays Before a Sonata.* Ives composed very few new works after 1921, and it seems that, as he presented these three major works to a public mostly ignorant of his music, Ives suspected that his days of composing major works were over. This trilogy, then, was a crucial means by which Ives began to promote his music and shape its reception.

114 Songs effectively conveys the eccentricities of its composer. *114* is a strange number (why 114?) and an imposing one (why so many? why trumpeted in the title?). Any logic behind the ordering of songs is difficult to discern. They are not ordered chronologically, as one might expect from a collection of a composer's life's work, nor are they arranged thematically or in any practical manner. Most provocative is the way the songs look on the page. In the *Essays,* Ives famously proclaimed, "My God! What has sound got to do with music!" (1961: 84), and in keeping with this spirit, the printed score invests the songs with a unique aura; like the *Essays,* it seeks to guide the reader toward the deeper aspects of music that transcend sound. Notational irregularities abound, and while many are surely due to carelessness or miscommunications, this is only part of the story: Ives often used notation evocatively or symbolically, more concerned with the appearance of notes on the page than with communicating unambiguous instructions to the performer.

Consider, for instance, page 1, the first page of the song "Majority," derived from Ives's choral work *The Masses* (the top half of the page is reproduced in Example 0.1). Ives wrote twenty tone clusters, each spanning about two octaves and encompassing a continuous block of white or black notes, and each enclosed in a box. The clusters are impossible to play by any traditional means; Ives recommended calling upon a second pianist or, apparently, using a stick. In his critical edition of the song, H. Wiley Hitchcock represented only the outer notes of each cluster, connected by elongated stems, but this simplification destroys the visual impact of Ives's notation, which bombards the reader with impressive masses of noteheads and ties, obvious analogues to the "Masses" which form the subject of the song. The rhythmic values of these clusters often have nothing to do with the rhythm of whatever else is happening simultaneously: in several instances, the

1
Majority

Example 0.1. "Majority," p. 1/1–2.

performer is forced to ignore the rhythm of the clusters to avoid irreconcilable contradictions.

Ives commented on the visual effect of this first page and how it influenced his decision to feature the song at the beginning of his collection:

> Another instance of how opinions, remarks, etc., which to the recipient seem either stupid or unfair, will cause one to do something that his better judgment knows it's not quite best perhaps to do—was the way some of the "old ladies" purred out about playing the piano with a stick—"and how just terribly inartistic to have octaves of all white or black notes as chords of music!" The book of *114 Songs* was to start with the second one on page 6, Milton's *Evening*. But the "ta-tas" etc., above, made me feel just mean enough to want to give all the "old girls" another ride—and then, after they saw the first page of *The Masses* as No. 1 in the book, it would keep them from turning any more pages and finding something "just too awful for words, Lily!" I know for a fact that this is exactly what one lady did—and her wastebasket, not mine, was the one right place for that book! (1972: 126–27)

Stuart Feder claimed that this prime positioning of "Majority" occurred at the "last minute" (1992: 313), but this interpretation makes too much of Ives's dramatization of the switch: I suspect that the decision was more measured than Ives let on. "Majority" supplies an arresting opening for the collection, its first page, and initial gesture in particular, closely resembling that of the *Concord* Sonata. Both openings are emphatic, marked *forte* and "Slowly"; the right and left hands begin in contrary motion, generating imposing pillars of sound that establish the vast musical and expressive spaces the following music will inhabit. With the opening page of "Majority," Ives is setting the terms for the song and the entire collection, positioning himself as a surrogate for Emerson as described in the first paragraph of Ives's "Emerson" essay: "America's deepest explorer of the spiritual immensities—a seer painting his discoveries in masses and with any color that may lie at hand—cosmic, religious, human, even sensuous," and discoverer of the "wondrous chain which links the heavens with earth" (1961: 11). The text of the song, one of several that Ives wrote himself, conveys this vast scope:

> The Masses! The Masses have toiled,
> Behold the works of the World!
> The Masses are thinking,
> Whence comes the thought of the World!
> The Masses are singing,
> Whence comes the Art of the World!
> The Masses are yearning,
> Whence comes the hope of the World.
> The Masses are dreaming,
> Whence comes the visions of God!
> God's in His Heaven,
> All will be well with the World!

Surely, this initial outburst of metaphysical extravagance has turned some away from the collection of songs, just as Ives hoped. Those so disinclined would be surprised, however, to jump to the end of the collection and encounter a much different choice for the ultimate song, one that serves as a fitting antidote to the first. "Slow March" is the first song that Ives ever composed, dating from 1887 or 1888, when Ives was around thirteen years old. An elegy to the Ives's family cat, Chin-Chin, it is simple, short, quiet, and tonal—the very antithesis of "Majority." Its text, apparently a collaborative effort of the Iveses and Charles's uncle, Lyman Brewster, is as unabashedly homey and modest as the text of "Majority" is existential and profound:

> One evening just at sunset we laid him in the grave;
> Although a humble animal his heart was true and brave.
> All the family joined us, in solemn march and slow,
> From the garden place beneath the trees and where the sunflowers grow.

As with "Majority," the positioning of this song seems purposeful: not only did Ives eschew a chronological arrangement of his songs, but he placed the earliest song last. Endings are the primary sites of spiritual transcendence in Ives's music, and it is entirely characteristic of Ives to elevate personal memories in this way. Ives claimed that he discovered the score for "Slow March" in his cellar in May of 1921 (1972: 176). Just as the young Ives might have imagined the soul of his pet ascending to heaven, the musical memorial, unearthed by its composer many years after its composition, is positioned to ensure its own immortality.

It is telling that Ives, as made clear by his remarks about the "old girls" cited above, envisioned his public paging through his song collection like a book. Al-

Song nos.	Dates
1–32	1920–21
33–52	1912–21
53–56	1894–96; 1919
57–102	1892–1910*
103–05	1921
106–14	1888–96*

*roughly in reverse chronological order

Table 0.1. Dating of *114 Songs* (as in the printed score).

though Ives surely did not intend the songs to be performed in order, he does seem to have conceived of the collection as something more than an anthology. A trajectory is implied by the bookends of *114 Songs,* reinforced by the intervening 112: musically, the collection travels from the innovative and difficult to the conventional and straightforward; thematically, from the grand and universal to the quaint and personal. There is also a strong sense of temporal trajectory. If *114 Songs* is a "scrapbook" of Ives's career, as Hitchcock has suggested (Hitchcock 2004a: lxviii), we are guided, against convention, from the recent past to the more distant.[1] The dates provided in the score outline this trajectory, as shown in Table 0.1.

More significantly, many of the songs themselves are about the passing of time, including the bookends. "Majority" moves from past to present to future via evolving verb tenses: the Masses *have* toiled, the Masses *are* thinking (and so on), all *will be* well with the World (see Broyles 1996: 133). The final line, significantly, modifies the ending of Robert Browning's short poem *Pippa's Song:* "God's in His heaven—All's right with the world!" Union with God in heaven, an explicit theme in other works of Ives's and many of the hymns he liked to borrow, is the implicit goal, what the Masses yearn for and dream of; it is symbolized musically with functional tonality, which makes its triumphant appearance in the final two systems. In "Slow March," the temporal orientation is more straightforward: the song points toward the past, recalling the life and burial of the family pet, and borrowing liberally from the "Dead March" in Handel's oratorio *Saul,* music that predates the vast majority of Ives's subsequent borrowings. And so, not only do the framing entries of the *114 Songs* turn conventional chronological ordering on its head, but they compound the effect with their musical style and subject matter: the songs imply a trajectory from the music of the future to that of the past, and from a forward-looking vision to a backward one.

In the passage cited above, Ives acknowledged the significance of beginning his song collection with "Majority," and he certainly was aware of the irony of ending with the very first song of his youth. If these two songs do imply a trajectory, might Ives have thought of them in tandem, as a pair? This possible pairing tells us nothing about Ives's composition of "Slow March," but it may have influ-

Example 0.2. "Majority," p. 5/2–3.

enced his composition of "Majority," and it certainly could have influenced his decision to place the two songs at opposite ends of the collection. Imagine these songs as a frame that can be extracted and juxtaposed: "Majority" ends with an anomalous cadential progression in F major (see Example 0.2), and "Slow March" takes up this key and inhabits it fully. Larry Starr has suggested that "Majority" actually concludes in C major, and that the final two chords represent an incomplete plagal cadence, whose "'missing' C-major chord . . . can occur only in the imagination" (1992: 138); this interpretation was approved by Broyles (1996: 133) and Tick (1997: 155). The notion of a C-major tonic is appealing: C major, the key of white notes, is Ives's preferred tonal representation of God, the elemental, and the universal, an idea I return to numerous times in the following pages. But Starr's hearing is musically problematic. Most obviously, it ignores the clear metrical hierarchy of the final two chords, which emphasizes the latter as a point of arrival. Furthermore, an F-major triad with an added sixth emerges repeatedly from the midst of the piano's white- and black-note clusters in the previous measures, p. 5/2/1–p. 5/3/1, its third, A, powerfully reinforced through solemn repetition in the vocal line. This emphasis establishes an immovable context for

Slow March

Inscribed to the Children's Faithful Friend

(1888)

Example 0.3. "Slow March," mm. 1–8.

the final three measures, which affirm F major with a IV–V–I progression. The subdominant clashes with the vocal line ("All"), whose B♮ implies a secondary-dominant harmonization, and it is separated from the dominant by interpolated harmonies; but the final two chords arrive simply, quietly, and unadorned, their white-note purity a symbol of cosmic harmony.

Not only does the tonality of "Slow March" follow seamlessly from this cadence, but other details make the beginning of the song musically satisfying as a follow-up to "Majority." In this imagined pairing, the sudden decrescendo at the end of "Majority" functions as a dynamic modulation to the *pianissimo* of "Slow March"; the repeated melodic A's that begin "Slow March" (mm. 1–3) echo "God's in His Heaven"; and the stepwise descending thirds that punctuate the introduction of "Slow March" (B♭–A–G in mm. 3–4, C–B♭–A in mm. 7–8) echo "well with the World!" The songs could be successfully programmed as a pair, with the final chord of "Majority" eliding with the first chord of "Slow March." In this scenario, the meaning of "Slow March" changes: the song becomes a demonstration of the closing lyric of "Majority," "God's in His Heaven, All will be well with the World!" This judgment now applies to the Masses and all the Chin-Chins of the world alike, distant but connected rings on that "wondrous chain which links the heavens with earth." And a hint of this sentiment at the end of "Slow March" is amplified, as though an echo of the spiritual elevation that concludes "Majority": the image of growing sunflowers, which resemble the sun while reaching toward it, and the final benedictory plagal cadence.

Ives's fascination with Emerson helps to account for the apparent paradox of the visionary ending of "Majority" functioning as prelude to a song consumed by memory. "Emerson tells, as few bards could, of what will happen in the past, for his future is eternity, and the past is a part of that," Ives wrote in his "Emerson" essay, one of many instances in which Ives's prose teeters perilously between the profound and the nonsensical (1961: 12). But Ives was grasping at an idea that is crucial to our understanding of his music and thought, an understanding of time strongly influenced by the philosophy of Emerson and Thoreau. Ives referred to Emerson's supertemporal lessons as "revelations." "Revelation is concerned with all time," he wrote; "It is prophecy with no time element" (12). Emerson's "symphonies of revelation begin and end with nothing but the strength and beauty of innate goodness in man, in Nature and in God" (35). If the conclusion of "Majority" finds its fulfillment in "Slow March," then perhaps Ives saw himself, too, as a prophet of revelation, "telling of what will happen in the past," the former song's prophecy realized in the latter's memory. More broadly, this Emersonian notion of time understands past, present, and future as Earth-bound elements of a more fundamental, and atemporal, state: eternity. For Emerson, the experience of eternity could be achieved in the present, what he referred to as the "everlasting Now" (Emerson 1902: 399). Emerson's writings—and Thoreau's as well— are shot through with this idea,[2] one that is compatible with the Christian view of God's time, another strong influence on Ives with deeper roots in his psyche. To conceive of time in this way is to eradicate normal ideas of time and chronology—hence, Ives's nonchronological ordering of his songs and the seemingly backward temporal trajectory from the first to the last. Most importantly for Ives, this conception of time could undo the pastness of the past, moving it from the realm of what-has-been into the realm of what-will-be, and ultimately simply what-is. And for an intensely nostalgic composer profoundly alienated from his own time, recovery of the past was everything.

Moving in Many Directions at Once

When describing Ives's music, scholars typically begin with two fundamental characteristics: it is eccentric, eclectic, inventive, and modern; and it incorporates once-familiar tunes, mostly taken from nineteenth-century American popular music and Protestant hymns. To put it in the simplest terms, innovation and derivation are among the music's most essential and obvious qualities. Importantly, these qualities stem from the opposite temporal impulses illustrated above: Ives's music reaches toward the future while looking backward to the past.

Many writers have considered the specific sources and aims of this dual temporal focus. On the first page of the second and much shorter of his two biographies of the composer, Stuart Feder wrote of how "times past inhere in the music, informed by the profound nostalgia Ives felt for the nineteenth-century Danbury of his boyhood and earlier. As for the future, a paradox: despite being rooted in the earlier century, Ives's innovative music looks forward to modernism and even post-modernism. He has influenced generations of new composers. Beyond this was Ives's seeking for a music of the future which would encompass not only his single life, but *all* life" (Feder 1999: xi). Feder is hardly alone in identifying, and seeking to resolve, the apparent paradox of Ives's simultaneous orientation toward the past and future. But the problem is illusory, in part a product of misguided comparisons between Ives's approach to composition and his worldview. Ives's primary means of expressing nostalgia—musical borrowing—was in fact among his most notable innovations. Furthermore, Ives's novel compositional techniques and frequently old-fashioned musical sources were linked in their opposition to the music of the present. The connection is clarified in relation to the expressive purposes of these compositional features. Ives's profound sense of alienation from the modern world led to his preoccupation with the remembered past and hoped-for future. These sentiments were not unique to Ives but shared by many of his contemporaries and arguably a defining aspect of modern consciousness: nostalgia and utopianism are important strains of modernism. Ives's music registers the desire for temporal transcendence, drawing on music of the past to create the music of the future. In this way, Ives's views of past and future are complementary, not paradoxical.

Ives's growing dissatisfaction with the historical moment in which he lived is well documented. It has been identified convincingly by Gayle Sherwood Magee as a primary factor in his health crisis of 1918, which seems to have precipitated Ives's steep decline in compositional productivity after 1921. Magee argued that Ives suffered from what was known as "neurasthenia," a nervous condition that stemmed from "a fear of modernization . . . in the social, economic, and industrial spheres" (Sherwood 2001: 574). This worldview led Ives increasingly to seek stability in his life. "Ives yearned for a simpler, preindustrial time," Michael Broyles has explained: "Later in life Ives saw modern civilization itself as degenerating, and he responded with self-imposed isolation. He refused to read newspapers or listen to radios, and he fled New York City as soon and as much as he could. . . . [His political rhetoric] directly reflected his frustrations and disillusionment with the present. It was an expression of the tension he felt between the world in which he lived and the past he wanted to reclaim. Ives's rhetoric was the conflict between memory and reality" (1996: 134).

Substitute "music" for "political rhetoric" and you have a convincing rationale for much of Ives's compositional activity. Ives lamented the lost wholeness of the past, and he sought to restore it through music. As Leon Botstein wrote, comparing Ives with Mahler, "One easily might hear in the music . . . the clash between an idealized world and culture associated with an embattled rural landscape of the past and the urban, industrial, and technological facts of modern times" (1996: 43). From a more hermeneutically suspicious point of view, Lawrence Kramer formulated this clash in Ives's later music in terms of problematic hierarchies in which "the value accorded hegemonic status affirms a social order that is rural, white Protestant, patriarchal, and premodern. Formal and ideological unity is achieved through the exclusion of radical heterogeneity" (1995: 189).[3] The threatening heterogeneous elements of early twentieth-century America implied by Kramer are those of a social disorder that is urban, multicultural, feminist, and modern. Ives was more ambivalent about each of these aspects of the evolving world than is suggested by Kramer's cut-and-dried characterization, but the essential idea is accurate: Ives's valuation of diversity was more narrow than many of his champions would like to think, and thus the gap between the world as he knew it and as he wished it to be was great. There is an aggressive, at times violent side to Ives's music, heard in the pounding clusters of "Majority," the cacophonies of his wildest orchestral collages, the disorienting interruptions that seem to rob the music of continuity and coherence; these, in many instances, are the sounds of frustration with a world going wrong.

But there is a much gentler side to Ives's music, a peaceful side, one that grew more prominent in his later works as well. Ives increasingly brought pieces to tranquil conclusions that attempt to resolve any preceding tensions, suggesting the transcendence of worldly problems. In Ives's mature works, such endings are typically characterized by relatively static textures built on one or more layers of ostinati or other repetitive material. Prominent examples of such ostinato-codas include the final movements of large-scale works such as the "Thoreau" movement of the *Concord* Sonata, the *Largo maestoso* movement of the Fourth Symphony, "Thanksgiving and Forefathers' Day" from the *Holidays Symphony*, "From Hanover Square North, at the End of a Tragic Day, the Voice of the People Again Arose" from *Orchestral Set no. 2*, and "The Call of the Mountains" from String Quartet no. 2, as well as single-movement works such as *Psalm 90*. Whatever conflicts are registered during these pieces, they end with visions of community, natural order, and eternal harmony.

The world as it is versus the world as it once was and will be again, human existence as experienced in the present versus the faithfully held notion of God's eternity: these are the fundamental expressive poles of Ives's music. From early on in his compositional career, and increasingly as he grew older, Ives became focused on representing these poles and attempting to bridge the gap between them. His music strives to master time, to move freely among past, present, and future, and even to bring time to a halt, while at the same time revealing the difficulties of this endeavor. Music, as a temporal medium, is ideally suited to express relationships among past, present, and future, to evoke the passing of time and transcendence of time's passing. Yet the musical traditions Ives knew best were not, from his perspective, sufficiently versatile in their temporal organization to support the ideas and relationships he wished to express. Indeed, there were no precedents for many of the compositional strategies Ives employed. Simply put, Ives needed to reconceive the temporality of music.

This book proceeds from the premise that our existing conceptions of temporality in music during the time Ives was active as a composer—from the late nineteenth century into the early decades of the twentieth—are insufficient for understanding Ives's music. Musical temporality refers to the way musical ideas are organized in time and the relationship between this organization and musical experience. (For a similar definition, see Hatten 2006: 62.) Ives's music very often seems to lack linear direction and coherence relative to earlier or contemporaneous music of the Western classical tradition. Much of this quality is due to the extreme fragmentation that often characterizes his musical surfaces, where disparate ideas clash against one another with little or no warning of where and how such clashes might occur. This feature of Ives's music is well known. For example, in an oft-cited essay, Robert P. Morgan identified fragmentation as one of many "spatial" features in Ives's music designed "to negate as much as possible the succession of temporal sequence as the principal path for establishing musical relationships" (1977: 148). As an example, he noted how in Ives's song "The Things Our Fathers Loved," "it is almost as if the whole cause-and-effect pattern of traditional tonal music has been turned upside down" (149–50).

But in his characterization of Ives's music as spatial, Morgan overplayed his denial of the music's temporality. Temporal sequence and cause-and-effect relationships are essential, even in extremely fractured musical environments such as "The Things Our Fathers Loved"; they have not been negated, but reoriented. Ives's music contains a vast number of instances in which musical units are best heard as fragments dislodged from alternative, and more coherent, linear successions. Ives's treatment of preexisting music, as is well known, often works in this way. But fragmentation in Ives's music is hardly limited to his treatment of preexisting music. What of fragments with no relation to borrowed music—could these be understood to derive from more coherent successions as well? Scholars have rarely considered this question. But the fragmentation and reconfiguration of linear successions are critical aspects of Ives's music not only when Ives manipulates borrowed music, but also when the source material is of his own invention. The phenomenon is found in various forms. The remnants of disrupted successions range in size from short fragments to discrete sections or even separate movements or pieces. The mechanics of separation can be simple (interpolation) or complex (a network of multiple interwoven successions). The displaced continuation of a succession can be located later in a piece or earlier. Disrupted successions can be apparent or obscure; their presence may be confirmed by Ives's manuscripts or suggested by analytical evidence alone.

Most of Ives's music is fundamentally linear, but in the cases just outlined, its linearity is displaced; directed musical motion is not limited to the single plane of strict chronology. This music is best understood in terms of multiple temporal levels: the succession of ideas we hear in real time and the alternative successions we are encouraged to imagine. Indeed, the splintered musical surfaces encourage a listener to construct hypothetical, *a priori* successions by reconfiguring musical fragments, something of an aural equivalent of assembling a jigsaw puzzle. This mode of listening is modeled by Ives's notoriously chaotic musical manuscripts and associated compositional habits, as I consider in detail in chapter 6. Indeed, the process of aurally reassembling musical fragments is analogous to the process of sorting through Ives's fragmented manuscript sources to assemble a piece, which itself replicates aspects of Ives's own process of constructing pieces from fragments of borrowed and self-borrowed material.

Multidirectional motion is a widespread phenomenon in Ives's music from his undergraduate works to his mature compositions of the 1920s. A piece featuring such motion is best understood not merely as a single linear succession of ideas, but in terms of a network or web of multiple displaced chronologies. This book explores the presence of displaced linear successions in Ives's music, outlining their treatment and meanings, their contexts and ramifications. The pages that follow attempt to show that multidirectional motion was a key to Ives's expressive project. The interaction of actual and implied musical successions was both a primary means by which Ives represented temporal relationships—the distance between the lived present and the idealized past and future, and the distance between the real-world experience of time and God's eternity—and a means of expressing his desire to transcend these distances. Although analysis of the compositional phenomenon constitutes the core of the book, I present it not as an end in itself but rather as a jumping-off point, a way of opening up other analytical insights, addressing questions of musical meaning and expression, and situating Ives's music within broader historical, biographical, and intertextual frameworks.

Ives's treatment of musical chronology was not completely unlike any compositional practices that preceded it, whatever Ives's reputation as an innovator might lead one to assume. To take a simple example, the practice of parenthetical insertion had been common since the mid-eighteenth century—think of the insertion of a cadenza between the cadential $^6_4$ and its resolution onto the dominant in a traditional concerto. Indeed, *"Parenthese,"* on various scales, was a basic eighteenth-century compositional principle.[4] More complex manipulations of linearity have occasionally been identified in music of the nineteenth century, particularly in Beethoven's late music (see Kinderman 1988; Kramer 1973; and Ratner 1980: 234–36). Edward T. Cone was often inclined to hear these sorts of relationships in nineteenth-century music, as displayed in his provocative analyses of Schubert and Brahms (1982, 1995). More recently, Robert Hatten has discussed what he called the "troping of temporality" in the context of music by Beethoven, Schubert, and others, which involves "the reordering of temporally coded events" resulting in "unexpected relationships between the expected location of musical events and the actual location where they appear, relative to one another and to their plausible dramatic sequence" (Hatten 2006: 62). Hatten emphasizes how such relationships can generate meaning, a perspective that is fundamental to my study as well. Despite these apparent precedents, however, it rarely makes sense to regard instances of reconfigured linear successions in Ives's music as extensions of practices from the tonal era. As I try to show, multidirectional motion was for Ives an ad hoc means of expression, frequently used to convey his central musical and philosophical ideas. His experiments with musical time may in some cases resemble those of much earlier composers. But as Karol Berger has convincingly argued, temporality in Western music of the late eighteenth and nineteenth centuries is best conceptualized in terms of an arrow moving continuously from past to present to future (Berger 2007); in Ives's music, the arrow has multiplied and broken.

In the music-theoretical literature, the best means of accounting for Ives's displaced linear successions is provided by Jonathan Kramer's notion of "multiply directed linear time," as he outlined in his unconventional and engaging study *The Time of Music.* My concept and term are both indebted to his. Kramer defined multiply directed linear time as a "time sense" associated with

> pieces in which the direction of motion is so frequently interrupted by discontinuities, in which the music goes so often to unexpected places, that the linearity, though still a potent structural force, seems reordered. . . . A graphical analogy

(comparable to a straight line for goal-directed linear time or a meandering line for nondirected linear time) for multiply directed time would be a multidimensional vector field. . . . I am suggesting not only that some passages can progress in more than one direction at once but also that their continuations need not follow them directly. When some processes in a piece move toward one (or more) goal(s) yet the goal(s) is (are) placed elsewhere than at the ends of the processes, the temporal continuum is multiple. (1988: 46)[5]

There are some crucial differences between Kramer's concept and the related phenomenon under consideration here. The displacement of linear successions, when it occurs in Ives's music, is not necessarily a pervasive feature of individual works; it occurs in isolated instances as well. Kramer, however, was interested in defining and categorizing the various "temporalities" established by individual works, temporalities that were by nature pervasive. He defined nonlinear time, for instance, in terms of "principles permanently governing a section or piece" (20). Like Kramer, my conclusions are informed by close musical analysis; I also place a high value on Ives's actual compositional process, which I focus on most carefully in the final chapter. Kramer, however, was much more comfortable with broad generalizations that go beyond close analysis, often creating the impression that multiply directed time is something that can be perceived aurally with ease. He wrote, for instance, that he found "relatively few examples" in music of the twentieth century, and none in neo-tonal music (48) (his primary example of multiply directed time is the first movement of Beethoven's Op. 135 quartet). My study can thus be understood as filling what in Kramer's book was a curious and ultimately unexplained gap.

Although this is the first study of Ives's music to address multidirectional motion from an analytical perspective, the idea was actually articulated briefly by Henry and Sidney Cowell nearly fifty years ago. In chapter 1 of their biography of Ives (the first biography of the composer), the Cowells provided a memorable summary of the nature of Ives's music:

> [Ives] pondered the relations of things, testing out music by life and life by music, and building abstract musical structures like concrete events. This makes his particular kind of program music, in which the flow of musical relationships derives from the patterns of activity he saw around him. The music therefore records not a *thing* that happens but the *way* things happen. Because events don't move by singly, but carry memories and forecasts with them, colliding and conflicting with other events too, Ives's music moves in many directions at once and is built on many levels, in the way that experience comes to the mind. (Cowell 1969: 6–7)

There is much to admire in these sentences, even if the third, and arguably most memorable, was lifted from Ives himself (Ives 1961: 42). The Cowells alluded to the dual focus on past and future—"events . . . carry memories and forecasts with them"—and emphasized the synergy between lived time and musical time in Ives's music, one of its defining features. Ives, like many of his contemporaries, experienced time both as "flow" and as "collision/conflict," and the Cowells set up this central opposition in Ives's music as well; the former experience is both privileged and elusive relative to the latter. Perhaps most intriguing, however, is the Cowells' image of both music and experience "mov[ing] in many directions at once . . . on many levels." This statement comes across as intuitive, if somewhat vague; but my analyses will suggest just how apt it actually might be.[6]

Because multidirectional motion implies the fragmentation of a priori linear successions, it is especially useful to conceptualize the phenomenon in relation to Ives's treatment of borrowed music. As is well known, Ives drew freely and liberally upon various musical genres, weaving portions of American popular tunes, Protestant hymns, and classical works into his own pieces; this borrowed music generally surfaces in modified fragments, with complete statements of borrowed melodies reserved for the ends of pieces. Ives could assume that his listeners would be familiar with many of his borrowed sources (to the extent that he believed his music would be listened to at all). But there is no such aid to hearing a fragmented succession whose actual or implied derivation is newly composed, and thus such successions have largely gone unnoticed. As will be evident from the analyses that follow, instances of multidirectional motion range widely in their perceptibility. Some are fairly obvious and not difficult to hear, whereas others seem to be hidden, available only intellectually as a result of close analysis. But Ives was committed to what he called "ear stretching": composing music that challenged his listeners to develop their auditory capacities. As with his myriad musical borrowings, he designed nonchronological relationships to be heard.

A characteristic way that Ives incorporated borrowed material in his music is what J. Peter Burkholder has called "cumulative setting," the most elaborate and significant treatment of borrowed material that Burkholder outlined in his landmark study of borrowing in Ives's music, *All Made of Tunes* (1995: 137–266). Cumulative setting is a means Ives developed for organizing a piece around the gradual, climactic revelation of a borrowed or paraphrased tune. The tune is encountered first in fragments, which gradually coalesce into a statement of the complete (or near-complete) tune near the end of the piece. When the main theme is not borrowed, Burkholder uses the more general term "cumulative form," and this term has frequently been used by scholars for borrowed and original themes alike; I favor this more inclusive term as well.

The effectiveness of cumulative form hinges partly on a listener's ability to recognize the tune from its fragments and to anticipate its completion. Each fragment conjures up the tune until ultimately it manifests itself in full. But even in the numerous pieces where borrowed tunes are never realized in their entireties, the fragments work in the same way on the listener who recognizes them, pointing toward their original sources. For such a listener, these fragments cannot simply be encountered in their immediate musical context but must be heard in relation to their *a priori* contexts as well. And so, in this way, multidirectional motion and Ives's borrowing practices are conceptually quite similar.

The expressive meanings of multidirectional motion are also enlightened by Ives's borrowing practices. Surprisingly, given the breadth of his study of cumulative setting in *All Made of Tunes,* Burkholder did not provide any broad outlines for the interpretation of its potential symbolic meanings in a piece. James

Hepokoski, in a short but penetrating essay, was much more concerned with hermeneutic lines of questioning. In Hepokoski's view, cumulative form provided Ives with a means of recovering the composer's own past:

> In short, Ives' music may also be heard as his attempt to recapture or shore up what he believed his own experience of adulthood and the routinised, rapidly decentering modern world were inexorably eroding away. His fragments, distortions, and interfering dissonances can easily be taken to stand for a perception of a current loss of innocence in a changing, more socio-culturally diverse age. When the "whole" and once-secure past could no longer be confidently grasped in the here and now, only memory-splinters of original meaning remained. Ives' best hope, it would seem, was to reassemble the splinters into larger patterns in the hope of providing "a sentiment, a leaven, that middle-aged America needs nowadays [1920] more than we care to admit." (1994: 750, quoting Ives 1961: 47)

As can be gleaned from this quotation, Hepokoski tended to interpret Ives's recovery missions somewhat negatively as confrontations with a largely irretrievable past; the title of his essay, "Temps Perdu," neatly summarizes this view. Burkholder, on the other hand, has generally interpreted Ives's music in a much more positive light, as a site of joyful reconnection with the past. For instance, in his discussion of *The Fourth of July,* the third movement of Ives's *Holidays Symphony* and one of Burkholder's examples of "collage," Burkholder characterized the piece as a marvel of psychological representation, "a wonderfully true musical evocation of the way human memory works" (1995: 380). Compare this assessment with the concluding words of Hepokoski's essay, which reference the same piece: "That such memory-fragments are to be fleetingly lit up through the medium of music—the art that is as vivid and ephemeral as a skyrocket—could not be more appropriate. But for Ives it may also have been that the 'real music,' much feared, lay in the emptiness of the framing silence—after the ashes fall" (1994: 751). Similarly, David Metzer heard the "memory-edifice collapsing" at the end of this movement (2003: 22).

Do Ives's recovery missions succeed or fail? My interpretations of Ives's music highlight the music's tendency to leave this important question unresolved. But whatever one's judgment may be about the relative success or failure implied by Ives's memory pieces, the basic idea that this music seeks to reconnect with the past is hardly controversial and has informed a wide range of interpretive commentary. As many authors have noted, however, Ives's music is often specifically concerned not simply with the past, but the *music* of the past. Ives has been said to write "music about music"; this turn of phrase has been used by Swafford (1998) and Feder (1999: 93), and the basic idea informs Burkholder's writing as well (1994: 268–86, 346). Likewise, the most direct impression of Ives's cumulative settings is not of a struggle to regain the past, but of a struggle to resuscitate its music.

When Ives drew upon preexisting music, he tended to juxtapose musical fragments associated with different historical eras, styles, and genres, including non-borrowed music pointing to the era of the composition itself, or beyond it. Ives's irregular, piecemeal presentation of this music was aggressively modern and could easily be heard as a sonic analogue for the sensory overload of urban life. Yet, at the same time, Ives seems to have used these textures to evoke the free-associational mechanisms of memory and the desire to return to the remembered past. Thus Ives's treatment of borrowed music serves two opposing functions, evoking the present while striving to recover the past. Lawrence Kramer has cast this opposition as a tension between Ives's "urban-modernist collage" techniques, where diversity and commotion reign, and his "pictorial ideal" of the rural New England of years past (2008: 473). Ives attempted to reconcile these two aspects of his collages, Kramer argued, by superimposing his fragments over "acoustic horizons" (464), the static and cyclical textures that serve as a musical backdrop for many of his pieces. In so doing, he was able to "recover the spiritual and social wholeness that the alienated modern age had lost, but that its technical sophistication could help make recoverable, at least in art" (463).

Kramer's idea of urban modernity presenting Ives with both a problem and its solution is an appealing way of addressing the central paradox of Ives's music being at once modern and anti-modern. Although the compositional features under consideration in this book are different, Kramer's basic interpretative framework applies. Multidirectional motion was thoroughly modern as a compositional principle, and its disruptions of musical time indicate parallel aspects of temporal experience and other elements of modern life. Yet it gestured toward a higher musical level in which dissociated fragments could form coherent linear successions, providing Ives with a means of projecting an image of the more continuous temporality of the past and, ultimately, the timeless realm of God's eternity.

Dualities

Multidirectional motion involves fractured musical surfaces that point toward unified ones. As I have suggested, the fundamental purpose of this relationship between actual and implied music is to represent actual temporal experience and to suggest its transcendence. Ives's music is rooted in a basic temporal distinction between real-world relationships—those among past, present, and future events—and a philosophical/spiritual notion of an everlasting present, where all of these events coexist and where time holds no sway. In the simplest terms, his music is founded on the opposition between *eternity* and *time*. These categories stemmed from a worldview instilled by Ives's Protestant heritage, refined by his studies of Transcendentalist philosophy, and heightened in significance as a direct result of his encounters with urban modernity. The role of Transcendentalism should not be overemphasized, as Ives's ideas about time were shaped first and foremost by the ideas and events of his own historical moment, as I explore in chapter 5. But the Transcendentalists provide helpful and elegant formulations of these ideas as Ives conceived of them at least as early as his composition of the *Essays*. I quoted from Emerson above, but Thoreau was a strong influence as well, as the *Essays* make clear. Thoreau, like Emerson, conceived of a dichotomy between human time and the supreme "everlasting Now," and he sought to shift his experience as much as possible toward that latter. As he memorably put it in "Walden": "In any weather, at any hour of the day or night, I have been anxious to improve the nick of time, and notch it on my stick too; to stand on the meeting of two eternities, the past and future, which is precisely the present moment; to toe that line" (Thoreau 2004: 16). Much of Ives's music has this same aim: to capture time, particularly time lost, and hold onto it in the present.

Any consideration of binary oppositions in Ives's music must of course address the famous "duality" laid out in the *Essays,* "substance" vs. "manner." As Ives explained: "The higher and more important value of this dualism is composed of what may be called reality, quality, spirit, or substance against the lower value of form, quantity, or manner" (1961: 75). As this statement and many others in the *Essays* suggest, the duality amounts to the familiar opposition between content and form, but with content taking on a spiritual element—it "comes form somewhere near the soul" (1961: 77)—and manner tagged as an "under-value"; to be overly concerned with manner is to be superficial and morally suspect.

A host of subdualities are sprinkled over the pages of the *Essays,* most synonymous with substance/manner or highlighting a particular aspect of this duality. Some of these are suggested by the above quotation: reality/appearance, quality/quantity, content/form. But substance/manner itself may best be regarded as a subcategory of the more inclusive duality eternity/time. Strong support from this view is found in the *Essays.* Before offering the rough definitions of substance and manner cited above, Ives warmed up to his topic by describing the changing nature of manner and the permanent nature of substance. "There may be an analogy," he wrote, "between both the state and power of artistic perceptions and the law of perpetual change, that ever-flowing stream, partly biological, partly cosmic, ever going on in ourselves, in nature, in all life" (1961: 71). In other words, there may be an analogy between *time* (the "ever-flowing stream") and the evaluation of artworks: both seem to change continually. Musical value, like human life, appears impermanent, which, Ives conjectured here, would explain why Wagner's music had increasingly been exposed as morally deficient over the years. But then Ives rejected his analogy as imperfect. His reason was the existence of composers such as Bach and Beethoven whose music is timeless in value (1961: 73). So now the original analogy can be refined: musical value that is subject to the forces of time is grounded in manner, whereas musical value immune to such forces—*eternal* value—is grounded in substance.

Eternity/time, then, is usefully regarded as a master duality with a strong and deep-seated presence in Ives's thought and musical expression; substance/manner, based on categories that came to structure Ives's thought about music and also a tension he sought to express through music, is one of many secondary dualities subsumed within it. Among these subdualities, most relevant to this book are those that form the "substance" of Ives's music. Whereas substance/manner is concerned with musical expression in general, I am most interested in dualities that enhance understanding of how and what Ives's music expresses, particularly with regard to the fundamental issue of temporal relationships. Three subdualities are of particular relevance, not as absolute categories but as heuristics that facilitate interpretation:

1. *God/Man.*[7] This subduality stems naturally from the master duality eternity/time: God is immortal but human life is ruled by time. It is relevant in pieces incorporating explicitly Christian themes or texts, most common in Ives's earlier music (most of his psalm settings, for instance), as well as those with a more inclusive or ambiguous spirituality, where some sort of supreme being or cosmic presence, perhaps referred to as "God," is positioned on an elevated plane in relation to worldly affairs. Such is the case in *The Unanswered Question,* for example, as I consider in chapter 4. Heaven/Earth is a closely related duality that in some cases receives equal or greater emphasis.
2. *Community/individual.* The relationship between the individual and the larger community was critical for Ives, and it draws attention to an important inner conflict. The small-town New England values and way of life whose erosion Ives mourned were strongly community-oriented, but Ives, a notorious recluse, can hardly be said to have sought out such a community in his own adult life, even if accounts of his isolation have been exaggerated. Ives felt strongly the disconnective effects of modernity, but these feelings were largely self-imposed. Ives was no doubt aware of this tension, as the advantages and disadvantages of the solitary life were grappled with by Emerson and Thoreau, notably in Emerson's essay "Society and Solitude" and the chapter "Solitude" in Thoreau's *Walden,* both of which Ives knew (see Ives 1961: 25, 52, and 69). But however much Ives may have shared Thoreau's preference for solitary contemplation over social interaction, his music tends to portray isolation negatively in relation to communal experience. The latter is typically associated with the common folk of New England, but Ives was also concerned more generally with the Common Man—what he would come to refer to as "the Majority" (as opposed to "the Minority," those who possess political power). As he wrote in his 1920 essay, "The Majority": "God is on the side of the Majority, . . . He has made the Common Heart, the Universal Mind, and the over-soul greater than the individual heart, mind, and soul" (1961: 144). The Majority, as suggested here, transcends the mortality of the individual, and Ives's musical portraits of New England imagine these communities in the same way.[8]
3. *Intuition/expression.* The third subduality concerns thought, action, and artistic creation. A central component of Transcendentalist philosophy, intuition, according to Emerson, pertains to "ideas . . . which did not come by experience, but through which experience was acquired" (1990: 102). Intuitions are God-given, and thus eternally true; one should strive to understand and act upon them. Although he was not entirely consistent in his deployment of the terms in the *Essays,* Ives tended to pit intuition against *expression,* the means by which an intuition is translated into art.

Expression, in Ives's view, is often inadequate to the original intuition—"A true inspiration may lack a true expression" (1961: 6)—and to be overly concerned with expression is necessarily to pay insufficient attention to the intuition. The terms are closely linked to the substance/manner duality. Whereas substance and manner are elements of artworks, intuition and expression are their sources; intuition is the wellspring of artistic substance. When Ives articulated these dualities in the *Essays* his most active period as a composer was nearing its end, and it is difficult to say to what extent he thought in these terms earlier in his career. But generally when Ives parodies an idiom and places it in negative relation to his "own" musical style, he is asserting the importance of remaining faithful to intuition and not succumbing to empty expression. And thus this duality both reflects a way that Ives thought about artistic creation and was an idea that he sought to express musically.

As the preceding summaries make clear, just as substance and manner exist in a hierarchical relationship—an "over-value" paired with an "under-value"—so do each of these subdualities. Man strives to be one with God; the community is stronger than the individual; expression can only produce imperfect representations of intuition. But in addition to sharing the same basic structure, these pairs are connected to one another via nested relationships. The under-value of one duality encompasses both values of the next: community/individual is a duality of Man; intuition/expression is a duality of the individual. This structuring of dualities reinforces the link between intuitions and God fundamental to Transcendentalist thought. In discussing substance and manner, Ives seems to have implied a similar chain of relationships:

> Substance in a human-art-quality suggests the body of a conviction which has its birth in the spiritual consciousness, whose youth is nourished in the moral consciousness, and whose maturity as a result of all this growth is then represented in a mental image. This is appreciated by the intuition, and somehow translated into expression by "manner." (Ives 1961: 75)[9]

The key terms here are "spiritual," "moral," and "mental image," whose referents can be identified as God, behavior in society, and intuition, respectively; Ives added the final under-value, expression, to extend the chain further. The overarching metaphor is temporal—specifically, life itself in all of its stages. The metaphor stalls at "maturity," but the logical conclusion is death, which, the passage implies, is brought on by the conversion of an artistic intuition into actual art by expression. Ives hinted at these associations elsewhere in his writings: "As soon as music goes down on paper, it loses something of its birthright!" (1972: 189), for example. The entire scheme of nested dualities, incorporated with the temporal metaphor, can be visualized as in Table 0.2.

Ives, as mentioned, often wrote "music about music," and the process of artistic creation, as characterized here, is thematized or even dramatized in many of

God	Man		
	Community	Individual	
		Intuition	Expression
Birth →	Youth →	Maturity →	Death

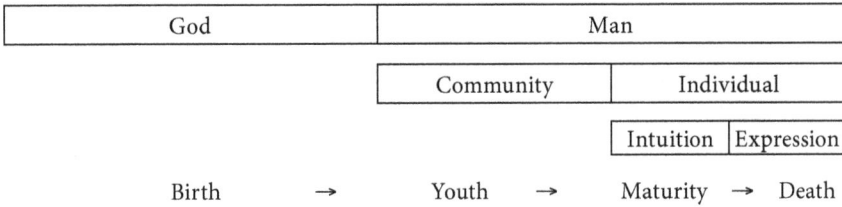

Table 0.2. Nested relationships of three subdualities, with Ives's temporal metaphor.

his pieces. An example will be helpful to show how Ives's music reflects and represents his ideas about the creative act, as expressed in the above quote, and how the subdualities outlined above might structure meaning in a work. The third and last movement of Ives's *Orchestral Set no. 2,* "From Hanover Square North, at the End of a Tragic Day, the Voices of the People Again Arose" (c. 1919), is a musical response to an experience that Ives recounted in detail in *Memos:*

> There's a personal experience behind [the movement], the story of which I will now try to tell. We were living in an apartment at 27 West 11th Street. The morning paper on the breakfast table gave the news of the sinking of the Lusitania. I remember, going downtown to business, the people on the streets and on the elevated train had something in their faces that was not the usual something. Everybody who came into the office, whether they spoke about the disaster or not, showed a realization of seriously experiencing something. (That it meant war is what the faces said, if the tongues didn't.) Leaving the office and going uptown about 6 o'clock, I took the Third Avenue "L" at the Hanover Square Station. As I came on the platform, there was quite a crowd waiting for the trains, which had been blocked lower down, and while waiting there, a hand-organ, or hurdy gurdy was playing on a street below. Some workmen sitting on the side of the tracks began to whistle the tune, and others began to sing or hum the refrain. A workman with a shovel over his shoulder came on the platform and joined in the chorus, and the next man, a Wall Street banker with white spats and a cane, joined in it, and finally it seemed to me that everybody was singing this tune, and they didn't seem to be singing for fun, but as a natural outlet for what their feelings had been going through all day long. There was a feeling of dignity all through this. The hand-organ man seemed to sense this and wheeled the organ nearer the platform and kept it up fortissimo (and the chorus sounded out as though every man in New York must be joining in it). Then the first train came and everybody crowded in, and the song eventually died out, but the effect on the crowd still showed. Almost nobody talked—the people acted as though they might be coming out of a church service. In going uptown, occasionally little groups would start singing or humming the tune.
>
> Now what was the tune? It wasn't a Broadway hit, it wasn't a musical comedy air, it wasn't a waltz tune or a dance tune or an opera tune or a classical tune, or a tune that all of them probably knew. It was (only) the refrain of an old Gospel Hymn that had stirred many people of past generations. It was nothing but—*In the Sweet Bye and Bye.* It wasn't a tune written to be sold, or written by a professor of music—but by a man who was but giving out an experience.

This third movement is based on this, fundamentally, and comes from that "L" station. It has secondary themes and rhythms, but widely related, and its general makeup would reflect the sense of many people living, working, and occasionally going through the same deep experience, together. It would give the ever changing multitudinous feeling of life that one senses in the city. (1972: 92–93)

The musical element of "From Hanover Square North" most obviously related to this program is Ives's treatment of "In the Sweet Bye and Bye," a favorite hymn that turns up frequently in his music. Ives's incorporation of the hymn shapes the movement's fairly simple form. The movement begins with a "Distant Choir" of horn, chimes, harp, piano, unison vocals, and strings, playing alone, offstage (Example 0.4). Its music is amorphous and indistinct, comprised primarily of layered ostinati, except for an intoned passage from the *Te Deum:* "We praise Thee O God, We acknowledge Thee to be the Lord, All the Earth doth worship Thee." After singing this text, the voices depart, never to be heard from again. Soon thereafter the main orchestra enters, immediately incorporating fragments of the featured verse from "In the Sweet Bye and Bye." These are subsequently heard in various forms and combinations while the main orchestra slowly makes its way from the hushed atmosphere of the opening to a *fortissimo, tutti* rendition of the complete chorus near the end of the movement, completely obscuring the music of the Distant Choir along the way. The shared source of the overlapping fragmentary statements of the hymn becomes increasingly evident as the movement progresses, and in retrospect the form can be heard as cumulative.[10] Immediately following the fortissimo climax, the second violins restate the hymn chorus at *pianissimo;* but the repeat fades away, and the second violins blend in with the music of the main orchestra, now amorphous and amelodic. From the resulting void, the Distant Choir emerges once again, reasserting its immutable presence as the piece ends.

All three subdualities outlined above figure prominently in Ives's program and its musical realization. Most obviously, the idea of the individual finding strength through community is essential to the program and seems to grow naturally from the hymn: the commuters converge on the platform as though enacting the heavenly reunion of which they sing ("We shall meet on that beautiful shore"). Ives invites us to imagine this convergence though the cumulative formation of the *fortissimo* chorus, the gradual coming together of various instruments and melodic fragments. This process is not only a musical representation of the commuters' congregation on the platform, however, but also a nonliteral representation of their coalescing vocal utterances; we are hearing a loose sonic portrait of the episode. Ives's use of cumulative form, a metaphor for the creative act, indicates that this portrait be interpreted similarly; the commuters' creation of the chorus, as though from scratch and with little effort, models an idealized compositional process of developing inchoate ideas into musical forms. In other words, "From Hanover Square North" dramatizes the mysterious process by which intuition is translated into expression. Recall Emerson's idea that intuition is not obtained through experience, but rather makes the acquisition

Example 0.4. "From Hanover Square North," mm. 1–11 (Charles Ives, *Orchestral Set no. 2,* used by Permission of Peer International Corporation).

of experience possible. Likewise, Ives notes that "In the Sweet Bye and Bye" was composed "by a man who was but giving out an experience." Passed on to the commuters, this hymn provided "a natural outlet" for their emotions.

Intuition comes from God, and his presence is suggested at the beginning of the movement by the *Te Deum* and the omnipresent backdrop of ostinati. His proxy is the hand-organ man, who initiates the events while remaining in the background. This street musician's playing of "In the Sweet Bye and Bye" has no literal analogue in the movement: for Ives to have included it would have required the full-fledged tune to be heard too soon. But its presence can nonetheless be heard, channeling a divine one, in the circling repeated figure that runs through the entire movement, evoking the hand organ's continually turning crank. Interpreted in this way, the figure conforms to the broad outlines of the program: first played by the viola (see Example 0.4), it is prominent at the beginning of the movement, becomes obscured for most of the remainder by the main orchestra, but resurfaces briefly at the very end, when the passengers have boarded their train. These passengers are the vehicles of expression, and it is suggestive that, according to Ives's program, their song "dies out" almost as soon as it materializes. Expression, in the formulation above, is the death of intuition, and we hear the inevitable recession of the original musical impulse in the fadeout of the second violins. But the substance of "In the Sweet Bye and Bye" is immutable, as Ives emphasized with his list of styles that the commuters did *not* sing—"Broadway hit," "musical comedy air," etc.—all of these highly fashionable, impermanent forms of expression. And thus as the tune fades away, it blends into the background texture, and the main orchestra and the Distant Choir for the first time become difficult to distinguish.

Whereas Ives's treatment of "In the Sweet Bye and Bye" is most obviously understood in direct relation to the program, as a representation of a musical/social happening, the text of the hymn suggests a supplementary interpretation that extends beyond the program. Although Ives did not cite it in his commentary and chose not to have it sung, the hymn text clearly informs the movement. As other scholars have noted, the hymn seems to have been hand-picked for the occasion, the repeated line "we shall meet on that beautiful shore" a promise to those victims who drowned in the Atlantic. In the company of these associations, the undulating ostinati of the Distant Choir, particularly the repeated figure that runs through the entire movement, evoke the steady, constant undulations of the sea. But Ives, I would suggest, has transposed heaven from the shore to the sea itself. Sublime, seemingly limitless, and immune to the trials of Man, the sea is a natural analogue for the afterworld, and Ives approximates these attributes in the music for the Distant Choir. The intoned *Te Deum* helps to establish the association, positioning the backdrop of ostinati as God's heavenly dwelling, or a cathedral dedicated to his worship: at the end of Ives's program, when the passengers board their train, they act "as though they might be coming out of a church service."

When the voice of the people arrives in the guise of the main orchestra (m. 20), it enters without warning or nuance, disconnected, uncertain, and separated physically from the offstage ensemble. All these features suggest Man's separation from God, as though the tragedy has temporarily borne existential dismay ("the people . . . had something in their faces that was not the usual something"). The remainder of the movement is occupied with overcoming this separation. The melodic summation achieved at the climax points toward divine deliverance, just as the fellow commuters, in coming together on the platform in song, prefigure their coming together with the Lusitania victims in heaven, as promised by the hymn: "There's a land that is fairer than day, and by faith we can see it afar; For the Father waits over the way, to prepare us a dwelling place there." The passengers even enact their heavenly reunion in the very manner described by the hymn, *in song*: "We shall sing on that beautiful shore, the melodious songs of the blessed." When the echo of the triumphant *tutti* chorus fades back into the music of the Distant Chorus, we can hear the voices of the people blending with the humming backdrop of God's eternity, as though an image of the reunion to come.

Having interpreted the musical narrative of "From Hanover Square North" in terms of Ives's dualistic pairings, a new layer of interpretation can be added by mapping these dualities onto the temporal metaphor outlined at the bottom of Table 0.2. The tune is born in the "spiritual consciousness" (God), stemming from the sacred space established by the *Te Deum* and the Distant Choir at the beginning of the movement (the womb of the sea, the hand organ's crank). It is "nourished in the moral consciousness" (community), as the commuters gather on the platform and the hymn begins to coalesce. It grows into an "image" (intuition), the crystallization of the full chorus. And then, having been translated (expression), it immediately dies away. As the piece ends, the spiritual realm remains to engender ideas into perpetuity.

In sum, "From Hanover North" brings to life Ives's metaphor for the creation of substantive artistic ideas. To be of substance was to be of eternal value, and Ives wished to attach this quality securely to the commuters' impromptu hymn sing, to the hymn itself, and to his own piece. For Ives, the happening at Hanover North, and the tune that constituted its focal point, were emblems of the interconnectivity of the present and an idealized past and future. Generations had been united, and temporal distinctions erased, in a single moment by a timeless tune. Spatial distinctions seem also to have been negated: "The chorus sounded out as though every man in New York must be joining in it." Ives conceived of this moment on a grand scale. His reference to "the ever changing multitudinous feeling of life that one senses in the city," though confined to the explicit locale of the program, points toward the greater cosmos as well, echoing Ives's earlier description of the subject matter of the *Universe Symphony*: "incessant myriads, for ages ever and always changing, growing, but in ages ever always a permanence" (Austin 1997: 186). The program takes these workers and businessmen who have put their normal urban existences on hold to contemplate and immerse themselves fully in the present moment, and it pits them against the temporal experience of the overly time-conscious society of urban modernity. The latter is signified by Ives's identification of the time (6:00 PM) early in his program and by the train itself, whose rigid schedules and ability to disrupt one's sense of space-time relationships made it a quintessential symbol of the new mechanization of time. In Ives's telling of the happening at Hanover Square North, what enabled the travelers to rise above this suffocating aspect of modernity, whether they embraced it as businessmen or were its victims as workmen, was the hymn. An inherent duality was essential to the hymn's significance: its text pointed forward to eternal rest and promised reunion for those whose lives were torn apart by the war, but its cultural significance pointed backward to the nineteenth century and the rural lifestyle and values whose loss Ives so profoundly felt. By pointing both directions at once, the hymn reached toward eternity, transcending time.

* * *

The remainder of the book is structured in two parts, each consisting of three chapters. Each chapter is devoted to the analysis of one or two individual pieces, with the exception of the final chapter, which deals with a group of closely related pieces. Every piece or group of pieces involves multidirectional motion, and each of my analyses seeks to show how recognition of this aspect of the music expands the interpretive frameworks through which the music can be understood. In the studies of Part I, analysis and interpretation are limited, relatively speaking, to matters directly related to the pieces under consideration; Part II opens up the discussion to include a broader range of issues. Altogether, these chapters address a wide variety of pieces ranging from the beginning to the end of Ives's active period as a composer. The six analyses of Part I are arranged roughly in chronological order and grouped according to the three subdualities outlined above. The layout is not intended to demonstrate the absolute authority of these categories, however; for any given piece, more than one subduality is potentially relevant. The chapter headings are simply designed to focus attention on the primary strain of dualistic thinking critical to the interpretation of each piece. As already shown, the subdualities should not be regarded as mutually exclusive but as closely interrelated.

Chapter 1 focuses on the God/Man duality as expressed in two works for chorus, the early hymn *I Come to Thee* and Ives's setting of *Psalm 14,* both based on texts that thematize the desire for union with God in heaven. The latter piece provides an especially lucid example of Ives's experiments with musical chronology, one that features what Philip Lambert has described as Ives's penchant for "systematic" compositional thinking, where musical ideas "can be rigidly organized, exactingly contrived, formulaic" (1997: 4). The two instrumental works under consideration in chapter 2, Sonata no. 1 for Piano (particularly the scherzo movements) and String Quartet no. 2, both highlight the duality between community and individual. Its presence is explicit in the case of the quartet, for which Ives outlined a short programmatic narrative in which four men, separated by their opinions, find common spiritual ground through their experience of nature. I interpret the piano sonata through the lens of Ives's programmatic commentary as well, in conjunction with the texts of numerous borrowed tunes; together, these suggest the story of a young man's separation from and reunion with his family and community, a scenario that, at a more abstract level, lies at the heart of much of Ives's music.

Chapter 3 features two mature entries from *114 Songs,* composed in close proximity to the publication of the *Essays* and exhibiting a concern with some of the same issues Ives was working out there, particularly the duality between intuition and expression. "Nov. 2, 1920" concerns a bereaved old man who laments the diminishing will of the American people in the wake of Warren Harding's election as president. The man's tirade, as Ives rendered it both textually and musically, seems spontaneous and rough—positive qualities that Ives associated with the orational modes of Lincoln and Emerson and increasingly emulated in his own music. But when reflecting the sources of the old man's bitterness, Ives's setting often gestures toward musical idioms he regarded as shallow, specifically ragtime and the music of Debussy. The latter is an explicit target in "Grantchester," in which Ives sets a portion of Rupert Brooke's eponymous poem. The song features a musical critique of Debussy and Wagner, whom Ives described disparagingly as "sensual" composers (1961: 24–25, 82, 101), and uses this to advance his ideas about the proper sources and modes of artistic expression.

The dualities emphasized in chapters 1–3 recede into the background in Part II of the book, but they quietly underlie the chapter organization here as well. In *The Unanswered Question* (the subject of chapter 4), the divide between God and Man is cast in terms of a cosmological struggle in which the mortal search for the meaning of existence is met by silence from the heavens. "The Things Our Fathers Loved" (discussed in chapter 5) concerns a subject who, as in so much of Ives's music, mourns the loss of a rural community—one in which music-making is part of everyday life and intimately connected to societal values. And the evolution of Ives's "Emerson" music (chapter 6) can be understood as Ives's lengthy, and increasingly unsuccessful, struggle to recapture and find adequate expression for an esteemed artistic impulse from his most productive compositional phase.

The primary objective of this part of the book is to introduce new interpretive contexts and methodological approaches, exploring these in greater depth than in Part I. Ives's music is grounded in human experience, and multidirectional motion provided him with new ways for music to tell stories and convey ideas about this experience at a time when many artists were seeking new ways of representing the modern world and life within it. His innovations paralleled contemporaneous developments in the arts and reflected an experience of modernity that Ives, despite his oft-noted isolation, shared with many. Chapter 4 considers *The Unanswered Question* using the model of narrative as an interpretive framework. This model is suggested not merely by the obvious storytelling impulse in this and many other works of Ives's, but by the relationship between Ives's treatment of musical successions and the presentation of stories in literary and filmic narratives, as well as by the coexistence of a primary level of musical action and a higher level of commentary. Film provides an especially useful model for conceptualizing multidirectional musical motion, one that is historically apt:

film was evolving into a narrative medium at the same time that Ives was maturing as a composer, and some of Ives's compositional techniques bear striking resemblance to those of the cinema. Chapter 5 pursues this connection, using the
emerging techniques of film as an entry point for thinking about new concepts
of time in the early twentieth century. More specifically, it addresses the growing fixation on the present moment and how Ives's music reflected this modern
preoccupation. I explore these ideas through the song "The Things Our Fathers
Loved," in which the vocal persona attempts to reconstitute in the present moment the lost values and way of life of an earlier America.

Finally, chapter 6 examines the complex compositional history of the
"Emerson" movement of the *Concord* Sonata, from the incomplete *Emerson Overture* (c. 1910–14) through the second edition of the *Concord* (1947). Ives mined the
overture for music upon which to build the *Concord* movement and numerous
other pieces, in some cases literally cutting and pasting fragments from one score
to another. Drawing upon my own comparison of the relevant scores, recordings, and manuscript sources, I offer the first concise outline of these interrelationships, using as a conceptual model Burkholder's notion of cumulative form.
Ives's treatment of what he referred to as the "human-faith-melody" in the *Concord* mirrors the evolution of his Emerson music from numerous partial adapta-
tions of the original overture sketches to his 1933 recording of the first "Emerson"
transcription, a nearly complete reconstruction of the first section of the overture
from its various offshoots. In other words, the ways in which Ives seems to fragment and reconfigure musical successions within individual pieces can be seen
to operate at a higher compositional level: his continual revising and recycling of
music over time. Taking this idea further, I suggest that Ives's struggle to restore
the form of his original overture in the recording studio can be interpreted similarly to his treatment of fragmentary material in individual pieces, as an attempt
to resuscitate music of the past and to preserve it for the future—an endeavor
that, as in so many of Ives's later works, was ultimately shrouded by a profound
sense of loss. And thus this chapter makes a fitting conclusion, showing how the
compositional processes considered throughout the book encapsulate the larger
expressive project of Ives's music.

Part I: Three Dualities

1 God/Man:
I Come to Thee and *Psalm 14*

I Come to Thee

In his aesthetic history of Ives, J. Peter Burkholder divided Ives's life and compositional career into six periods (1985: 43–44). These continue to provide a useful and influential means of thinking about Ives's artistic development. The music of the first two phases, "boyhood" (1874–94) and "apprenticeship" (1894–1902), was relatively traditional. As Burkholder described, Ives composed primarily "sentimental parlor songs, pieces for his father's band, and organ and chorus pieces" during his Danbury youth and "large romantic works in the mold of his teacher [Horatio] Parker" while at Yale and during his first years in New York (1985: 43). Seeking to serve justice to the eclecticism that characterized Ives's music from early on, however, Burkholder also stressed Ives's early experimentalism, inherited from his father. As Burkholder noted, the radical techniques that the young Ives was developing often found their way into pieces that are not generally considered experimental: "Ives later incorporated many of the ideas he had first developed in his 'memos in notes' into his music for public performance, first in his church music. . . . Yet in these pieces, the new techniques were often less rigorously handled than in the experimental works, for in his concert music Ives was concerned not with technique for its own sake but rather with musical and emotional effects" (1985: 49).

The notion that Ives, in his more conventional early works, employed experimental techniques in limited, strategic ways toward expressive ends is useful for making sense of the idiosyncratic blend of convention and experiment that often characterizes these pieces. It would be natural to understand this interplay between traditional and innovative compositional techniques as merely the byproduct of a composer developing his own distinctive musical voice, but, as Burkholder suggested, this aspect of Ives's development was more purposeful: from an early stage, and more and more throughout his career, Ives used the tension between tradition and innovation as a means of expression.

An excellent example is *I Come to Thee,* a short devotional piece for SATB choir which Ives composed around 1896–97, or possibly as early as 1889 (Sinclair 1999: 289–90). My analysis is based on Ives's pencil sketch and ink score (f5927–32); John Kirkpatrick's critical edition (Ives 1983) takes some problematic liberties with these sources, as I discuss below. The first page of the pencil sketch, which contains Ives's setting of the first two stanzas, is reproduced in Example 1.1.

Example 1.1. *I Come to Thee*, pencil sketch (f5927).

The text derives from a hymn by Charlotte Elliott:

> God of my life! Thy boundless grace
> Chose, pardoned, and adopted me;
> My rest, my home, my dwelling-place!
> Father! I come to Thee.
>
> Jesus, my hope, my rock, my shield!
> Whose precious blood was shed for me,
> Into Thy hands my soul I yield;
> Saviour! I come to Thee.
>
> Spirit of glory and of God!
> Long hast Thou deigned my guide to be;
> Now be Thy comfort sweet bestowed!
> My God! I come to Thee.
>
> I come to join that countless host
> Who praise Thy name unceasingly;
> Blest Father, Son, and Holy Ghost!
> My God! I come to Thee.

Elliott's hymn adopts a similar theme as "In the Sweet Bye and Bye," the faithful anticipation of union with God in heaven, but from an individual rather than collective perspective. Each of the first three stanzas juxtaposes past and present tenses; the fourth uses only the latter. The implied trajectory is from the past (the persona was chosen, Jesus's blood was shed for her, etc.), to the present ("I come to Thee"), to the future (the imminent union) and, ultimately, eternity ("praise Thy name unceasingly").

The structure of the hymn implies a simple strophic setting: each stanza scans similarly and ends with the words of the title. Ives did not set out to compose a straightforward hymn, however, but instead to construct his own idiosyncratic form. Thus he was not wedded to the original text. Whereas he took few liberties with Stanzas 1, 3, and 4, Ives reordered and built upon the lines of Stanza 2, discarding the original rhyme scheme in the process. His version places greater weight on the stanza in relation to the others and emphasizes in particular the name of Jesus and his act of self-sacrifice:

> Jesus, whose blood was shed for me,
> Jesus, whose precious blood was shed for me,
> Jesus, Jesus, my strength, my faith, my hope, my rock, my shield,
> Into Thy hands my soul I yield, my life, my all,
> I come to Thee, I come to Thee.

The adventurousness of Ives's musical setting of this stanza stands apart from the others as well. Overall, Ives's setting of the hymn rests fairly comfortably in the familiar chromatic tonal idiom of nineteenth-century Protestant hymns, with F major an unequivocal tonal center. But Ives's intention to depart from the associated musical conventions of such hymns is evident by the end of the

——Stanza 1——	——————————Stanza 2——————————		
mm. 1-7 (F Major)	mm. 8-16 (unstable tonality)	mm. 16-24 (————F Major————)	mm. 24-27

——Stanza 3——	——————————Stanza 4——————————	
mm. 28-35 (F Major)	mm. 36-43 (unstable tonality)	mm. 43-47 (F Major)

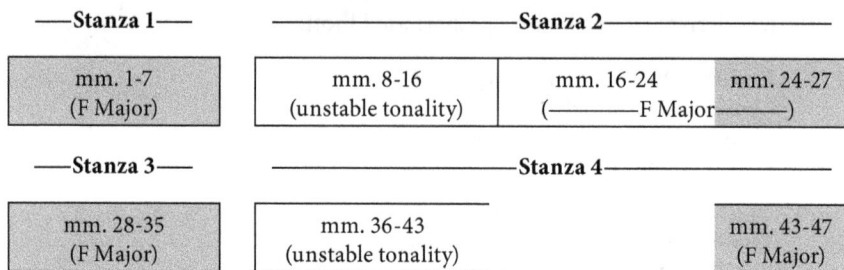

Figure 1.1. Form of *I Come to Thee*.

first stanza. Rather than affirming F major with a tonic cadence at the end of the textual refrain, as one would expect in a traditional strophic setting, the titular words are set to a half cadence (m. 7), implying, perhaps, a consequent phrase. The music of the second stanza (mm. 8–27) then veers away from that of the first in its tonality and proportions. F major is temporarily abandoned in favor of harmonic ambiguity and unusual chromatic voice leading (mm. 8–16), and the duration of the entire stanza is about three times that of the first. But the music of Stanza 2 turns out to be an aberration: the remainder of the piece is stylistically consonant with the opening phrase. Stanza 3 (mm. 28–35) reprises the music of Stanza 1, and whereas the fourth stanza strays from F major, it is not marked by the harmonic and melodic eccentricities of the second and its proportions are extended only slightly. Figure 1.1 summarizes the overall form of the piece, giving a sense of its skewed proportions; passages that are essentially identical musically are shaded and aligned vertically.

From his early works onward, Ives's musical forms tended to be situational, determined less by preexisting musical conventions than by the form of the ideas or experiences he wished to express. This attitude shaped Ives's approach to text setting as well; his setting of *I Come to Thee* seems to have been informed not by the abstract form of the text itself, but rather by the meaning of the words. For instance, Ives clearly structured the piece around the arrival of the line "Blest Father, Son, and Holy Ghost!" in Stanza 4, where the members of the holy trinity, isolated in Stanzas 1–3, are brought together. This line is sung in mm. 39–41 and immediately repeated in mm. 41–44, where the piece reaches its registral apex (m. 42), as well as its highest dynamic (*fff*) and fastest harmonic rhythm (mm. 42–43). Mm. 8–16 hardly seem to belong in the same composition as this grandiose and gaudy climax. The passage is transcribed in Example 1.2, along with the subsequent transition back to F major in mm. 16–18. The horizontal slashes in most of the measures were Ives's means of notating the absence of one of the voice parts from the texture. In this passage, Ives seems to have been drawn to the fleeting reference to the crucifixion, featured prominently in his recasting of the text of Stanza 2, as shown above. The convoluted chromaticism evokes the pas-

Example 1.2. *I Come to Thee*, mm. 8–18, with key annotations.

sion, and the descending semitonal gestures of mm. 11–12 and 15–17 respond with cries of lament.

The episode is not only musically anomalous but actually set off from the rest of the piece as though parenthetical. The A-major music at m. 8 shifts abruptly away from the F-major half cadence that ends m. 7, but a much more conventional continuation can be generated by simply eliminating mm. 8–18 and proceeding directly from m. 7 to m. 19, where F-major tonality returns. Numerous musical connections make this alternative version logical and satisfying. These are outlined in Example 1.3, which juxtaposes the final two measures of Stanza 1 (mm. 6–7) with mm. 19–20; a dotted barline indicates the hypothetical connection between these passages. As highlighted by numbered brackets on the example, the latter two measures take up the ascending stepwise bass of m. 7 (1), echo the ascending minor seventh C to B♭ in the soprano and the rhythm of "I come to Thee" (2), and echo the accented chromatic neighbor that decorates the arrival on the dominant in m. 7 (3). These connections are so prominent in the recomposed version that it is easy to conceive of this version as having actually existed at some earlier stage in Ives's compositional process. At this hypothetical stage, Ives would not have yet decided to alter the text of Stanza 2—it would begin with the words "Jesus, my hope, my rock . . ." essentially as they appear in mm. 19–20—and the music of mm. 19–27 would provide a consequent phrase to balance that of mm. 1–7.

Embedded within the interpolation of mm. 8–18 is another, shorter interpolation, Ives's setting of the word "Jesus" in mm. 11–12. This particular utterance of Jesus's name is set off both melodically and harmonically. The soprano momentarily drops out, replaced by the bass, creating a void where the melody had been. Kirkpatrick, in his edition, felt it necessary to correct this oddity, adding a

Example 1.3. *I Come to Thee*, linear and motivic connections between mm. 6–7 and 19–20.

melody in an "implied" organ part. As he explained in his commentary, "The two sources have no organ notes at all, but in m. 11–12 and 15–18 the quartet clearly sings accompanying chords that require organ phrases, which probably varied the soprano phrase in 10–11" (1983: 3). The chords that Kirkpatrick refers to are as disorienting as the absence of the soprano line. As indicated in Example 1.2, they imply the key of D♭ major, a complete non sequitur in the A-major context established in mm. 8–11 and an apparent tonal dead-end. The pair of chords can be heard as a tonal displacement of a normative progression: transposing the pair of chords up a minor sixth would create a straightforward path to a reprise of m. 8 as a consequent phrase via a modified descending-fifths progression. Not only are the chords harmonically disruptive, but they are metrically disruptive as well, inserting four beats into a 3/4 scheme; in a normalized version of the passage, beat 2 of m. 11 would proceed directly to beat 3 of m. 12. Even the word "Jesus" is superfluous in this context: it could be omitted without sacrificing the coherence of the text.

The music reels after this disruption. The melodic motion immediately reverses course, slithering upward until returning to the same chord that had set the word "shed" in m. 10; see Ives's harmonization of "blood" in m. 13, an enharmonic respelling of the downbeat chords of mm. 9 and 10. The reversal can most easily be heard in the alto, in which the E–D–C♯–B–B♭ motion of mm. 10–11 is followed by the B♭–B–D♭–E motion of mm. 12–13. This reversal can be heard as a retracing of steps or, more provocatively, as a reversal of musical time. In either interpretation, the effect is of a retreat and correction, an attempt to overcome the misstep of mm. 11–12 and to regain the tonal stability of A major. In the process, the two-chord progression of mm. 11–12 is sealed off as an aberration—harmonically, metrically, and textually.

These two interpolations, one embedded in the other, are important stages in an ongoing tonal drama that is a crucial expressive element in the piece. Abstractly, the drama centers around departures from the home key and subsequent returns, as tonal dramas inevitably do. The first stanza establishes F major as the tonic; this key is abandoned in mm. 8–16 and restored in mm. 17–18. The abandonment is sudden when A major arrives in m. 8, but a logical overall tonal plan supporting F major is still available at this point, with A positioned to function as an altered mediant. Mm. 11–12 seem to lurch in the opposite direction, however, gesturing toward D♭ major, a major third *below* F, which balances the previous move from F to A. An attempted return to A major follows in mm. 12–13 via the reversal of mm. 10–11, but the move is unsuccessful; the chromatic motion becomes more convoluted and the tonality veers off to G♭ major (mm. 12–15)—an extremely distant key in the overall context of F major—as though infected by the sudden shift to flat-side tonality in mm. 11–12. Kirkpatrick once again felt obliged to correct Ives's idiosyncrasies, "clarifying" the score such that mm. 11–15 (beat 2) are notated entirely without flats. But this alteration obscures the developing tonal drama: the enharmonic respelling of the music from m. 10 in m. 13 is a symptom of the failed return to A major. The tonality has gone quickly and perilously astray.

But it rights itself with a quick sleight of hand. The progression of mm. 11–12, which evokes D♭ major, reemerges from G♭ tonality in mm. 15–16 where it is less tonally disruptive. The first of the two chords, when immediately restated in m. 16, is reinterpreted as a dominant of F, allowing F major to be restored as abruptly as it was lost in m. 8. The remainder of the piece is relatively devoid of conflict. Stable F-major tonality is maintained through Stanza 3, and Stanza 4, rather than recapitulating the tonal problems of Stanza 2, recasts them on more secure footing. Like Stanza 2, it begins with A-major harmony (m. 36), but now grounded more solidly in root position. A harmonic sequence in mm. 36–39 leads, via an assortment of applied chords (mm. 39–43), to a reprise of the strong cadence in F that ended Stanza 2 (mm. 43–47). In short, A major has been transformed from problem to solution, supporting F major rather than leading away from it.

The real "problem," to move away now from the abstract drama of key relations, is separation from God (and Jesus, and Holy Ghost) and the longing it engenders. Ives fixed upon the line in the original hymn that alludes most strongly to this separation, the reference to the crucifixion, in which Jesus, in suffering, awaited his own union with God. As we have seen, Ives increased the line's prominence, moving it to the beginning of Stanza 2, extending it through repetition, and calling attention to it via musical contrast. The relatively extreme nature of this contrast evokes both Jesus's separation from God and the persona's separation from Jesus, to be overcome only through death and resurrection. Ives's setting of the first two stanzas establishes the physical and temporal divide. The stability and purity of F major is associated with heaven, the persona's "home, rest, and dwelling place" where she is united for eternity with the holy trinity. (Recall the connotations of this key in "Majority" and "Slow March"; it is also the key of the triumphant chorus of "From Hanover North.") The ascending melodic lines highlighted in Example 1.3 reinforce the idea of the soul's resurrection. In stark contrast, the music of the temporal, earthly realm of Jesus's sacrifice, from which the persona is transported, is unstable, tonally diffuse, and weighted downward melodically; it strives for eternal union, and achieves it only in the divine harmonic transformation of mm. 16–17. The fact that we can plausibly imagine Ives having composed the F-major passages first and interpolating mm. 8–18 later enhances the sense that the relationship between the music of F major and the passage it envelops signifies the way in which God's eternity encompasses all that is temporal.

Within the larger interpolation of mm. 8–18, the setting of "Jesus" in mm. 11–12 invites its own interpretations. The musical isolation of Jesus's name creates a sense of grammatical isolation, as though the persona is calling out to Jesus, desperately longing for and attempting to hasten the union to come, just as Jesus himself had called out to God from the cross, a moment evoked by the reference to bloodshed in the text. The absence of a soprano line here and the shift to flats, both "corrected" by Kirkpatrick, effectively evoke absence and separation, the persona's isolation from Jesus and Jesus's from God. As the persona contemplates Jesus's suffering, and as we behold its musical image, she seems to wish to undo it, as the music reverses its course in mm. 12–13. But she looks forward as well, and her cries for union with God, linked with those of Jesus across time, are answered in m. 17 when the reprise of the interpolation from mm. 11–12 brings about the return to F major. This moment carries double weight, integrating the short interpolation while closing off the larger excursus of mm. 8–16. In sum, *I Come to Thee* uses the arrangement of musical ideas in time to express the temporal relationships of its subject matter: Jesus's suffering in the past, the persona's praise of God in the present, her expectancy of union with God in the future, and God's existence above time. By encouraging us to hear not only its actual chronology but also to imagine its implied, reconfigured chronologies, the music grants us access to a higher spiritual realm, one Ives increasingly sought to represent.

Psalm 14

Ives set numerous biblical psalms for choir, directed to this genre by his work as a church musician. Many of the settings are notably experimental. Among these is *Psalm 14,* one of several settings Ives composed around 1902 and revised about a decade later (c. 1912–13).[1] The text, adapted from the King James Bible, describes a world corrupted by atheism and sin, awaiting salvation. Ives's full text reads as follows:

1. The fool hath said in his heart, There is no God. They are corrupt, they have done abom'nable works, there is none that doeth good.
2. The Lord looked down from heav'n upon the children of men, to see if there were any that did understand, and seek God.
3. They are all gone aside, they are all together become filthy: there is none that doeth good, no, not one.
4. Have all the workers of iniquity no knowledge? who eat up my people as they eat bread, and call not upon the Lord.
5. There were they in great fear: for God is in the generation of the righteous.

	Choir I	Choir II
Verse 1	opening key: — closing key: CM (spans both)	
Verse 2	opening key: CM closing key: CM	
Verse 3		opening key: gm closing key: gm
Verse 4	opening key: d♭m closing key: CM	
Verse 5		opening key: a♭m closing key: G♭M
Verse 6	opening key: — closing key: gm (spans both)	
Verse 7	opening key: E♭M	opening key: b♭m
	closing key: E♭M + b♭m (spans both)	

Table 1.1. Formal overview of *Psalm 14*

6. Ye have shamed the counsel of the poor, because the Lord is his refuge.
7. Oh that the salvation of Israel were come out of Zion! when the Lord brin-
   geth back the captivity of his people, Jacob shall rejoice, and Israel shall be
   glad. [Amen.]

Ives set each verse as a distinct musical section, and he differentiated these from one another in several ways. The psalm is scored for two choirs, often heard in isolation in individual verses. Some verses mostly adhere to functional tonality; others do not. Most verses end with a clear tonal cadence, establishing a key that is immediately abandoned by the following verse. These differentiating elements are summarized in Table 1.1. The table shows how the verses are distributed between the two choirs, an organization that is straightforward until Verse 7, which features several alternations between the choirs followed by their union in the final measures. The tonality of each verse (or relative lack thereof) is simplified in the table, which shows only the key areas with which each verse begins and ends. In Verses 1 and 6, the initial tonality is ambiguous and thus omitted from the table; Verse 7 ends with a bitonal cadence that superimposes the two keys featured earlier in the verse.

As with *I Come to Thee*, Ives's setting of the text seems to have been designed to represent the separation of Man from God and their ultimate union. This basic idea is evident in the text itself. It is laid out clearly from the onset in Verses 1 and 2, and Ives makes it even more obvious in his setting of these verses. Verse 1 is disjointed rhythmically and largely incoherent tonally; this is the music of earthly corruption. Verse 2 is God's music: fluid, melodic, and firmly grounded in C major. The text of these verses fits naturally into Ives's dualistic worldview and seems to have inspired its particularly vivid expression in this piece. The text of the subsequent verses is not so neatly divided between the realms of God and Man, but Ives maintains a set of dual relationships, juxtaposing major and minor keys, tonality and atonality, rhythmic fluidity and disjunction, and the two choirs—not as part of any simple, uniform scheme, but primarily in ad hoc relation to the text.

The emphatic bitonal conclusion to the piece, where both choirs sing together, emerges as the inevitable musical expression of the corresponding text and its image of salvation and jubilation: "Jacob shall rejoice, and Israel shall be glad." At the simplest level, what makes this conclusion effective is Ives's split-choral scheme and the way it maps onto the basic narrative of separation and union. The choirs sing together in Verse 1, and the expectation of their eventual reunion hovers over the rest of the piece. This reunion is achieved in the penultimate verse, but the effect is not one of resolution; the text focuses not yet on salvation but on shame, and the music reflects this with the most tonally incoherent music of the piece. The text turns optimistic in Verse 7, but now the separation of the choirs is intensified: this is the only verse that features internal alternations between the two choirs. The alternating segments grow increasingly shorter in duration, however, until ultimately the choirs join one another, uniting for the final bitonal cadence.

The effect is not so much of a gradual coalescing of the choral forces as of a powerful collision. Each shift between choirs is marked by blunt tonal and registral disjunctions—that is, by the sort of fragmentation that characterizes much of Ives's music. This disjointed texture is disorienting and may even seem chaotic, an apparently odd means of setting the final line of text. But understood in terms of compositional design, its meaning becomes clearer. Verse 7 derives completely from Verses 2 and 3, which feature the most straightforwardly tonal and linear music of the piece. Verse 2 (the Lord in heaven) is in C major, and Verse 3 (his wayward children on Earth) transposes this music to G minor. In Verse 7, Ives reprises this music, transposed up a minor third to E♭ major and B♭ minor and divided between the choirs in the same way. But rather than simply reprising the music of Verse 2 followed by the music of Verse 3, he intercuts segments derived from each, jumping back and forth from one verse to another until the concluding union of the choirs. Example 1.4 summarizes, showing only the soprano lines in the interest of concision. The example reproduces Verses 2, 3, and 7 in their entirety, illustrating the derivation of Verse 7 by superimposing Verses 2 and 3.[2]

The example stops just short of the merging of Choirs I and II at the end of Verse 7. Here, Ives superimposes two cadential progressions that affirm the to-

Example 1.4. *Psalm 14,* derivation of Verse 7 from Verses 2 and 3.

nality of each choir: V–I, V–IV–I in the soprano and alto, affirming Choir I's E♭ major, and v–i, v–iv–i in the tenor and bass, affirming Choir II's B♭ minor (m. 59–end). These progressions do not correspond exactly to the ends of Verses 2 and 3, but they evoke those endings by cadencing on their respective tonics.

This derivation of Verse 7, once noticed, is clear and unmistakable, and it points toward similar stratifications of material elsewhere. Specifically, Verses 2–5 seem to be the product of intercutting in a manner analogous to Verse 7's derivation from Verses 2 and 3. Verses 2–5 are organized as two pairs. As mentioned, Verse 3 transposes the music of Verse 2 from C major to G minor—down a perfect fourth with a change of mode. Verses 4 and 5 introduce new material, organized in a similar way. Verse 4 begins in D♭ minor but quickly veers away, eventually finding its way to a C-minor cadence; Verse 5 transposes this music down a perfect fourth, maintaining this transpositional interval until the last two measures (mm. 40–41), where it stretches to an augmented fourth. As a result, where Verse 4 had descended a semitone from the initial key of D♭ to the concluding key of C, Verse 5 descends two, from A♭ to G♭. The analogous tonal relationships of Verses 2–3 and 4–5 are reinforced by the scoring: Verses 2 and 4

Verse 2 → Verse 3:	C major → G minor (mm. 18–19)
Verse 3 → Verse 4:	G minor → D♭ minor (mm. 25–27)
Verse 4 → Verse 5:	C minor → A♭ minor (mm. 33–35)
Verse 5 → Verse 6:	G♭ major → non-tonal harmonies (mm. 41–42)

Figure 1.2. *Psalm 14,* tonal shifts between verses.

are sung by Choir I, Verses 3 and 5 by Choir II. (Verse 6, scored for both choirs, stands outside of the scheme.) The choral shifts are underscored by jarring tonal shifts from the final cadence of one verse to the opening tonality of the next, as summarized in Figure 1.2. In all cases, successive verses are set off from one another by the juxtaposition of distantly related keys, and no overarching pattern of key relations is evident. In other words, in scoring and tonality, these verses are differentiated in the same way as the fragments of Verse 7; the final verse accelerates a process begun much earlier in the piece.

Furthermore, as with the fragments of Verse 7, when Verses 2–5 are realigned according to choirs, a much more logical tonal organization emerges that encompasses not only these four verses but Verse 7 as well. Figure 1.3 demonstrates, separating out the verses sung by each choir. In this reconfiguration, connections between verses are forged either by semitonal root motion (Verse 2 → Verse 4, Verse 3 → Verse 5) or by close key relations (Verse 4 → Verse 7, Verse 5 → Verse 7). In all cases, these connections are reinforced by parallel voice leading, as illustrated in Example 1.5. Overall, the music of Choir I is organized around parallel and relative key relations, as indicated on the example. The key structure of the music of Choir II is similar but not identical. Presumably, Ives thought it critical to maintain the tonal relationship of Verses 2 and 3 in the reprise of this music in Verse 7: the final verse transposes the music of Verses 2 and 3 up a minor third, as indicated on the example. But because Verse 3 inverts the mode of Verse 2, Ives could not organize the music of Choir II around parallel and relative key relations, as with the music of Choir I, and still end up at B♭ minor in Verse 7. Likely for this reason, the parallel and relative relations articulated by Choir I are not similarly articulated by Choir II.

Choir I:

| End of v. 2 → beg. of v. 4 (m. 18 → m. 27): | C major → D♭ minor |
| End of v. 4 → beg. of v. 7 (m. 33 → m. 47): | C minor → E♭ major |

Choir II:

| End of v. 3 → beg. of v. 5 (m. 25 → m. 35): | G minor → A♭ minor |
| End of v. 5 → beg. of v. 7 (m. 41 → m. 50): | G♭ major → B♭ minor |

Figure 1.3. *Psalm 14,* realignment of Verses 2–5 and 7, according to choirs.

Example 1.5. *Psalm 14*, connections between verses within each choir.

Example 1.5 shows that Verses 2–5 and 7 can be heard as the product of two interwoven musical trajectories, a larger-scale instance of the phenomenon that accounts for the disjointed music of Verse 7 itself. As outlined above, Verses 2 and 3 set up the braided texture of Verse 7: we hear in advance, and in their proper chronology, the interlocking components of Verse 7. Whereas the piece provides no such primer for the larger-scale hearing proposed in Example 1.5, it does condition this hearing in subtle ways. The C minor → E♭ major motion of Choir I (Verse 4 → Verse 7) is prefigured by the actual motion between the final chord of Verse 4 and the upbeat chord of Verse 5 (C minor → E♭ minor); and the G minor → A♭ minor motion of Choir II (Verse 3 → Verse 5) is prefigured by the actual motion between the final chord of Verse 3 and the upbeat harmony of Verse 4 (G minor → A♭ major). These associations with earlier portions of the piece make the displaced connections easier to perceive, and suggest that Ives's treatment of the interlocking choirs in Verses 2–5 was systematically planned.

To summarize: the form of *Psalm 14* is driven by linear musical successions whose constituent parts are separated from one another but gradually coalesce. From this point of view, the design bears a remarkable resemblance to the compositional strategy that Edward T. Cone outlined in his essay "Stravinsky: The Progress of a Method." Cone posited a three-phase compositional method that would account for the musical organization of works from all stages of Stravinsky's career, what he called "stratification," "interlock," and "synthesis":

> By stratification I mean the separation in musical space of ideas—or better, of musical areas—juxtaposed in time; the interruption is the mark of this separation.
> ... Since the musical ideas thus presented are usually incomplete and often apparently fragmentary, stratification sets up a tension between successive time segments. When the action in one area is suspended, the listener looks forward to its eventual resumption and completion; meanwhile action in another has begun, which in turn will demand fulfillment after its own suspension. The delayed satisfaction of these expectations occasions the second phase of the technique: the interlock. To take the simplest possible case, consider two ideas presented in alternation: A-1, B-1, A-2, B-2, A-3, B-3. Now one musical line will run through A-1, A-2, A-3; another will correspondingly unite the appearances of B. ... The most interesting phase of the

process, the synthesis, is the one most likely to be overlooked. Some sort of unification is the necessary goal toward which the entire composition points, for without it there is no cogency in the association of the component areas. . . . The diverse elements are brought into closer and closer relation with one another, all ideally being accounted for in the final resolution. (1962: 19–20)

This model is not broadly applicable to Ives's music, given the specificity of the three-stage process.[3] And whatever Cone's characterization of the process may imply, the actual musical connections between disparate musical fragments that he showed seem to be based much less on ordered linear connections than on unordered, associative ones. But putting aside Stravinsky's compositional practice, the theoretical model as Cone describes it fits *Psalm 14* remarkably well, and his analysis of the progression from fragmentation to unification provides an apt way of understanding the dynamics of Ives's psalm. The distinction between succession and simultaneity is critical and provides an important insight about Ives's unusual setting of the text. Just as the children of men strive for salvation, the music of Verses 2 and 3, firmly oriented in linear musical time, strives to transcend this temporal limitation when it returns in Verse 7. Ives's Verse 2 had been the music of God looking down on Earth, Verse 3 the music of the depraved inhabitants he saw there. Verse 7 attempts to erase this existential divide through the fragmentation and juxtaposition of the musical settings, bringing the music of each verse into closer contact and undermining their linearity, and thereby undermining their associations with worldly time. As the alternated segments become shorter, the sense of linear time is diminished until it is completely abolished in the final bitonal chords.[4] Separation gives way to synthesis; the mortal dissolves into a simple image of eternal harmony.

2 Community/Individual: Sonata No. 1 for Piano and String Quartet No. 2

Sonata No. 1 for Piano

Ives's first piano sonata is rooted in his experiences of late nineteenth-century New England life and his later idealization of that time and place. The basic program, according to two retrospective commentaries, concerns young men growing up and leaving their distressed families behind. As Ives wrote in *Memos*:

> What is it all about?—Dan S. asks. Mostly about the outdoor life in Conn. Villages in the '80s & '90s—impressions, remembrances, & reflections of country farmers in Conn. farmland.
>
> On page 14 back [of the first movement], Fred's Daddy got so excited that he shouted when Fred hit a home run & the school won the baseball game. But Aunt Sarah was always humming *Where is My Wandering Boy*, after Fred an' John left for a job in Bridgeport. There was usually a sadness—but not at the Barn Dances, with their jibs, foot jumping, & reels, mostly on winter nights.
>
> In the summer times, the hymns were sung outdoors, Folks sang (as *Old Black Joe*)—& the Bethel Band (quickstep street marches)—& the people like[d to say] things as they wanted to say, and to do things as they wanted to, in their own way—and many old times . . . there were feelings, and of spiritual fervency! (1972: 75)

This written scenario is compatible in its broad outlines, if not in all details, with an even shorter one remembered by John Kirkpatrick. According to Kirkpatrick, Ives once related to him a "possible aspect of the scenario" for the five movements of the sonata, a narrative of separation and reunion: "the family together in the first and last movements, the boy away sowing his oats in the ragtimes, and the parental anxiety in the middle movement" (1972: 75).

As implied by this summary, the sonata's five movements are arranged symmetrically. The outer movements are dramatic and weighty, the third is slow and subdued, and the second and fourth are set apart by their ragtime rhythms. Each of the ragtime movements is divided into two parts, numbered IIa and IIb, IVa and IVb. Although I discuss the sonata as a whole, my primary focus is on these ragtime movements, particularly IVb. These movements are largely derived from Ives's *Four Ragtime Dances* for theater orchestra, a set of short pieces that

Ragtime Dances	Sonata no. 1
No. 1	IIb
No. 2	IIa
No. 3	—
No. 4	IVb

Table 2.1. Derivation of Sonata no. 1 for Piano, scherzo movements, from *Ragtime Dances*.

in many ways resembles a single through-composed work. Ives recalled composing the *Ragtime Dances* during the years 1902–11; he assembled the sonata years later (c. 1915–16, 1921). Table 2.1 outlines the relationship between the two pieces. Most of the music in Movements IIa, IIb, and IVb of the sonata corresponds with music from the dances, whereas Ives composed IVa mostly of new material; the positions of the first and second dance are reversed in the sonata. Overall, the structure of the sonata can be understood in terms of a traditional four-movement sonata with an added scherzo. Given the derivation of Movements II and IV from the *Ragtime Dances,* however, these movements are better regarded as "a single scherzo, interrupted by the central third movement," as Dennis Marshall suggested (1968: 46). Significantly, both of these conceptions of the sonata's form regard one of the movements, either the slow movement or a scherzo, as an insertion that reconfigures the traditional four-movement sonata structure.

Marshall's notion of Movements II and IV as a single, interrupted scherzo suggests a radical formal concept, a view strengthened by the clear sense of a thematic process instigated in Movement II and completed in Movement IV. This process derives from the *Ragtime Dances* and is best understood in relation to it. Each of the four dances is structured as an extended "verse" followed by a short chorus. The "verse" sections do not resemble actual verses in any evident way; they earn this title mainly by virtue of preceding the choruses, which do function more or less like choruses, albeit unusually dramatic and inconclusive ones. The verse sections develop freely and intermittently the melody of the protestant hymn "Bringing in the Sheaves." Marshall and Burkholder cited the hymn "Happy Day" and the related tune "How Dry I Am" as borrowed sources as well, but if these tunes are referred to at all—Marshall and Burkholder provide little evidence—their roles are clearly much less significant. The choruses are taken from the refrain of another hymn, "I Hear Thy Welcome Voice," which they preserve in easily recognizable forms. One implication of this verse/chorus structure is that the entire set of dances can be conceived of as the hybrid of a multi-movement work and a strophic hymn.

But the analogy with strophic hymns is a loose one: each movement treats its source hymns differently, and the overall form is dynamic, not predictably repetitive. As in so much of Ives's music, closure is attained via melodic completion. In the first three dances, both of the source tunes are heard as incomplete.

Example 2.1. Ragtime Dance no. 4, mm. 103–04.

"Bringing in the Sheaves" is developed in fragments, whereas the refrain of "Welcome Voice" always stops short of its final cadence, ending on a hanging, unresolved dominant—V/G major in the first two movements, V/A major in the third. The fourth dance brings both hymns to completion. The verse section culminates in a boogie-woogie rendition of "Bringing in the Sheaves," featuring a triple-*forte*, tutti chorus (see mm. 63–93);[1] for this reason, Burkholder considered the piece an example of cumulative setting (1995: 212–14). As if to celebrate the long-awaited statement of the full tune, the final F-major tonic is extended as a wild, syncopated vamp for several measures (93–103), but now with a prominent added E♭, suggesting a functional change from tonic to dominant. At m. 103, the dominant is cut off abruptly, and after a brief pause, the music is suddenly calm (see Example 2.1, which converts the full score to two systems but maintains the full orchestral texture, save for the drum set). Immediately, the F dominant resolves, as the chorus of "Welcome Voice" returns once more, now in B♭ major (mm. 104–08). For most of the piece, the two source hymns had been kept separate and seemed to have little to do with one another, but now they are fused together harmonically. As though a symbol of this connection, the hymns are combined contrapuntally for the first time: the main melody of "Bringing in the Sheaves" is added as a countermelody to the "Welcome Voice" chorus. The final cadence extends the relationship, punning on the melodic cadence shared by the two choruses, î–ŝ–ẑ–î (Marshall 1968: 53). All has been brought into balance, and the final chorus, after the aborted attempts of the first three dances, cadences on the tonic, bringing the piece to an end.

In adapting the dances for the piano sonata, Ives reversed the order of the first two dances and eliminated the third, as outlined above. He replaced the third movement with a shorter one (IVa) that features relatively dissonant music and bears no obvious relationship to the other scherzo movements, aside from its syncopated rhythms. Each of the other three scherzo movements shares the verse-chorus structure of its respective dance, with the choruses following the same key scheme. Also following the dances, the choruses of IIa and IIb do not cadence, and IVb brings closure to the scherzo group with a statement of "Welcome Voice," in counterpoint with "Bringing in the Sheaves," on the tonic. Of these three movements, IIb differs most from its correlate in the *Dances;* Movements IIa and IVb share almost all of their sketch material with Dances Nos. 2 and 4, respectively. Nonetheless, because of the incomplete nature of much of this material, there is no definitive form for these movements. As James Sinclair has explained: "Ives did not personally rework his early ragtime materials for mvts ii[a] and iv[b] of this sonata. . . . Lou Harrison [one of the editors of the original 1954 edition of the sonata] . . . had to cope with sketches that were unfinished and which presented to him multiple options for some passages. Any performing version of these two sections necessarily must be considered merely provisional" (1999: 191).[2]

In some cases, comparison of the printed editions of the *Ragtime Dances* (edited by Sinclair) and the piano sonata draws attention to the "multiple options" to which Sinclair referred. For instance, aside from instrumentation, the most substantial discrepancy between the fourth dance and Movement IVb is the presence of an additional seven measures near the end of the sonata movement (mm. 150–56), wedged between the F dominant and its resolution as shown in Example 2.1, and set off from the surrounding music by double barlines on each side. Example 2.2 reproduces the ending of Movement IVb, beginning with the tail end of the sustained dominant.[3] By this point, the dominant has been prolonged for ten measures and is brimming over with frenetic energy and forward propulsion. As shown in the example, rather than resolving onto the B♭ tonic of the "Welcome Voice" chorus, the F dominant proceeds without pause to a non sequitur: a bastardized version of the chorus, with "Welcome Voice" played not in B♭ but in B major. The tune is accompanied by a mischievous bass line that vacillates between B and B♭ tonality; but the metrical treatment of the bass line combined with the B-major orientation of "Welcome Voice" in the right hand preserve a clear sense of an overriding B-major center. This deviant chorus, having undermined the triumphant tone of the preceding music, stomps to a brusque conclusion (m. 156), and a caesura sets up the true, B♭ chorus that had concluded the fourth ragtime dance. The chorus is slow and quiet, features that lacked a clear rationale in the *Ragtime Dances,* but now arise more naturally as consequences of the insertion and its negation of the force of the F dominant.

Ives's reworking of this ending can be observed in his sketches, particularly the last page of his ink sketch, f2480, reproduced in Example 2.3. The page is

Example 2.2. Sonata no. 1 for Piano, Movement IVb, mm. 144–62 (Charles Ives, Sonata no. 1 for Piano, used by Permission of Peer International Corporation).

Example 2.3. Sonata no. 1 for Piano, Movement IVb, ink sketch (f2480) (Charles Ives, Sonata no. 1 for Piano, used by Permission of Peer International Corporation).

dominated by sketches for the F dominant, with original indications for this dominant to proceed directly to the B♭ chorus; see the lower-right corner, where a sign points toward the B♭ chorus as sketched elsewhere. Ives crammed a draft of the B-major version of the chorus on this same page, however; see the right-hand side of the second and third systems. The chaotic nature of the insertion is reflected by the great number of scribbles and looping arrows Ives needed to convey his new conception of the passage.

The B-major insertion is striking for the way it pulls out the rug from under the seemingly inevitable resolution of the emphatic F dominant of the preceding measures. According to the script of the *Ragtime Dances,* m. 150 should instigate large-scale closure by forging at long last a harmonic and melodic connection between the two borrowed hymns and, as a symbol of this union, by allowing "Welcome Voice" to cadence properly. But the sonata systematically weakens the cumulative force of the final dance and its ending through a series of interpolations and substitutions: first, Movement III, which divides the dances into two isolated pairs; next, Movement IVa, which abandons the verse-chorus pattern and the identifiable borrowings of the other ragtime movements; and finally, the B-major insertion in Movement IVb.

The conclusion of Movement IVb can be heard in at least two different ways. In one hearing, the unexpected B-major tonality arrives as a botched resolution of the F dominant pedal: the attempted resolution is one semitone too low, a musical mistake that accounts for the unsettled character of the false chorus. The real chorus follows as a correction, one that essentially ignores or undoes the error. A sense of struggle between the false and real resolutions is projected by the bass line of the B-major passage, which staggers back and forth between the competing tonics. In the second and more provocative hearing, the dominant does resolve properly to the B♭ chorus, but at a different temporal level. The compositional history of Movement IVb encourages this nonchronological hearing over the other. The F dominant did, in fact, proceed directly to the B♭ chorus at one stage of Ives's sketches, as preserved in the fourth *Ragtime Dance;* thus, in this hearing, the B-major parody-chorus of Movement IVb is a literal interpolation.

In sum, Ives's sonata places various complications upon the processes of melodic completion that define the form of the *Ragtime Dances,* inserting two essentially unrelated movements (III and IVa) and disrupting the climactic cadence. To understand why, it is essential to turn to Ives's programmatic commentary and the tunes he chose to incorporate in the sonata. Both sources of meaning raise tricky methodological issues. Burkholder addressed the significance of the sonata's retroactive programs in relation to the sonata's cumulative settings. After listing several ways in which the programmatic details are ill suited to the music they purport to elucidate, he concluded that "the only relation between either of these 'programs' and the piece itself is one of overall mood or character, the evocation of certain kinds of music and certain states of feeling"; retroactive programs "should be understood as explaining only the character of the music, not its structure, form, or meaning. What happens in these pieces is based on musical rather than programmatic ideas, and primarily on the formal plan of cumulative setting" (1995: 248–50).

The limits Burkholder placed around the significance of *ex post facto* programs may have been a reaction against scholars who have taken Ives's programmatic impulse and adopted it indiscriminately, seeking concrete stories that help to "explain" any or all of Ives's esoteric musical forms. But surely the simple fact that Ives's programmatic interpretation of a piece postdates its composition does not necessarily exclude it from a role in the compositional process. Why couldn't a program have informed Ives's formal plan for a piece, regardless of when—or if—Ives chose to tell anyone about it? Consider Kirkpatrick's recollection that the scherzo movements of the sonata concern a "boy sowing his oats." This turn of phrase is suggestive, given that the music of these movements features a cumulative setting of the hymn "Bringing in the Sheaves," whose first verse features the following lyrics:

> Sowing in the morning, sowing seeds of kindness,
> Sowing in the noontide and the dewy eve;
> Waiting for the harvest, and the time of reaping,
> We shall come rejoicing, bringing in the sheaves.

In conjunction with this text, Ives's comments to Kirkpatrick suggest that the sonata evokes and contrasts two kinds of "sowing"—one wholesome, one not—and forges a musical narrative from the tension between them. Furthermore, this association between two senses of "sowing" suggests a link between Ives's minuscule program about familial separation and reunion and the now-familiar notion of reunion with God that is central to "Bringing in the Sheaves." If these suggestions are valid, the programmatic idea likely *preceded* the music, influencing Ives's selection of the hymn, and perhaps informing its cumulative setting as well.

In addition to cautioning against the use of Ives's retrospective program notes to make interpretive claims, Burkholder has been similarly circumspect about incorporating the texts of borrowed tunes in interpretive studies: "It is typical of Ives's uses of borrowed tunes from [the first string quartet] on that, although the overall character of the tune is important and the subject or spirit of the text may be as well, the specific words tend not to be" (1995: 74). Once again, however, Burkholder's stance is too limiting. In the scherzo movements, Ives makes prominent use of familiar tunes, and it is not a simple matter to "turn off" the associated lyrics while listening, nor is there any reason to think that this would be desirable. More generally and more importantly, when confronted with borrowed music, it is not clear why close readings of the associated texts should be discouraged. Surely Ives would have been familiar with these texts, and I assume that their "specific words" informed his sense of their "subject or spirit." If we hope to discern the latter, we should attend to the former as well.

Several borrowed tunes feature prominently in the sonata. Although the scherzo movements are my primary focus, it would be difficult to interpret them convincingly in isolation, and so I will consider all five movements.[4] As Burkholder has outlined in detail (1995: 187–92), the first movement features a cumulative setting of the Baptist hymn "Lebanon," better known as "I Was a Wandering Sheep." The tune, with a decorated cadence, emerges clearly during an extended passage at the end of the movement (beginning with the last system on p. 9). The text uses the wandering sheep as a metaphor for Christians who lose their faith only to have it restored by Jesus, charting a temporal journey from remembered past to present. This trajectory is evident from the first and last stanzas:

> I was a wandering sheep, I did not love the fold;
> I did not love my Shepherd's voice, I would not be controlled.
> I was a wayward child, I did not love my home;
> I did not love my Father's voice, I loved afar to roam.
>
> [...]
>
> No more a wandering sheep, I love to be controlled;
> I love my tender Shepherd's voice, I love the peaceful fold.
> No more a wayward child, I seek no more to roam;
> I love my heavenly Father's voice, I love, I love His home!

The first movement also seems to incorporate the opening snippet of "Where Is My Wandering Boy?" by the hymnist Robert Lowry, as Burkholder (1995: 187–91) and several others have argued; see the upper system of m. 101, beginning at the *agitato* marking, for the two potential references to the tune. The borrowing is questionable from a purely musical perspective, but is strengthened considerably by the connection between the texts of "Wandering Sheep" and Lowry's song. In the latter, the wandering subject has grown up, left home, and is mourned after by his mother:

> O where is my boy tonight?
> O where is my boy tonight?
> My heart o'erflows, for I love him, he knows;
> O where is my boy tonight?

The idea of Christians returning to their heavenly father, explicit in "Wandering Sheep" and perhaps metaphoric in "Wandering Boy," has evident similarities to the themes of "Welcome Voice" and "Bringing in the Sheaves."[5] The refrain of "Welcome Voice," featured in Movements 2 and 4 as we have seen, is about coming home to God:

> I am coming Lord!
> Coming now to Thee!
> Wash me, cleanse me in the blood
> That flowed on Calvary!

And "Bringing in the Sheaves," using farming as a metaphor, celebrates the reward in heaven that stems from Christian sacrifice on Earth (see the first verse above).

Nestled in the center the sonata, the third movement features a peaceful cumulative setting of the hymn "Erie" (Burkholder 1995: 188–89, 192–93), better known as "What a Friend We Have in Jesus," whose verses all address the troubles of life and the solace to be found in Jesus. Verse 3 provides a representative example:

> Are we weak and heavy laden, cumbered with a load of care?
> Precious Savior, still our refuge, take it to the Lord in prayer.
> Do your friends despise, forsake you? Take it to the Lord in prayer!
> In His arms He'll take and shield you; you will find a solace there.

Finally, in Movement V, a portion of "I Was a Wandering Sheep" surfaces once again, briefly, in mm. 5–9 and 207–12 (Burkholder 1995: 244). The finale eschews extended or obvious instances of borrowing, however, in favor of the development of abstract motivic cells; the clandestine returns of "Wandering Sheep" seem mainly features of the symmetrical movement structure as opposed to programmatically significant events.

Despite the relative absence of borrowed music in the finale, the prominence of hymn tunes in the other movements clearly suggests an overarching sacred theme. More specifically, a recurring aspect of the texts of these hymns is the idea of the Earth-bound soul returning to God. The sonata seems to reflect this idea through a sacred/secular duality: in the ragtime movements, Ives gives his hymns a secular treatment that flirts with sacrilege, whereas in Movements I and III he treats them with appropriate reverence. Furthermore, the cumulative settings of Movement I, Movement III, and the composite scherzo of Movements II and IV, each driving toward melodic completion and closure, convey persistent spiritual striving. Cumulative setting is a versatile form that lends itself to a variety of expressive strategies, but the dominant theme of wandering and returning to God in this sonata helps to bring the meaning of the form into focus. This is particularly the case in the scherzo movements, where "I am coming Lord!" is the call of each chorus, ultimately provided a peaceful setting in its final utterance.

Considered in conjunction with the borrowed hymns and their employment in the sonata, Ives's programmatic commentary suggests ways to build upon this understanding of the sonata in relation to the theme of wandering and return. This commentary should not be applied to the piece uncritically, but given its apparent connection to the themes established by the borrowed music, it would be a mistake to ignore it. Both the short program cited by Kirkpatrick and the longer one related by Ives in *Memos* bear obvious relation to the texts of the borrowed music. The boy's departure from and return to his family in the shorter program, like the allegory of "I Was a Wandering Sheep," emphasizes the theme of separation from and return to God featured in each of the hymns. The boy of the Kirkpatrick program would seem to be the wandering boy away from home, the wayward soul drifting from God, sowing his oats rather than seeds of kindness. His journey back to his family follows the spiritual journey so prominent in the hymns, particularly that of "I Was a Wandering Sheep"; his return home is a return to the community of God. In the program from *Memos,* Ives gave the wandering boy a name (Fred) and a reason for leaving home (a job); he also tied his absence explicitly to the hymn "Where Is My Wandering Boy."

These basic themes and programmatic ideas do not enable any sort of comprehensive interpretation of the sonata: the music is much too complex and unruly to be summed up so simply. But they do suggest ways of understanding many critical musical moments and aspects of the quasi-symmetrical five-movement structure. The emphasis on wandering in the music Ives chose to borrow suggests that the oats-sowing boy, rather than his family and community back home, is the programmatic focal point of the sonata. It is difficult to find convincing representations of familial togetherness in the outer movements, for example, but there is a strong sense of departure at the end of the first movement, of a journey begun. The first movement ends with a protracted statement of "I Was a Wandering Sheep" in B major (beginning at p. 9/5), but it is interrupted and never cadences satisfactorily. Although the melody ultimately resolves on the tonic, this resolution is undermined by the supporting harmonic progression, E major → A major (IV–VII) in the left hand, and a lower third, G#, harmonizing the arrival on B in the right. The ending is thus decidedly open tonally. If one hears the hymn text in the background, the first verse ("I was a wayward child, I did not love my home") is much more appropriate than the last ("No more a wayward child, I seek no more to roam"). The melody wants to roam no more, but the harmony, lacking any clear tonal direction through much of the first movement, will not comply. And thus continues the boy's wandering—and the soul's.

If sowing oats is the primary subject of the scherzo movements, then the prominence of ragtime in these movements suggests that the pursuits are undertaken within the seedy culture of bars and brothels in which this music was typically played. A cue pointing toward this meaning is the subtitle of Movement IIb, "In the Inn." Yet the presence of the family back at home never fully recedes into the background. "Bringing in the Sheaves," a song of proselytizing, serves as a frequent reminder of the family's desire to bring the boy back to his community and to God, and the recurring chorus, "I am coming, Lord!," tells of the boy's eventual return. But this return is continually delayed by the non-resolving choruses of Movements IIa and IIb and the digression of Movement III. The latter can be heard narratively as a cutaway—"meanwhile, back at home . . ." This movement may concern "parental anxiety," as the Kirkpatrick program suggests, but this anxiety seems to have been confronted and controlled. The music is prayer-like in temperament, its peacefulness a reflection of constant faith. As the source hymn advises: "Are we weak and heavy laden, cumbered with a load of care? Precious Savior, still our refuge, take it to the Lord in prayer."

When the resolution of "Welcome Voice" finally arrives at the end of Movement IVb, having been further delayed by Movement IVa and the B-major interpolation, the chorus—always rowdy in its previous iterations—takes on the hymn-like tranquility featured in Movement III. The two principal themes of the ragtime movements are now united for the first time, as though the prayers have been answered. The sheaves have been brought in; the boy is home; the soul is at rest. It would be easy to mistake the ending of Movement IVb for the ending of the sonata—it is the equivalent, in fact, of the ending for the *Ragtime Dances*. But the pungent opening of Movement V annihilates the hard-won peace of the previous movement. In its higher level of abstraction, grander sense of proportion, and failure to participate in the patterns of musical borrowing established by the earlier movements, the finale seems to stand apart from or supersede the rest of the sonata. As Burkholder noted, Movement V is the only movement in the sonata that is not structured around a cumulative setting (1995: 243), and according to Sinclair, the movement "gave Ives particular problems."

The key to incorporating the last movement into a programmatic interpretation of the sonata, I would argue, is found in a section of the movement least representative of its overall character. Despite its bombast, Movement V has a soft core: the *Adagio cantabile* music of mm. 131–47, anchored over a C-pedal in the bass. The passage begins with a short melodic motive that derives from earlier movements: see the uppermost line of m. 131. Prominent incarnations of this motive earlier in the sonata include Movement I, mm. 3 and 21; Movement IIa, m. 1; Movement IIb, m. 73; and Movement III, m. 1. In its ultimate appearance, the motive emerges as though a revelation, stated simply in the key of C major after a prolonged transition away from the feistiness that characterizes the first half of the movement (see mm. 126–30; Ives added a performance indication instructing that "This passage to the Adagio cantabile should be a dissolving kind of thing"). The entire C-major passage feels like the culmination of the sonata's spiritual trajectory, given its position within the movement and the sonata as a whole; its key, which Ives associated with purity and transcendence; and its position at the end of a series of closely related motives that originated in the opening measures of the sonata. Contributing further to the sense of cyclical closure, the passage is strongly reminiscent of a parallel passage in Movement I, mm. 21–27. Both passages are quiet and dreamy, primarily diatonic, and characterized by rolling, Chopinesque arpeggiations in the left hand anchored over pedal points (C♯ in Movement I).

Ives adapted the C-major passage from (or possibly into) a self-standing "Take-Off" for piano solo that he called "Scene-Episode," a title that suggests something about its meaning here: this interlude, and the parallel one in the first movement, might offer the glimpse of familial harmony that is referred to in the Kirkpatrick program. More intriguingly, as part of the sonata's implied metaphysical program, this episode might be a musical image of the spiritual goal with which the sonata and its source hymns are concerned, the soul's reunion with God. In this regard, it is well worth noting the resemblance between Ives's C-major motive and the definitive tonic statement of the "Ideal Theme" in Richard Strauss's *Tod und Verklärung*. As shown in Example 2.4, the two figures are identical in pitch save for their penultimate notes. They are also metrically similar, despite their notation: Ives's initial G sounds like an upbeat because of the left-hand C coordinated with the following note. Strauss's tone poem builds to the "soaring of the soul upward into heavenly regions," as Strauss's sense of the program was characterized by Walter Werbeck (Hepokoski 1998: 611). This image comes through clearly with the work's title alone as an interpretative guide; if Ives knew *Tod und*

(a)

(b)

Example 2.4. (a) Ives, Sonata no. 1 for Piano, Movement V, m. 131; (b) Strauss, *Tod und Verklärung,* "Ideal Theme."

Verklärung, he no doubt would have appreciated the shared impulse to conclude a piece by reaching for the heavens, however he might have regarded Strauss at the time.

The symbolic importance of C major for Ives was not unlike its significance for Strauss (think of the opening of *Also Sprach Zarathustra*), and the absence of this key earlier in Ives's sonata points toward an ongoing drama of key relationships. If C tonality is the apotheosis of the drama, C♯ is the beginning, similarly nestled in the middle of the first movement (mm. 21–27), but dominated by black keys rather than white, the point of furthest remove that marks the beginning of the spiritual journey in the same way that C major marks its end. There is no easily identifiable path between the two in the sonata, but the sonata does seem to be occupied with negotiating this tonal space. The C♯ mixolydian scale (six sharps) featured in the middle of Movement I, for instance, is succeeded by B major at the end of the movement (five sharps), and E major at the end of Movement III (four sharps), all suggesting a gradual movement toward C major: 6♯→5♯→4♯→[. . .]→0♯. Interspersed with this trajectory, however, are the ending choruses of Movements IIa and IIb, in G major (one sharp) and A major (three sharps), respectively. The latter trajectory moves in the wrong direction, a danger heightened by the unexpected intrusion of B major near the end of Movement IVb: 1♯→3♯→5♯. The B♭ chorus that follows as a corrective serves to stop the wrong-way progression of sharps by shifting to the flat side: now, if the whole-step ascent continues, it will lead directly to C: 2♭→0♭. The B♭ chorus accomplishes this redirection of tonal motion while preserving a sense of directed key relationships among the three "Welcome Voice" choruses: as in the *Ragtime Dances,* it completes a chain of tonics rising by steps, G–A–B♭, that lends added cohesion to the scherzo movements and constitutes another component of the implied spiritual journey.

The B-major interpolation, then, occupies the crux of two opposing tonal motions, one toward the black keys, one toward the white. These motions can be heard to signify, at the most concrete programmatic level, the opposing paths taken by the boy, his literal and spiritual journeys. The interpolation itself can be understood in multiple ways, each with a distinctive temporal meaning—specifically, as present-, future-, or past-oriented. If priority is given to the symbolic weight of the oscillation between B♭ and B that characterizes the bass line, the boy's future can be heard to lie in the balance, as he struggles to choose between two divergent paths in the present moment. Understood in this way, the deviant quality of this passage is an expression of temptation, the dark forces at work on the protagonist, threatening to derail his journey home in its final moments. But the lack of a linear thread connecting the interpolation to its musical surroundings undermines this interpretation. The interpolation essentially ignores the music that precedes it, and the following chorus responds to the interpolation in the same way, as though the detour never happened—which, of course, at an earlier compositional stage, it didn't. Further weakening any sense that the interpolation participates in the representation of a linear sequence of events, the passage is not actually tonally ambiguous; despite its unstable bass line, B♭ is clearly subsidiary to B, as explained above.

For these reasons, the interpolation is better regarded as anachronous with regard to its narrative meaning. By reinvigorating the succession of keys associated with the earlier choruses, G major–A major–B *major,* and by preserving the ragtime rhythms of these choruses as well, the interpolation might suggest a glimpse into an alternative future where the boy's rabble-rousing continues, a future that is not revealed as false until the true resolution of the F dominant arrives to supersede the incorrect one. B major is also the key of the final section of the first movement, in which the boy's roaming is just beginning; the return of this key brings the boy's journey full circle. This connection suggests, alternatively, that the boy takes a final look back at his oats-sowing period before leaving it behind. In this view, the interpolation is a memory, a flashback. This interpretation might be the most convincing, and it is enhanced by what happens after the interpolation: the B♭ chorus looks back to the end of the first movement as well. Just as the final B-major cadence of Movement I is undermined by a suspended A-major triad, so is the final B♭-major cadence of Movement IVb colored by the same suspended triad (see Example 2.5). The effect is quite different, however. The A-major triad is cut off prior to the B♭ tonic, and thus there is no sense of the resolution being weakened, of the boy's return being called into question. The triad is subsumed within the inner register as well, locked within the B♭ triad analogous to the way the B-major interpolation is locked within the key of B♭ (A and B are in fact balanced around B♭ semitonally). Nonetheless, the A-major chord of Movement IVb contributes to the sense of retrospection, casting its gaze on a specific moment, the final chord of Movement I.

Ultimately, the most compelling argument for hearing the B-major interpolation as retrospective is the overall nature of the sonata. Composed in the early twentieth century, the sonata records "impressions, remembrances, & reflec-

Example 2.5. Sonata no. 1 for Piano, Movement IVb, end.

tions" of Connecticut farmers from the end of the twentieth, as Ives described it in *Memos*. As with so much of Ives's music, the sonata is best understood not simply as music that represents the past, but as music that represents the act of examining the past. Retrospection is staged by the music, which frames the past from the vantage point of the present. Musically, retrospection is evoked systematically at the ends of movements. Each ending lacks either force or stability, an effect Ives often associates with temporal fluidity, memory, and nostalgia. When the first movement concludes with a hanging, isolated non-tonic triad, for instance, we can hear not only Aunt Sarah's sadness at Fred and John's departure for Bridgeport, but the solitary modern subject—or Ives himself—recalling the vibrant communal experiences of his youth. Similarly, the interpolation of Movement IVb is best understood not only as a remembrance of boyhood, but as a representation of a young man's looking back at his youthful adventures at the onset of adulthood, and as part of Ives's larger meditation on his own youth and on mortality in general. In his preface to the published score, the pianist William Masselos wrote: "I came to realize performer and copyist were both archaeologists . . . working at the piece's very inception, its *arche*" (1990: iii). He might have gone even further: the sonata's composer, as he so often did, was working as an archaeologist of his own personal and cultural history.

String Quartet No. 2

According to Ives, he composed the second string quartet intermittently between 1907 and 1913; the completed score dates from c. 1913–15. It is the only multi-movement work Ives completed after *The Celestial Country* (1898–1902) whose movements all belong to an "original grand conception," as opposed to being partially or completely culled from earlier pieces (Burkholder 1985: 88). This special status—which it would have shared with the *Universe Symphony,* had the symphony's conception not proved too grand to realize—can be taken as encouragement to listen to and analyze the quartet somewhat differently from Ives's other multi-movement pieces, with an ear more open to connections among movements.

As usual, Ives provided some indications of the inspiration for the piece and its meaning, which strengthen the notion that Ives conceived of the quartet movements as integrated components of a single musical narrative. The three movements are subtitled "Discussions," "Arguments," and "The Call of the Mountains." Ives fleshed out these programmatic clues with a note on the first page of his pencil sketch of the piece, suggesting the topic of controversy with which the first two movements are concerned, and illuminating the cryptic title of the third: "SQ for 4 men—who converse, discuss, argue in re 'Politick,' fight, shake hands, shut up—then walk up the mountain side to view the firmament!" Years later, Ives's comments in *Memos* explained his impetus for composing the piece:

> It used to come over me . . . that music had been, and still was, too much of an emasculated art. Too much of what was easy and usual to play and to hear was called beautiful, etc.—the same old even-vibration, Sybaritic apron-strings, keeping music too much tied to the old ladies. The string quartet music got more and more weak, trite, and effeminate. After one of those Kneisel Quartet concerts in the old Mendelssohn Hall, I started a string quartet score, half mad, half in fun, and half to try out, practise, and have some fun with making those men fiddlers get up and do something like men. (1972: 74)

Ives is characteristically argumentative regarding the "emasculation" of music, one of his numerous diatribes on the subject. Here and elsewhere, Ives used sexist conceptions of the masculine and feminine as means of establishing a dichotomy between tradition and innovation in music. One of his clearest articulations of the tension between the two—in this case mostly free of gender stereotyping—is found in *Memos,* in a short section that begins with an account of his conventional musical education at Yale. Ives argues for an extended concept of tonality based on a less constrained and more imaginative understanding of the natural basis of music:

> Look at a fugue. . . . So, if the first statement of the theme is in a certain key, and the second statement is in a key a 5th higher, why can't (musically speaking) the third entrance sometimes go another 5th higher, and the fourth statement another 5th higher? . . . "Because Bach didn't do it," Rollo says, "and that's the best reason I know." The reasons of the others are not as good as Rollo's. One Mus. Doc. [music doctor] says, "Because it destroys tonality." Having four nice different men playing tennis together doesn't always destroy personality—tonality is more of a man-made thing than personality. Then the Musdock says, "It violates the true, fundamental, natural laws of tone." Does it? What are the true, fundamental, natural laws of tone? The people who talk and tell you exactly what they are, who teach them explicitly, who write treatises about them—ipso facto,—know less about them than the deaf man who wonders! They measure a vibrating string and want to tie your ears to it. When it's easy to catch the vibration, then it's "natural," and they smile. When it's hard, then they scold or get mad, or go to sleep. (1972: 49–50)

In both quotations, Ives lambastes regressive compositional perspectives. In the first, his pun on the word "strings" suggests that he regarded the quartet genre itself, with its four instruments each featuring a quartet of vibrating strings, as particularly old-fashioned—hence his choice of the string quartet as the genre via which to stage his re-masculation/de-feminization of music. Although the second quotation does not refer specifically to the genre, it does concern four-part writing and vibrating strings, and the odd analogy of four tennis players evokes not only a quartet but also, with its emphasis on the individual personalities of the players, Ives's last contribution to the quartet genre. Additionally, his comments about scholars who defend music's "natural laws" resonate strongly with the narrative of the "Arguments" movement, as I suggest below. Ives's idea of organizing fugal entrances in a sequence of perfect fifths is realized in the same movement: see the fugue that begins in mm. 42–46, with successive entrances on G, D, A, and E. These entrances evoke the tuning of the violin, and the natural tuning of string instruments is a recurring reference point in the quartet. All this calls into question the primacy of his identification of "Politick" as the topic of his fiddlers' debate; the much more pressing issue would seem to be "Musick."[6]

Perhaps the strongest link between the above passage from *Memos* and the second quartet is the presence of "Rollo," a recurring character in Ives's prose (particularly in *Memos*) whom Ives drew from a popular series of books for adolescents and regarded, as Kirkpatrick explained, as "a symbol of the literal mind unable to imagine anything beyond what he'd been taught" (Ives 1972: 26–27). Rollo is the embodiment of the emasculated musician in the second quartet, and Ives refers to him several times in his marginal notes on the pencil score. Most concretely, Rollo emerges in portions of the "Arguments" movement, identified with the second violin. At m. 31, in the midst of an aggressively dissonant *tutti* vamp, the second violin unexpectedly begins an effusive, tonal (albeit tonally unfocused) melody that eventually brings the other instruments to stunned silence (m. 34). Ives labels this melody a "burlesque cadenza" with the performance indication "Andante Emasculata" ("pretty tone, Ladies!"), and the other instruments twice respond in angry outbursts, the first marked triple-*forte* and "Allegro con fisto Cut it out! Rollo!" (m. 37).[7] Eventually, Rollo coaxes his colleagues into a short "Largo sweetota" in A♭ major (m. 40), or perhaps they merely mock him. Either way, they abruptly reject this sentimental lapse with a third "con fisto" outburst (m. 41), leaving the dominant of A♭ to hang unresolved. This is one of the most memorable and best-known passages in the quartet, and it is supercharged with the composer's very real hostility: here is a rare instance of Ives's homophobia and related frustration with contemporary musical culture taking center stage in his music.

Ives's objections to Rollo's music are twofold: Rollo displays virtuosity for its own sake, and his tastes are melodramatic. The *con fisto* responses of the other instruments, on the other hand, are to be heard as pure Ives: rugged and dissonant, no-nonsense music. The chasm between Rollo's and Ives's music is indicated by the stark and unmediated clashes between them and the apparent complete lack of influence of either perspective on the other. Rollo is not the least bit deterred by the other players' fists of fury, which seem to have been shaking almost continuously from m. 1. After each interruption of his cadenza, he takes

Example 2.6. (a) String Quartet no. 2, "Arguments," mm. 36–37 (*Allegro con fisto*); (b) embedded stack of fifths.

up where he previously left off, on the most recently sounded pitch or pitch class; see the B♮s of mm. 36 and 37 and the A♯ and B♭ of mm. 39 and 40, respectively. The three *con fisto* responses are all essentially the same, consisting of repetitive triple-*forte* chords that crystallize the pitch material of mm. 1–34; the first response is excerpted in Example 2.6 (a). (This and subsequent examples reduce the quartet score to two staves for concision; first violin and viola are represented by upward stems, second violin and cello by downward.) Embedded within these chords, as shown in part (b) of the example, is a stack of perfect fifths corresponding to the cello's open strings, with the upper two pitches transposed up an octave. This particular stack of fifths recurs as a motive throughout the quartet. In the "Discussions" movement, for instance, see mm. 25, 37, and 41; the fugal entrances of mm. 42–46; and, most obviously, the open fifths of the final two measures, marked "Andante con scratchy (as tuning up)." See also "The Call of the Mountains," mm. 28 and 117. In "Arguments," the C–G–D–A skeleton remains stable throughout the first two *con fisto* passages, with D and A sustained in counterpoint with their chromatic displacements in different registers: B♭ and G♯ sound above A in the first violin, and C♯ and E♭ below D in the viola and cello. Thus, the strings' harsh and aggressive chords are structured around a simple and harmonious core, suggesting that Ives is more interested here in extending the "natural laws of tone" than in musical chaos.

The antagonism between the second violin and the other instruments mostly subsides after the "Largo sweetota" and the final *con fisto* response. For the remainder of the movement, despite evident tensions within the ensemble, the second violin is not singled out for ridicule in any obvious way.[8] The pointed and fairly specific conflict of mm. 31–41, which had no precedent in the "Discussions" movement or the first thirty measures of "Arguments," is left hanging for the remainder of the piece in favor of a more general sense of conflict and resolution within the ensemble. But the "Largo sweetota" is not quite so isolated a moment as it seems. This interrupted cadential gesture in A♭ major has its counterpart early on in the first movement, mm. 9–10. The two passages are closely linked,

Example 2.7. String Quartet no. 2, hypothetical connection between (a) "Arguments,"
mm. 40–41 ("Largo sweetota"), and (b) "Discussions," mm. 9–10 (actual and
recomposed versions).

despite their separation in performance time. They are the only passages in the
quartet to invoke the key of A♭ major, and among the very few instances in which
Ives makes extended use of functional tonality at all. There are strong melodic
similarities as well. The viola lines are nearly exact permutations of one another
and feature similar triplet figures beginning on the downbeats of their respective second measures; and the first violin's distinctive downward leap F–G in the
"sweetota" is embedded in the "Discussions" passage, with the same rhythm and
metric position.

In addition to these associative connections, however, the most striking relationship between the passages is linear, based on harmonic syntax. As shown in
Example 2.7, mm. 9–10 of "Discussions" provide a continuation and near resolution of the "sweetota" gesture. The resulting harmonic progression is straightforward, as indicated on the example, and the second pair of measures balances
the first. The only wrinkle—a significant one—is the failure of the second pair
to cadence on the tonic: the anticipated but unrealized cadence is shown on the
lower system of the example. The effect of this linear connection is much different
from that of the associative one; the "sweetota" does not simply recall the earlier
passage but envisages a return to it.

These two forays into A♭ major are crucial moments in the narratives of their
respective movements. "Discussions" is concerned in part with the relative merits

of tradition and innovation in music, particularly of traditional tonality and the more flexible and adventurous forms of musical organization that Ives espoused. The movement is predominantly atonal but features numerous attempts—often non sequiturs—to establish C, the cello's grounding string, as a tonic or tonal center: for a few examples among many, see mm. 18–19, 40–41, 78–82, and 125–32. The opening chord of the movement establishes the main topic of the conversation. A sustained C-minor triad in the violins and viola is pitted against an atonal melody beginning on F♯ in the viola. Atonality pervades the polyphonic texture of the first eight measures, and m. 9 arrives as a return to the tonal perspective suggested in m. 1, as the A♭ major triad creates an audible link to the opening sonority: with a single semitonal shift, C–E♭–G becomes C–E♭–A♭, with no changes in register. But the new key cannot gain traction. The A♭ progression fails to cadence and leads back instead to a reprise of the opening chord (end of m. 10). After this earnest attempt at traditional closure fails, subsequent attempts in the movement are often ironic, beginning with the forced arrival on C-major in m. 19. The movement ends essentially where it began, settling back on the opening sonority (m. 131). The circularity of the first ten measures has been replicated on the large scale, and the implication is clear: the discussions have achieved nothing.

The stage is now set for the second movement, where any hope of a simple tonal resolution has been abandoned, and the ironic veneer has only grown thicker. In his sketch of the piece, at the onset of the white-note passagework in "Arguments," mm. 74–76, Ives mocked the key: "Join us again Prof. M 'all in key of C. you can? Nice and pretty, Rollo.'" C major, Ives's favored symbol of purity and transcendence, has been completely trivialized in Rollo's hands. And thus the Largo sweetota's recollection of the first movement (mm. 9–10) can be understood as a jaded look back at a less contentious stage in the ongoing drama, when it seemed possible that tonality could be defended and preserved as a foundation for meaningful music. The possibility of actually returning to that earlier moment, as it is illustrated in Example 2.7, offers nothing more than a dead end, continued cycling through the fruitless "discussions" and the inevitable impasse of their emblematic sonority.

Later in "Arguments," in response to the "nice and pretty" C-major music of mm. 74–76, the players again display their disdain for this kind of music, this time with an outburst marked *"Allegro con fuoco (all mad)"* (mm. 77–81), a varied reprise of the opening of the movement. Ives's pencil score abandons the character of Rollo from this point in the quartet onward, and now all four instruments are united in their rage, although suddenly isolated musically; each unleashes its short tirade in turn. What happens next is subtle but critical. The ensemble reunites (mm. 81–82, marked *rit.* and *meno mosso*), and Ives provides a glimpse of the resolution to come, the ostinato-layered apotheosis of "The Call of the Mountains" (mm. 123–40 of the third movement). The latter section is anchored by whole-tone scales descending from D in the cello, and this scale begins to materialize in m. 84 of "Arguments," moving from D down to F♯ (with a corrected false step to B♮), as though the ensemble's shared anger has yielded a

Example 2.8. String Quartet no. 2, hypothetical connection between (a) "Arguments," m. 84, and (b) "The Call of the Mountains," m. 123; compared with (c) "The Call of the Mountains," mm. 122–23.

fleeting epiphany. In addition to the cello's foreshadowing of its whole-tone osti-nato, both the cello and first violin preview the musical path via which the osti-nato section will be reached: the violin's E–F♯–G motion (m. 84) returns in "The Call of the Mountains" (m. 122) and continues to A, the uppermost pitch of the D-major triad with which the ostinato section begins (m. 123). In the same move-ment, in contrary motion to the violin, the cello's whole-tone descent continues past F♯ (m. 122), where it had stalled in "Arguments," ultimately landing on D to anchor the arrival on D major.

Thus, m. 84 of "Arguments" can be heard as a premature attempt to achieve the apotheosis of the following movement. This hearing is modeled in Example 2.8, which compares a hypothetical succession from m. 84 of "Arguments" to m. 123 of "The Call of the Mountains"—the attempted maneuver—with the actual musical succession from mm. 122–23 of the latter movement. The outer-voice

Example 2.9. String Quartet no. 2, harmonic progression from (a) "Arguments," m. 84, to (b) "The Call of the Mountains," m. 123.

motions that link the imagined and actual successions are highlighted on the example. The hypothetical succession is strengthened by the presence of a strong directed harmonic motion toward D major. Specifically, the F♯ to G motion in the first violin is harmonized by two whole-tone chords, each comprising a complete whole-tone collection and together comprising the chromatic aggregate with no repetitions. Were this upper melodic motion to proceed to a D-major triad, as it does in "The Call of the Mountains," the whole-tone chords would provide strong harmonic support, analogous to a V⁷/V→V⁷→I progression. This progression is shown in Example 2.9, with arrows highlighting the idiomatic resolutions of the primary tritones, D–G♯ and C♯–G (the accidentals have been respelled to emphasize the functionality of the progression). Note that in m. 84 of "Arguments," the whole-tone chord that harmonizes the first violin's G is prolonged through the remainder of the measure by the meandering lines of the upper three instruments, as shown with dotted slurs in Example 2.8; for this reason, I have bracketed off the last portion of m. 84 in the example as ancillary to the progression from the second whole-tone chord to the D-major triad.

In sum, embedded within "Arguments" are two pathways out of the tensions of the movement, one backward to "Discussions," one forward to "The Call of the Mountains." Because the quartet implies a temporal narrative, as encapsulated by the movement titles, these pathways can be understood respectively as attempts to revisit the past or race into the future. More specifically, in terms of Ives's program, the backward trajectory suggests an attempt to revisit tonality as a solution—not Rollo's saccharine tonality, but the earnest, unaffected tonality explored near the beginning of the quartet. Or perhaps the players are on the verge of pessimistic resignation to this tonality. The forward trajectory reaches not only toward a peaceful agreement but also toward music that epitomizes Ives's transcendental ideal of unity in diversity, four musical layers that are rhythmically and melodically independent but together forge a continuous tonality that evokes timelessness and eternity. These are Ives's "four nice different men playing tennis together"; they do not "destroy tonality" but bring it back to life. In both cases, the implied trajectories within the piece signify comparable temporal trajectories outside of it: the tonality that emerges briefly in "Discussions" is the music of the past, and the apotheosis of "The Call of the Mountains" is Ives's own music of the future.

The layers of ostinati that emerge near the end of the quartet's final movement are rich with associations. The communal act with which the program ends is signified by the balance between instrumental independence and cohesion. The four debaters maintain their individuality yet form some sort of consensus as a means of peaceful coexistence; the opposition between individual and community is resolved. The four men's communion with nature on the mountaintop is evoked by the first violin, which reaches higher on its E-string than most composers or players of the time would have dared to attempt, as it paraphrases the hymn "Nearer My God to Thee" (mm. 123–27), the title suggesting the ultimate object of the ascent up the mountain. God's eternity is rendered by the circularity of each of the lower three instrumental layers, whose ostinati repeat at different periodicities. In the cello, for instance, the whole-tone scale repeats in seven-beat groups, undermining the metric hierarchy implied by the notated 4/4 meter. The scale itself supplies a tonal analogue for eternity, its equal divisions of the octave destabilizing any sense of tonal hierarchy that might be suggested by the emphasis on the D-major triad throughout the passage.

The first violin, unlike the other instruments, is not organized around a repeating pattern, but instead follows a gradually descending trajectory that begins with the references to "Nearer My God to Thee," morphs into the melody of the Westminster Chimes (mm. 127–34), and finally settles onto the sustained open fifth of its middle strings, D–A (mm. 136–40). Westminster Chimes is heard twice earlier in the movement (mm. 74–76 and 91–96), but in relatively unstable contexts, just as the cello's whole-tone scales are anticipated in mm. 56–67 but without a clear tonal center. The union of the two musical ideas at the end of "The Call of the Mountains" creates a clear sense of culmination despite the absence of cumulative form. In his interpretation of the end of the movement, Christopher Ballantine heard the sound of the cathedral bells suffusing the entire ensemble, suggesting that the passage "symbolize[s] the regular peal of four giant carillons, one for each instrument" (1979: 171). Along these lines, the four bells can be heard as a symbol of the equality achieved by the four men of Ives's program. The carillon tune consists of four pitches—here D, E, F♯ and A—fixed in register and rhythm but arranged in various orders. The permutability of this melody is another indication of the erasure of temporal distinctions as the four men ascend nearer to God, and it reflects the newfound possibility of a flexible and equal arrangement among four individual entities. As Ballantine expresses it, "The unity of man with his own kind, and the surpassing of the duality of man and nature, are to be perceived in terms of a privileged—indeed transcendental—moment of illumination" (1979: 172).

Ballantine referred to the key of this moment as a "visionary" one (1979: 171), and it is well worth considering the possible associational meanings of D major, a key that emerges without any obvious links to the various tonal centers featured earlier in the piece. The sustained D–A fifth in the first violin, mm. 136–40, heard in relation to the C–G fifth of "Discussions," mm. 1–2, suggests that the quar-

Example 2.10. Comparison of (a) Ives, String Quartet no. 2, "The Call of the Mountains," mm. 129–30 (violin 1), and (b) Beethoven, Symphony no. 9, excerpt from "Ode to Joy."

tet's overall trajectory from C-centered to D-centered tonality affirms the natural fifths of the cello's open strings and the "natural laws of tone" they signify: Ives has achieved his goal to extend these laws and maintain their vitality. But I would like to pursue a complementary and more specific interpretation. One can hear in the conclusion of Ives's quartet echoes of another finale that celebrated fraternal harmony in the same key: Beethoven's Ninth Symphony. Beethoven was Ives's most admired composer, and Ives included the first three measures of "Ode to Joy" as one of the numerous eclectic borrowings in "Arguments," near the end of the movement (see mm. 96–97; Ives transposed the melody to A major). Ives's vision of men climbing a mountain to bring themselves nearer to God and thus to "view the firmament" from his perspective could have been taken directly from Schiller's ode: "Brothers—over the starry firmament / A beloved Father must surely dwell" (*Brüder—überm Sternenzelt / Muss ein lieber Vater wohnen*). And on a musical level, there seems to be a synergetic relationship between Ives's carillon and Beethoven's melody. One prominent motivic connection is suggested in Example 2.10, involving both of the permutations of "Westminster Chimes" that Ives incorporated.

In the Ninth Symphony, Beethoven's melody arrives, famously, as a rejection of the preceding music—"O Freunde, nicht diese Töne!"—and so does Ives's D-major apotheosis, an elevated alternative to various rejected musical paths that precede it, particularly those proposed by Rollo in "Arguments." Returning to the crucial passage analyzed above, Rollo's cadenza and the violent responses it provokes can now be understood against the backdrop of Beethoven's symphony as well. The final movement of the ninth begins with what Wagner referred to as a *Schreckensfanjare* (horror fanfare), and "Arguments" commences with comparable bluster. The harmony of Ives's *con fisto* passages even conjures the first chord of Beethoven's fanfare, with its distinctive clash of a minor ninth (B♭–A) in the upper voices; the two harmonies are juxtaposed in the first half of Example 2.11. The second half of the example compares Beethoven's second *Schreckensfan-*

Example 2.11. Comparison of two chords from Ives's String Quartet no. 2 and from Beethoven's *Schreckensfanfare:* (a¹) "Arguments," mm. 36–37, 39; (a²) Symphony no. 9, Movement IV, mm. 1–2; (b¹) "The Call of the Mountains," m. 119; (b²) Symphony no. 9, Movement IV, mm. 17–18.

jare chord (mm. 17–18) with a similar, and similarly dramatic, chord from "The Call of the Mountains" that closely precedes the D-major arrival near the end of the movement and initiates a false start of the cello's whole-tone ostinato (see m. 119). Again, both chords are characterized by a minor ninth (E♭–D) in the upper register.

The similarities do not end there. The horrific beginning of "Arguments" gives way to Rollo's "burlesque cadenza," much in the manner that Beethoven's *Schreckensfanfare* is silenced by the solo for cello and bass, "*Selon le caractère d'un Recitative.*" The first portion of Rollo's cadenza has notable motivic similarities to the first portion of the recitative, with the head motive and cadential gesture of the latter heard consecutively in the former, as shown in Example 2.12 (the head motive is labeled [1], the cadential figure [2]; an embedded reference to the cadential figure is labeled [2a]). The first portion of Beethoven's recitative is followed by a second fanfare, after which the cello and bass melody alternates with fragmented recollections of movements past, presenting these as the "tones" to be rejected. There is a sense of narration in this passage, enhanced by the way each portion of the recitative seems to take up where it last left off, in the manner of a running commentary that pauses periodically for aural illustrations. This effect is generated primarily by the pitch connections between isolated portions of the recitative, such as outlined above in the context of Rollo's cadenza: the cadential F of m. 16 is taken up in m. 25, the melodic cadence E♭–D–C–B♭ of m. 28 in mm. 38–40, and the cadential C of m. 47 in mm. 56–57. The argument between Rollo and his colleagues can in fact be heard as a telescoped version of the recitative and its interruptions in Beethoven's symphony. Table 2.2 suggests the specific correlations. Note in particular the shared "Presto" markings and the brief recollections of slow music in flat-side keys from previous movements.

Given these manifold connections, it seems plausible that Ives modeled his cadenza passage after Beethoven's symphony, adapting Beethoven's idea of an

Example 2.12. Comparison of (a) Ives's "burlesque cadenza" (String Quartet no. 2, "Arguments," mm. 31–36) and (b) Beethoven's cello and bass "recitative" (Symphony no. 9, Movement IV, mm. 8–16).

isolated pair of instruments presenting a musical vision in the face of violent resistance from the rest of the ensemble, and drawing upon specific aspects of Beethoven's musical implementation of the idea as well. At the same time, Ives's music maintains an ironic distance from Beethoven's. Rollo is an object of ridicule, not a messenger of profundities; Ives is firmly on the side of the shaking fists, whose fury we are meant to share rather than be horrified by. If Ives modeled aspects of the end of "The Call of the Mountains" on Beethoven's finale, he did so with a clear sense of historical distance from Beethoven as well. Where Beethoven's resolution of musical conflicts is triumphant and celebratory, Ives's is relatively tempered: it does not work itself into a state of ecstasy but instead recedes gradually into a meditative trance.

Many have found this ending profound and moving. In 1946, after attending one of the earliest performances of the quartet, Lou Harrison called its ending a "revelation": "It is hard to convey in words what every one present felt at this moment. Music of this kind happens only every fifty years or a century, so rich in faith and so full of the sense of completion" (Burkholder 1996: 345). Oddly, Harrison's account of the ending overlooks the final measures, as does Ballantine's and most others. What does it say about the "visionary" D tonality that it dissolves into a sustained F-major triad in the violins and cello (mm. 141–43)? Complicating matters further, this triad accompanies a fragment of "Nearer My God to Thee" in the viola in the key of C♯ major. No sooner has the duality between social cohesion and individual expression collapsed, it seems, than it is almost immediately reopened, as the harmonious tones of three players are heard against the solitary and incongruous melody of the fourth.

We are faced here with one of Ives's many so-called "open" endings that undermine closure, indications of Ives's refusal to suggest neat solutions to the problems his music addresses. After all of its musical and programmatic travails, the quartet's final gesture recalls its opening one, a similarly voiced C-minor triad sustained in the violins and cello, accompanying a tonally unrelated melody in

Ives, "Arguments"	Beethoven, Symphony no. 9, IV
Allegro con spirito (mm. 1–33)	Presto; "Schreckensfanjare" no. 1 (mm. 1–7)
Andante Emasculata (mm. 30–36); "burlesque cadenza"	Selon le caractere d'un Recitative (mm. 8–16)
Allegro con fisto (mm. 36–37)	"Schreckensfanjare" no. 2 (mm. 17–25)
Andante emasculata (m. 38)	Recitative (mm. 24–29)
Presto (m. 39)	—
Largo sweetota (mm. 40–41); A♭ major	Adagio cantabile (from Movement 3) (mm. 63–65); B♭ major
Allegro con fisto (m. 41)	—

Table 2.2. Comparison of "Arguments," mm. 1–41, and Symphony no. 9, Movement IV, opening section

the viola. The differences between these gestures are certainly significant. The major mode implies optimism, and the predominance of white notes in F major made this key, like C major, a frequent symbol of God and truth for Ives. And a fragment of "Nearer My God to Thee" obviously has very different connotations than an abstract atonal melody—in this case, suggesting that the men are both literally and figuratively nearer to God. But there are other similarities as well that serve as counterweights. The C-minor triad that opens "Discussions" makes tentative steps toward its submediant, A♭ major (m. 9), and this tonal relationship recurs at the end of "The Call of the Mountains," where F major and D♭ major (spelled as C♯) are heard together. The key of D♭ (C♯) major emerges in the viola as a semitonal slip from D major, a tonal move that in retrospect might be heard as preordained by the solitary atonal viola melody of the first movement's opening measure, D–F♯, D♭–F. In sum, the final transcendent vision of the second quartet is tempered with a dose of realism, the continued presence of the seeds of dissent with which the quartet began—characteristically, Ives leaves us with an ambiguous blend of the actual and the ideal.

3 Intuition/Expression:
"Nov. 2, 1920" and "Grantchester"

"Nov. 2, 1920"

Ives apparently began composing the song "Nov. 2, 1920" soon, and perhaps immediately, after the presidential election held on the date referred to in the title, making it among the last of the *114 Songs* that he composed. He developed the same music in an orchestral version with unison male chorus called *An Election*, which he completed in 1923. The thicker texture of this arrangement became the basis for a modified version of the original song, "An Election," which Ives included in his collection *Nineteen Songs*, published in 1935.[1] "An Election" differs from "Nov. 2, 1920" primarily in its occasional addition of contrapuntal lines derived from the orchestral version and notated with cue-sized notes. These lines usually move in parallel minor ninths above the bass: see, for example, mm. 1–2 and subsequent incarnations of this music (Ives 2004: 332–38). My analysis refers primarily to the cleaner, and conceptually clearer, version from *114 Songs*, but I consider one significant aspect of the revised version below.

The dramatic context for the song is provided in a short introductory note: "Soliloquy of an old man whose son lies in 'Flanders Fields.' It is the day after election; he is sitting by the roadside, Looking down the valley towards the station."

The election in question was Warren Harding's defeat of James Cox. Ives supported Cox as a successor to Woodrow Wilson and was angered by Harding's opposition to the United States' membership in the League of Nations. For this and other reasons, Ives was intensely invested in the election and distressed by its result. Michael Broyles went so far as to identify Harding's victory as a primary source of Ives's diminishing activity as a composer in the early 1920s (1996: 153–54). Not surprisingly, then, the soliloquy of "Nov. 2, 1920" reads like a rant from *Memos* or one of Ives's essays, albeit more manic and choppy:

> It strikes me that . . . some men and women got tired of a big job; but, over there our men did not quit. They fought and died that better things might be! Perhaps some who stayed at home are beginning to forget and to quit. The pocketbook and certain little things talked loud and noble, and got in the way; too many readers go by the headlines, party men will muddle up the facts, so a good many citizens voted as grandpa always did, or thought a change for the sake of change seemed natural enough. "It's raining, let's throw out the weather man, Kick him out! Kick him out!

Kick him out! Kick him out! Kick him!" Prejudice and politics, and the stand-patters came in strong, and yelled, "Slide back! Now you're safe, that's the easy way!"
Then the timid smiled and looked relieved, "We've got enough to eat, to hell with
ideals!" All the old women, male and female, had thier [*sic*] day today, and the hog-
heart came out of his hole; but he won't stay out long, God always drives him back!
Oh Captain, my Captain! a heritage we've thrown away; But we'll find it again, my
Captain, Captain, oh my Captain![2]

Based on this text alone, Ives's frustration (or that of his surrogate) would
seem to be aimed primarily at his compatriots, the majority of voters who took
"the easy way." But in a short note appended to the end of the song Ives gives a
different impression, distancing himself somewhat from the persona of his song:

> *NOTE:* The assumption, in the text, that the result of our national election in 1920,
> was a definite indication, that the country, (at least, the majority-mind) turned
> its back on a high purpose is not conclusive. Unfortunately election returns com-
> ing through the present party system prove nothing conclusively. The voice of the
> people sounding through the mouth of the parties, becomes somewhat emascu-
> lated. It is not inconceivable that practical ways may be found for more accurately
> registering and expressing popular thought—at least, in relation to the larger pri-
> mary problems, which concern us all. A suggestion to this end (if we may be for-
> given a further digression) in the form of a constitutional amendment together with
> an article discussing the plan in some detail and from various aspects, will be gladly
> sent, by the writer, to any one who is interested enough to write for it. *C. E. I.*

Harding's election, in other words, was not so much the fault of Americans as
it was the fault of their electoral system. This was a stubbornly optimistic view,
given that Harding's margin of victory was one of the greatest in U.S. history. But
it was in keeping with Ives's idealized notion of the American people, what he referred to as "the Majority." Ives's ideas on the topic are laid out in his longest essay, "The Majority," which he wrote in the years 1919–1920 (Ives 1961: 139–99).[3]
This essay provides a backdrop against which to understand the eponymous song
as well as "Nov. 2, 1920." The language and ideas of the text of "Nov. 2" are partly
derived from it: "The Majority" pits its subject, for example, against the "hog-
mind" of the "Minority" that holds economic and political power (156), and it
blames the Senate for "muddling up" U.S. entry into the League of Nations (182–
83). But in the song, the old man's faith in the Majority seems to be shakier than
Ives's, a disparity Ives was at pains to point out in his leavening postscript to the
song and its inconclusive "assumption." Together, the song text and the postscript convey Ives's own ambivalence, his struggle with the unavoidable implication of the election: that his views and those of the Majority were profoundly
out of synch. Put another way, the song foregrounds Ives's conflicting desires for
community and isolation. The old man is alone, with a demeanor likely to keep
him that way; yet he craves a community of like-minded thinkers and maintains
hope that the stand-patters will come to their senses.

The primary obstacle standing in the way of his fellow citizens, according to
the old man, is their own intellectual laziness. To represent the superficiality of

their views, Ives draws primarily on ragtime music, evoking its syncopations and textures and exaggerating its formulaic accompanimental patterns through repetition (as in p. 50/2/2–3, for example). This style dominates much of the song, particularly the large central portion from p. 51/3 to p. 54/3/1, and it is always associated with the negative portrayal of the electorate. Ives offered his largely dismissive opinion of ragtime in the "Epilogue" of the *Essays,* a passage that places some of his racial prejudices on full display.[4] He compared the musical value of ragtime to the nutritional value of ketchup and horseradish, and implied that American composers must provide the meat and potatoes (1961: 94). Ives called upon the words of a fellow composer, Daniel Gregory Mason, in support of these views. The quotation is germane to "Nov. 2" and may even have influenced the content of the song: "If indeed the land of Lincoln and Emerson has degenerated until nothing remains of it but a 'jerk and rattle,' then we at least are free . . . to insist that better than bad music is no music" (1961: 95). ("Jerk and rattle" refers to the sounds of urban America; see 1961: 252, note 49.)

"Nov. 2" is, in essence, a song about the disintegration of this "land of Lincoln and Emerson." If the ragtime music featured in the central portion of the song represents degeneration, the music evoking two of Ives's heroes, Lincoln and Emerson, at the beginning and end represents the struggle to reclaim what the country used to be. Ives derived the piano introduction (Example 3.1) from the end of another of the *114 Songs,* "from 'Lincoln, the Great Commoner'" (c. 1919–20), where it accompanies a poetic image of Lincoln's death adapted from Edwin Markham's poem "Lincoln, the Man of the People": "when he fell in whirlwind, he went down as when a Kingly cedar green with boughs goes down with a great shout, upon the hills!" (see p. 26/2–p. 26/3). In its original context, this music conveys the enormity of Lincoln's death, and for the old man, the present calamity is of comparable magnitude. But Lincoln provides a source of hope as well, which emerges when the end of the song evokes him more directly, coordinating a return of the music of "from 'Lincoln, the Great Commoner'" with a textual reference to Walt Whitman's elegy to Lincoln, "O Captain! My Captain!," a symbolically rich passage I return to below.

As in Mason's quote, Lincoln and Emerson are paired figures in "Nov. 2"; the grave opening bears notable resemblance to that of the "Emerson" movement of the *Concord* Sonata, a work that Ives was completing around the same time. The "Emerson" opening shares several features with the introduction of "Nov. 2." In addition to using registral extremes, the tempo indication "Slowly," and a loud dynamic, each is an epic instance of the "wedge," one of Ives's favorite textural structures: grand chords in the right hand fan outward in contrary motion against low octaves in the left.[5] (These are all features of the opening of "Majority" as well.) The first sonority of "Nov. 2" also shares with "Emerson" a solitary double-stemmed B3 in the right hand, a focal point from which the wedge emerges, eventually spanning nearly six octaves. The beginning of "Nov. 2" evokes the ending of the "Emerson" movement as well, featuring chromatically descending octaves in the bass similar to those that dominate the final pages of "Emerson" (p. 18/2–p. 19/3). Wilfred Mellers, in his discussion of the *Concord* Sonata, empha-

22
Nov. 2. 1920

Soliloquy of an old man whose son lies in "Flanders Fields"
It is the day after election; he is sitting by the roadside,
Looking down the valley towards the station.

Example 3.1. Opening of "Nov. 2, 1920" (p. 50/1).

sized the conflict at the heart of the "Emerson" movement: "Emerson is the hero of American Strife," he wrote, and the movement "deals with the fight of the ego with destiny" (1987: 48, 54). In "Nov. 2, 1920," the destiny at stake is America's, and the fight is waged by an ego determined to redeem it. The old man is a conduit for Emerson and Lincoln alike, his soliloquy channeling—both in its words and its musical setting—the raw, unfiltered truthfulness that Ives associated with both men and that he sought to emulate in his music.

The full fury of the American ego is on display at the beginning of the song, summoning the strength of the Masses and registering through its rage the full import of the strife at hand. Ives wrote "Down with Politicians & Up with the People!!" atop his pencil score for the orchestral version of the song, and this heading provides an apt interpretation for the mirroring trajectories of the song's piano introduction; the politicians drag the country down and the people struggle to pull it back up. The musical representation of this struggle is rooted in A dorian, the tonal center established firmly by the bass in m. 1 and the arpeggiation of an A-minor triad in the uppermost voice of the piano. The first chords in the right hand feature triadic extensions over the A bass, beginning with the initial ninth, B3, and continuing upward in diatonic thirds with D4–F#4–A4–C5–E5. When the voice enters (p. 50/1/3), the incorporation of A# and G# in the right hand gestures toward the whole-tone collection {C–D–E–F#–G#–A#} (hereafter WT$_c$). This whole-tone collection is not yet separated out from the diatonic elements in any evident way; but the brief co-presence of the two collections presages a pairing that takes on symbolic significance later in the song.

The sense of strife begins to lose its force when the voice enters; from this point on the song deals with how the people have dodged the present conflict and how they might come to face and surmount it. These concerns are suggested by the music and text in ways both blunt and subtle. As the introductory piano wedge is opening up to its registral extremes, the monologue begins tentatively with the words "It strikes me that"—"half spoken," as indicated by Ives, on a single mid-range E. A decrescendo brings the dynamic to *piano*, and the voice drops out of the texture, while the chromatic descent in the bass stalls on E♭. The music continues to drift away from the turmoil of the opening, as a series of chords waft downward above this bass note in an energy-dissolving, Debussyan transition inflected toward the other whole-tone collection, {C♯–D♯–F–G–A–B} (WT$_{c♯}$). The bass ultimately continues its chromatic descent to D (p. 50/2/2), which anchors the simple ostinato of the first ragtime passage ("Some men and women got tired").

The marked shift in tone in this opening passage can be attributed to the change of focus from the post-election woes to the pre-election circumstances and the corresponding shift of tense from present to past, where the text will remain for nearly the entire song. Ives's music generally looks to the past as an antidote to the present, but the recent past provides little relief here; instead, the light mood of ragtime reflects the false comfort of taking "the easy way." The score provides a visual representation of the shift from present- to past-orientation, with continuous ellipses connecting the words "that" and "Some" across the span of several beats (ninety-two dots in all, by my count). Ives often used the whole-tone collection to evoke the blurring of temporal boundaries, and it serves that purpose here, with the inherent lack of harmonic focus in marked contrast to the violent clarity of the opening A dorian and the mundane D tonality of the ragtime passage. Ives may also have regarded the whole-tone scale, when used in an airy sort of way, as an effeminate counterpart to diatonic scales, and thus here as a means of transitioning from the masculine confrontation of the opening to the feminine resignation of the ragtime music. This was a scale Ives no doubt came to associate with Debussy and what Ives referred to derisively as the composer's "sensual" musical language (as I examine later in this chapter), and Debussy's music may even have been a specific reference point in this passage. Although the masculine/feminine duality is not explicit, Ives's sexism rises to the surface elsewhere in the song, as in the line "All the old women, male and female, had their way today"; see also his comment about the emasculation of voters in the endnote on the last page of the score.

The whole-tone transition, then, serves as a temporal and moral free-fall transporting us from the crisis of the present to the failures that preceded it. The descending chromatic bass line E–E♭–D assists in this transition, preparing the slinking chromaticism that sets the word "tired" (p. 50/2/3). The latter vividly signifies emasculation, extending the coded lower trajectory of the opening wedge, a representation of the decline of American values. Yet the narrative of the opening is not quite this simple. Left out of my account of the descending bass line that spans the first two systems is a small backward step, the brief reversion to E inserted between the sustained E♭ of the whole-tone transition and the D of the ragtime interlude (see the end of p. 50/2/1). This E supports an E dominant, which emerges briefly, contained in register and at the tail end of a diminuendo. The am: V⁷   i

Example 3.2. "Nov. 2, 1920," hypothetical succession from p. 50/2/1 to m. 1.

chord sounds perfunctory, a simple reaffirmation of the tonality of the opening. But a more significant function lurks: as the dominant of A, it also activates a potential return to the strife of the opening. In addition to the potential dominant-tonic relationship, the downward motion of the right hand in p. 50/2/1 comes to rest on B3, recalling the angular dissonance of the very first sonority while providing a smooth pathway, as shown in Example 3.2. Thus, the E dominant can be heard as a musical path not taken, whose unused harmonic potential represents an act avoided, the country's "turn[ing] its back on a high purpose." Or, viewed more positively, while we witness the public's shrinking away from its responsibility, we can also detect a way out, a path of continued engagement.

The bass E♭ of the whole-tone transition provides the primary musical link between the strife music and the ragtime passage, and it reprises this role at the end of the latter, albeit with a much different effect. The bass note returns, suddenly and at *forte*, at the end of p. 50/2/3 ("of a"), once again supporting harmony based primarily on WT$_{c\sharp}$. This leads directly to a return of the strife music in all its furor ("big job"). The chromatic bass descent that follows stops abruptly on E, however, suggesting an *ascending* line D–E♭–E♮ that spans p. 50/2/2–p. 50/3/1, reversing the earlier E–E♭–D descent, and setting up the F♯ of p. 50/3/2. Accordingly, the old man's reflection on those who "got tired" now seems to arouse opposite, inspiring thoughts of tirelessly fighting American soldiers: "But, over there our men did not quit. They fought and died that better things might be!" Rather than descending weakly, the vocal line now rises in tandem with the reference to these soldiers, ascending through D5 ("over there") to E5 ("fought and died") to F♯5 ("better things").

But whereas the connotations of this rising vocal line are apparently straightforward, the musical details of this passage present a much more complicated picture. The setting of "over there our men did not quit" features a crunchy, dissonant polychord, repeated several times: tonic and dominant of B minor forged into a single harmony. The significance of this key is confirmed when the component triads fan out in another expanding wedge, marked *agitando* and with a crescendo (p. 50/3/3). This wedge grows naturally from the polychord, with transpositions of the B-minor triad in the right hand and parallel fifths stemming from the F♯-major triad in the left. The outer voices both conform to the key of B minor, with each voice strongly directed toward a coordinated resolution onto the tonic that would confirm this key.

In light of these melodic implications, the actual culmination of the wedge arrives as though a strenuous triumph over musical momentum. The word "fought" is set to a broadly voiced, *fff* C-major triad with added sixth (Cmaj$_6$). Its jolting force derives from the sudden shift of tonal center and mode, from B minor to C major; its consonance in contrast to the wedge harmonies, which all contain dissonant inner voices; and its broad voicing, with twelve notes in all. It also effects a sudden expansion of register, with the upper voice leaping from G#5 to E6. As partial compensation, a similar melodic gap is filled in by the voice, an octave lower, by the ascending line A#–C–D–E ("They fought"). This melodic segment and the outer voices of the wedge, D–E–F#–G# (upper voice) and F#–E–D–(Db)–C (lower), presage the chord that immediately follows the Cmaj$_6$, a rolled, *piano* aftershock built around the complete WT$_c$ collection. Cementing the connection, the intervallic spans of these melodic segments, A#–E, D–G#, and F#–C, are all isolated as intervals in the rolled whole-tone sonority.

The Cmaj$_6$ and its whole-tone partner are immediately repeated at a somewhat lower dynamic ("died"), and then give way to a variant of the B/F# major polychord, which instigates a short progression ("better things might be!") that is awkward and unfocused relative to harmonic motion in the rest of the song. The vocal line, too, is jagged and meandering, unlike the smooth lines before and after it. The left hand eventually returns to a C-major triad ("be!"), but now it forms the lower portion of an F minor/C major polychord. From here, the vocal line and its piano accompaniment all descend chromatically nearly an entire octave, continually growing slower, with the piano plodding through transpositions of the polychord ("Perhaps some who stayed at home are beginning to forget and to quit").

The short passage just described is highly charged, as were Ives's feelings about American involvement in World War I. The introductory note curiously provides the old man a short backstory: he has lost a son in the war. That knowledge is useful here, suggesting that when the old man refers to the fallen soldiers, his own son must be at the forefront of his mind. He has very personal incentives to believe that the deaths of American troops were not in vain, a possibility he seems to hold onto defiantly, as can be sensed from the setting of the Cmaj$_6$ chord, extreme in dynamic, register, and density. This chord and its whole-tone partner virtually stop the song in its tracks, drastically slowing down the rate of rhythmic activity sustained since the opening. In this way, the chords are marked for contemplation. The weightiness of the first suggests strength and heroism, and its associated key—highly symbolic in Ives's music—the divine status of the soldiers' deaths. Their souls are destined for heaven, and multiple features of the second chord suggest this transcendence of the worldly: the tonally ungrounded nature of the whole-tone collection; the arpeggiation upward, in juxtaposition with the firmly grounded Cmaj$_6$ chord; and the associated meanings of the whole-tone collection in other music of Ives's (including String Quartet no. 2, as well as

"Grantchester" and "The Things Our Fathers Loved," which I address later in the book).

The ending of "from 'Lincoln, the Great Commoner'" features the same pair, accompanying the word "hills" at the end of the song (p. 26/3/5). The image of the hill ties the basic meanings of the two chords together: hills are grounded and elemental, and they bring us closer to the heavens. Hills and mountains are sites of transcendence in much of Ives's music, and as such these hills symbolize the destination of Lincoln's soul, as well as his grandeur and strength, and the heroism of his death. Yet the final pianissimo chord, sustained for eight beats and followed by a fermata, suggests, in its ambiguous response to the firm tonality of the preceding chord, some combination of the eternal presence of Lincoln's spirit and the lingering ramifications of his premature death.[6] All these meanings can be transferred from Lincoln to the soldiers when these chords first occur in "Nov. 2."

In another of Ives's later songs, the Cmaj$_6$ chord seems to share with "Nov. 2" and "Lincoln, the Great Commoner" the specific purpose of asserting faith in God and the eternal life of the soul in the face of premature death. Like "Nov. 2," Ives composed "Immorality" in 1921 with a text of his own. The subject is the death of a child, revealed in the final lines: "Who dares to say our child is dead! If God had meant she were to die, She would not have been." The notion of the eternal soul is implied by these lines and made explicit by the song's title as well. The penultimate sentence is sung *più agitando,* with something of the stubborn insistence of the old man of "Nov. 2": compare this vocal line (p. 12/2/2–3) with Ives's settings of "our men did not quit" (p. 50/3/2–3) and "God always drives him back!" (p. 55/1), all of which share an emphasis on the descending motive D5–C#5. But the Cmaj$_6$ chord arrives as a ray of light (not unlike its first occurrence in "Nov. 2"), accompanying precisely the evocation of God's name in the final line of text (p. 12/3/1) and leading to a peaceful C-major conclusion to the song.

There is no such resolution when this chord first occurs in "Nov. 2," however. Its triumphant arrival gives way to the convoluted setting of "better things might be," calling into question whether the soldiers' deaths served a larger purpose. The old man's pessimism then returns in full force with the words "Perhaps some who stayed at home are beginning to forget and to quit," set to a long, chromatic descent that recalls Ives's earlier setting of "tired"—in both cases, weary music that represents the apathy of American citizens. Additionally, the descending polychords of the later passage recall the descending parallel fifths that led up to the Cmaj$_6$ chord, a passage that also featured prominently the word "quit." Both of these passages help to establish a stark contrast between the nobility of the American soldiers and the shallowness of their civilian counterparts at home, reinforcing the source of the old man's despair.

A potential linear connection contributes further to this contrast. The F minor/C major polychord that initiates the chromatic descent at "Perhaps" could function seamlessly as a continuation of the wedge that was disrupted by the Cmaj$_6$ chord, as shown in Example 3.3. In this hypothetical succession, the F-minor triad functions as a pivot around which the ascending line reverses

Example 3.3. "Nov. 2, 1920," hypothetical linear connection between p 50/3/3 and p. 51/1.

course, whereas in the left hand, the C-major triad links the chromatically descending fifths. And the ascending vocal line turns back from D to C♯ (bracketed in the example), reprising a melodic motive from p. 50/3/2–3 ("our men," "did"). Heard in this way, the displaced linear connection brackets off the paired chords and the subsequent ascent of the vocal line to F♯5 as a brief vision suspended by grim reality, a reality in which those who quit matter more than those who did not, in which climbing hopes collapse and fall away.

Whereas the Cmaj$_6$ chord, by both continuing and transcending the motion of the preceding wedge, suggests engagement with present circumstances and an eye directed toward the future—the better things that might be—the alternative path that follows is one of retreat. It is significant, then, that the descent beginning at p. 51/1 not only rejects the upward thrust of p. 50/3/3, but in some ways reverses it: the right-hand triads progress backward through those of p. 50/3/3, with added chromatic filler, as shown with brackets in Example 3.3. When the descent reaches B minor at "to forget," this triad is accompanied by an F♯-major triad in the left, restoring the original polychord, as highlighted on the example. The descent continues for three more chords, ending with an E–E♭ motion in the bass, as though continuing the reversal even further, through the F♯ of p. 50/3/2–3 and the E of p. 50/3/1, all the way back to the E♭ of p. 50/2/3.

The sense that the descending polychords supplant or reverse the preceding music has the effect of sealing off the climactic arrival of the Cmaj$_6$ chord as irrelevant or illusional; the hopeful look into the future it seemed to provide is not to return until the very end of the song. Instead, the bitter and resentful rehashing of the past that characterized the old man's first utterance returns; see, for instance, the reprises of the ragtime music at p. 51/3 and p. 54/2/2; the pat tonal cadences at p. 52/3 ("natural enough"), p. 53/3 ("that's the easy way!"), and p. 54/1/2 ("looked relieved"); and the mocking figure at the end of p. 54/2/1. The ironic tone predominates through the bottom of p. 54, reaching its low point at the "weak cheer" Ives identified at p. 54/3/1. By this point the suggestion of "better things" has faded to a blip. But the tone begins to shift, as does the old man's state of mind. "The hog-heart came out of his hole," he declaims, "but he won't stay out long," and the setting of the latter words recalls the *agitando* wedge of p. 50/3/3, with stepwise motion in the outer voices and block triads in the right hand, all building with a crescendo toward *fff*.[7] The word "won't" receives special rhythmic emphasis (p. 55/1), and its harmonization, a white-note chord anchored by C in the bass, brings the transcendent possibilities that followed the earlier wedge back into view. The outer voices seem ready to comply, briefly outlining a white-note wedge ("won't stay out"). But the upper voice missteps at the word "long," landing on C♯ instead of C. In so doing, it confirms the whole-tone tendencies of the vocal line, completing a whole-tone ascent of an octave that had been initiated on the word "hole." The accompaniment registers this shift between the white-note and whole-tone collections, supporting the voice's C♯ with a whole-tone chord (F aug/G).

This failed emergence of the white-note collection on C and its supplanting by the whole-tone collection throws the wedge off its course. The wedge continues to its climax on the next chord (with a change of register in the bass), the familiar B minor/F♯ major polychord of p. 50/3/2–3. The polychord now accompanies the word "God," an unsettling substitute for the Cmaj$_6$ chord; this dissonance between music and text conveys just how profoundly the country has drifted from its founding ideals in the old man's eyes. When the polychord first occurred in p. 50/3/2, it led to the building enthusiasm of the *agitando* wedge, but now it proceeds almost directly to another series of descending polychords, following the words "God always drives him back!" Once again, the music undermines the text's positive prognostications for America's future; by recalling the earlier passage about those "beginning to forget and to quit," the music calls into question the Majority's ability to rise to the occasion should God push the Minority out of power as promised.

Yet, there are signs of hope. At the end of p. 55/1, the sequence of chromatically descending polychords is broken into two segments of three chords each, differentiated by jumps upward in the right hand and downward in the left. There is a sense of a struggle against inertia here, an inertia that was on full display in the comparable passage of p. 51/1–2. The disruption of the descending pattern prevents the bass motion F♯–F♮–E from continuing to E♭, the same pitch upon which the bass line of the earlier sequence ultimately had come to rest, on the word "quit." Its avoidance points to a renewal of energy and resolve that drives the remainder of the song.

The song's ending returns to the beginning, reprising the strife music of the piano introduction and now adding a vocal line above it. The voice sings at full force, as it had in p. 50/3/1, on E5, a pitch it returns to several times in the remainder of the song. The text is derived from Whitman's well-known "O Captain! My Captain!" a response to Lincoln's assassination: "Oh Captain, my Captain! a heritage we've thrown away; But we'll find it again, my Captain!" Lincoln had steadied America's ship during the Civil War, and the old man calls out to

him now, attempting to conjure his spirit during the country's postwar turbu-
lence. Ives's setting of these words suggests a causal connection between this
tragedy and America's declining values. This is due in part to the way Ives adapts
the ending of "from 'Lincoln the Great Commoner'" and its musico-poetic depiction of Lincoln's death, drawing upon the vocal line as well as the piano part
from the earlier song. The imagery of the falling cedar in the source passage is
straightforward, as is its rendering by Ives. "Goes down" is sung with a descending minor seventh; the vocal line then rises to "shout," which is emphasized with
an accented grace note; "-on the hills" is set to an ascending minor tenth; and the
word "hills" is accompanied by the mountainous $Cmaj_6$ chord. The entire vocal
line through the word "shout" divides into two segments; the first ("Kingly cedar
green with boughs") is sung on sustained white notes, and the second ("goes
down with a great shout") comprises all but one note of WT_c. The latter segment
emphasizes the pitches F♯4–C5–E5, which recur as the upper three pitches of the
pianissimo whole-tone sonority that concludes the song. The sonority can thus be
heard as an echo of the "great shout," the sound of a fallen tree reverberating in
the forest—or, the great gunshot, the shouts it elicited, and the reverberations of
the event throughout the country's history.

In the equivalent passage from "Nov. 2" (Example 3.4), the notes of the vocal line are essentially unchanged; "Captain, my Captain!" is sung on white
notes, whereas "a heritage we've thrown away" outlines WT_c. The white-note and
whole-tone collections, juxtaposed harmonically by the paired "fought and died"
chords, here recur melodically in the same order, clearly differentiated as melodic
entities for the first time. The white-note collection is now associated with Lincoln, a Christ-like figure whose title is capitalized in the text and whom the old
man addresses as though in prayer, and the whole-tone collection is associated
with the destroyed social heritage. Ives's setting of the words "a heritage we've
thrown away" recalls the earlier reference to soldiers whose lives were thrown
away (p. 50/3/3): each vocal line comprises a whole-tone ascent to E5, decorated
by a grace note F. Whereas in the earlier passage, however, the arrival of E5 was
coordinated with the $Cmaj_6$ chord (on "fought"), in the later passage it is accompanied by an emphatic E dominant, signaling what will be a more deliberate approach to the $Cmaj_6$ chord. In the parallel moment from the introduction (the
third beat of p. 50/1/3), this dominant was passed over, giving way to the whole-
tone transition. That music had led to a staid ragtime vamp on D, but the music of
p. 55/3 arrives with a vigorous and dynamic D-major triad. Where the opening of
the song had depicted those who turned away from strife, the ending will provide
a vision of how they might face it in the future.

This vision is centered on a return of the paired chords of p. 50/3/3. The vocal line sets up this return through several musical connections. Most obviously,
the setting of "Captain, my" in p. 55/2/1 revives the E5–D5 motive of "fought
and died." The paired chords had been linked by the common tones C5 and E5,
and these two pitches are highlighted by the beginning and ending segments
of the vocal phrase spanning p. 55/2; once again, the C–E dyad is featured as a
shared element between the white-note and whole-tone collections. And the vo-

Example 3.4. Ending of "Nov. 2, 1920," p. 55/2–55/3.

cal setting of "a heritage we've thrown away" is linked sonically to the arpeggiated whole-tone chord by the upward motion from F♯4 to C5 and E5.

By invoking Lincoln, the old man has turned his thoughts once again to the great Americans who died for their country, and musically, the stage is now set for a return to the paired chords associated with this heroism. But whereas in the earlier passage, the music rushed into these chords, now it comes to a full stop. And whereas before, the chords were approached melodically via whole-tone motion, setting up the second chord of the pair, now the whole-tone motion of the vocal line is cut off. What follows instead is rugged diatonicism. This new lead-in features a bald D-major triad followed by an upward arpeggiated C-major triad in the voice accompanied by block chords in the piano ("But we'll find it again"). These triads are supported by a stepwise descent in the bass that continues the bass line of the preceding wedge, eventually making its way to A1 at the end of p. 55/3/1. This continuity, along with the continued emphasis on the dyads D–F♯ and C–E and the miniature wedge motion that concludes the measure, all suggest that p. 55/3/1 be heard as a continuation of the preceding strife music.

This music provides a new context in which to hear the Cmaj6 chord. As in the earlier passage (p. 50/3/3), its arrival is characterized by a breach, but there are strong elements of harmonic continuity as well. The C–E–G arpeggiation in the voice ("find it a-") is loosely coordinated with a chromatic bass motion from

C2 to A1, with A1 supporting a C-major triad (the last chord of p. 55/3/1). When this harmony proceeds to the Cmaj$_6$ chord, the voice leading is not smooth, but the harmonic connection between the two chords is strong: each is built around the pitch classes A, C, E, and G. The progression does not come across as a simple change of inversion, however, but as a profound transformation—specifically, a transformation of the strife music, the music of past conflict, into the Cmaj$_6$ chord, the music of future transcendence. By facing the country's crisis head-on, it can be overcome.

But such a victory, the music suggests, cannot be accomplished, or perhaps even imagined, without great strain. At the end of p. 55/2, the music pauses and then gathers force via the strong chords and slow, steady rhythm of p. 55/3/1. In most respects, this measure closely parallels the beginning of p. 55/1, as though the later passage revisits and attempts to correct the earlier one. It begins with the same word, has an anapestic rhythm, and returns to the future tense; its musical setting features heavy block chords, an expanding wedge, and emphatic rhythm. But whereas in the earlier passage, the brief attempt at establishing C-major tonality is disrupted by the whole-tone scale, the later one achieves its tonal goal. The sense of exertion this requires is conveyed most viscerally by the vocal line. The C-major arpeggiation (C4-E4-G4) leaps upward from G4 to E5, overshooting C5. The piano intensifies the disruption by jumping an octave higher to E6 in the uppermost voice. To the extent we expect an arrival on C5 in the voice, the reason is primarily external: the vocal setting of "But we'll find it again" paraphrases the beginning of "The Star Spangled Banner," "Oh say, can you see." As the anthem suggests, the old man, consumed with thoughts of Lincoln and his country's hallowed history, seems to be swelling with patriotism at this moment; and he is perhaps thinking again of the recent war and the wasted human lives, the heritage thrown away.

But he is also looking to the future—oh say, can you see?—and wondering what will become of his country. This may help to explain why the Cmaj$_6$ chord again requires a tear in the musical fabric—less disruptive than in p. 50/3/3, but still significant. The vocal line does not simply proceed to C5, as it would in the national anthem, but skips over a note, as though attempting to skip over the unfortunate moment in the country's history into an imagined future. The leap to E5 is another leap of faith, and "we'll find it again" is tinged by some of the same uncertainty that called into serious question the old man's faith in the utility of the war.

This uncertainty is communicated most powerfully by the presence of a second, catastrophic ending that lurks behind the actual one. All the factors that maintain a sense of struggle until the very moment the Cmaj$_6$ chord returns serve not only to place dramatic emphasis on the crisis that is being confronted and transcended, but to draw attention to the threat of an alternative future in which the crisis continues *ad infinitum*. This threat is conveyed by the ease with which p. 55/3/1 could cycle directly back to the strife music, as shown in Example 3.5. This connection is established in multiple ways: (1) harmonically, by the ascend-

Example 3.5. "Nov. 2, 1920," hypothetical succession from p. 55/3/1 to m. 1.

ing block chords in the right hand and their pitch-class content; (2) melodically, by the strong voice-leading continuity in the outer voices of the piano, with m. 1 supplying the missing word "see" from the national anthem; and (3) rhythmically, by the triplet groupings, which can be heard as a product of the meter of the national anthem. As with the first arrival of the paired chords in p. 50/3/3, the musical disjunction after p. 55/3/1 points to a displaced continuation with negative connotations. But whereas in the earlier passage the displaced continuation seemed to supplant the immediate one, in the later passage it looms as a future possibility taken from the song's past.

And thus, once again, the apotheotic arrival of the Cmaj₆ chord is undermined, its expressive implications called into question. The same is accomplished, but more directly, by the whole-tone chord, quietly but persistently raising doubts about its partner. The song concludes with five statements of the pair, each growing steadily quieter. The voice repeats its E5–D5 motive over the chords, and ultimately descends to C5 ("oh my Captain!"). This conventional 3–2–1 melodic closure, and the emergence of the E5–C5 interval as a unifying link between the vocal line and the paired chords, all reinforce the definitive nature of the old man's final declaration, but the whole-tone chord lingers with the voice as the last sound, raising doubts. Its meaning is multivalent and elusive, drifting away with the sound of the last chord itself.

Ives's song "In Flanders Fields" (c. 1917; rev. 1919), based on a poem by John McCrae, ends with a similar chord, a thick, rolled D-minor triad with an added G♯. In addition to the prominence of the interval D–G♯, it shares several other features with the whole-tone chord at the end of "Nov. 2": both are anchored by D2 in the bass, both are sounded five times, and both progress from *piano* to *pianissimo*. The earlier song ends with the text "If ye break faith with us who die We shall not sleep though the poppies grow in Flanders fields," and "Nov. 2," which refers in its introductory note to the same cemetery and to one of its inhabitants, ends by recalling these same soldiers through the established associations of the paired chords. The connection with the ending of "In Flanders Fields" suggests that the association is critical. The end of the song once again raises, and leaves unanswered, the question of whether the casualties of war will lead to "better things." Although the old man ends his soliloquy by looking into the future, one eye remains focused on the past—the war, the fallen soldiers, his son— a dual temporal focus reflected by the multidirectional possibilities as the song approaches its climax at p. 55/3/1. And like the final line of McCrae's poem, the paired chords that directly follow present two possibilities for the future well-being of the country, eternal rest or eternal restlessness.

As noted, the vocal setting of "a heritage we've thrown away" anticipates the upper portion of the second of the paired chords, and the judgment of these words can be heard lingering at the end of the song as well. But whether we hear the crisis fading away or looming as a future possibility is unclear. In "from 'Lincoln, the Great Commoner,'" the whole-tone chord had surfaced as an echo of the "great shout" of Lincoln's death, and perhaps that same echo can be heard at the end of "Nov. 2," sounding out through the leadership void that remains decades later, the void that forces the old man to call out to Lincoln in this moment of national need rather than to any living politician. The second stanza of Whitman's poem begins: "O Captain! my Captain! rise up and hear the bells; Rise up—for you the flag is flung—for you the bugle trills." In the five pairs of chords that end "Nov. 2," we might hear these beckoning bells, pealing regularly with faintly echoing overtones, a call unanswered.

But the summons at the conclusion of the song, although addressed to Lincoln, is ultimately directed at the American people, the Majority—*we've* thrown it away, but *we'll* find it again. Despite his profound disappointment with his fellow citizens, the ending of the song suggests that the old man, like Ives, believes in their inherent goodness. "God is on the side of the Majority," Ives wrote; "He has made Men greater than Man, . . . He has made the Common Heart, the Universal Mind, and the Over-soul greater than the individual heart, mind, and soul" (1961: 144). For Ives, the Majority was closely associated with God and the universal, and C major, so often a symbol of the latter in his music, is often associated with the Majority as well. This meaning can be discerned in "Nov. 2" when the Cmaj$_6$ chord is first heard in conjunction with the masses of soldiers who died in the war, as well as later in the song, when it suggests that a similar sacrifice is needed and forthcoming from the Majority. The song "Majority" provides strong support for hearing the Cmaj$_6$ chord in this way. Like the beginnings of these two songs, characterized by imposing wedges, their endings are closely related. Recall from the Introduction how "Majority" concludes with a joint image of God and his Masses; the words "God's in His Heaven" are accompanied by four sets of booming white-note clusters in the piano, each culminating in an Fmaj$_6$ chord (Example 0.2). Above these clusters, however, four black-note clusters are played by a stick or other means, as in the introduction of the song. These black-note clusters are roughly equivalent in function to the whole-tone chords of "Nov. 2," participating in a similar duality with the white-note collection and preventing any simple meaning to emerge.

"Majority" ends with a V–I final cadence in F major, affirming the prophecy "All will be well with the World!" and reflecting the final words of the accompanying essay, where Ives tells of how "as [the Majority giant] approaches maturity, there will come, we believe, a radiance such as the world has never seen!" (1961: 199). In contrast, there is no affirmative gesture in "Nov. 2" to eliminate the aftertaste of the whole-tone chord. Instead, it lingers as a reminder of how "the majority-mind turned its back on a high purpose," as Ives put it in his endnote. Another passage from Ives's essay "The Majority" seems appropriate here: the end of the first section, which ties together many of the themes from "Nov. 2." In an odd metaphor, Ives envisions the masses as an evolving giant "strolling down through the ages":

> He has seen Christ slain for his cause. He has see Ferro and Moore and Lincoln slain for his cause. He has seen martyr after martyr slain for his cause until his eyes have become dim. And he now proposes to stop the slaughter, for he is approaching a poise of mind, a strength of heart, that begin to come somewhere near the expression of his soul. How long before the few, the group, the hog-mind, the lower value, the Minority, will see the stupidity, the futility, of opposing this God-given power, and learn in accepting it to do a man's share in bringing the world, the Majority, the People, nearer a truer inheritance?!

Unlike the end of the essay, this passage ends with a question—or rather, a question/exclamation. At the risk of over-interpreting this detail, might it suggest a mixture of uncertainty and enthusiasm, or a conflict between doubt and confidence? Perhaps the paired chords of "Nov. 2" similarly project a dual image of the Majority's future, but with the punctuation reversed—a white-note exclamation followed by a whole-tone question. Perhaps Ives's melodic reference to the national anthem was inspired by the similar equivocation of its refrain, which, despite the anthem's triumphalism, raises a question about the future of American values.

In his revised version of the song, titled "An Election," Ives modifies the ending slightly, further muddying the interpretive waters. He adds a countermelody in the left hand beginning at p. 55/3/1 of "Nov. 2" that emphasizes D♭3 on the downbeat of the following measure. This D♭ clashes with the Cmaj$_6$ chord in its first three occurrences, significantly detracting from its diatonic purity and therefore diminishing its positive connotations as well. If this change reflects Ives's growing political pessimism, however, another one perhaps suggests his continued faith in his country. Ives adapted several other songs for unison choir, including "Majority" and "from 'Lincoln, the Great Commoner,'" but his choral arrangement of "An Election" is striking given the solitary identity of the song's vocal persona. In listening to the choral arrangement, we can hear the old man supported by the masses, speaking not for them but with them, the final line no longer a desperate expression of hope but a resolute expression of solidarity.

"Grantchester"

Ives's 1920 song "Grantchester" derives its text from a passage in Rupert Brooke's "The Old Vicarage, Grantchester." Brooke penned his poem in May 1912 while away from his native England, traveling in Berlin. His Grantchester is a paradise remembered and envisioned from afar. The persona, "sweating, sick, and hot," longs for his home, where spring is in full bloom. Brooke describes his Eden in luscious detail, and as the poem develops, the time frame stretches. We learn of past inhabitants of the village, among them Tennyson, Chaucer, and various creatures from Greek mythology. One can witness and commune with these spirits, for Grantchester, we are told, is a place where "the centuries blend and blur." And thus the persona can wonder if, on his return, he will find everything preserved just as it was when he left. The poem ends with a series of hopeful questions, including the famous last couplet, "yet Stands the Church clock at ten to three? / And is there honey still for tea?"

This image of a frozen instant, and the corresponding idea of centuries blending and blurring within it, seems ready-made for Ives, particularly the Ives of 1920, who was immersed in the philosophy of Emerson and influenced by his ideas about time. "The spirit sports with time,—'Can crowd eternity into an hour, Or stretch an hour to eternity,'" wrote Emerson (quoting Byron) in "The Over-Soul" (1990: 155), and it was with words like these at the forefront of his mind that Ives latched onto Brooke's poem. The specific portion Ives chose, though embedded in the interior of the poem, is a distinct section, set off by ellipses and framed by the lulling phrase "in Grantchester, in Grantchester":

> . . . . . . would I were
> in Grantchester, in Grantchester!
> Some, it may-be, can get in touch
> with Nature there, or Earth, or such.
> And clever modern men have seen
> a Faun a-peeping through the green,
> and felt the Classics were not dead,
> To glimpse a Naiad's reedy head
> or hear the Goat foot piping low . . . . . .
> But these are things I do not know
> I only know that you may lie
> day long and watch the Cambridge sky,
> and, flower lulled in sleepy grass,
> hear the cool lapse of hours pass,
> until the centuries blend and blur
> in Grantchester, in Grantchester . . . . . .

Ives set off the final three couplets as a coda marked *lento con grazia* and *slowly and calmly*. The music, comprising several layers of monotonous pitch material with little rhythmic articulation, is amorphous and hypnotic. These features help to evoke the washing away of temporal distinctions, the intermingling of centuries described in the text. The persona presents this experience, it seems, as a memory—he sings "you may lie...," not "I am lying...," as he would like. But we might also sense that the persona is reliving his earlier experience in front of us in some way, overcoming spatial separation in the same manner that Grantchester allows one to overcome temporal separation. As the final words linger, "in Grantchester, in Grantchester," their grammatical context fades and they can be heard as simple markers of place, as though the persona has been transported both in time and in space.

Several other codas of Ives's are similar to this one in their musical characteristics, most notably the "Emerson" movement of the *Concord* Sonata. As in "Grantchester," the "Emerson" coda is dominated by half-note octaves descending by step in the piano's left hand, leaping upward only out of necessity when approaching the lowest register of the piano (see p. 18/4/2–end of the 1920 edition). Also as in "Grantchester," the bass line ultimately makes its way to F1, above which the last of several hushed minor-third chimes is sustained in the right hand, dissonant with the bass as though distant overtones. In "Grantchester," there are three such chimes, as though emanating from the bell tower of the Grantchester church as the hour reaches three.

The musical similarities between the endings of these pieces point toward the "Emerson" chapter from Ives's *Essays*, published the same year that he composed "Grantchester," as the source of additional clues about the ideas behind the song. In an extended passage defending the "spiritual" beauty of Emerson's work (its substance) against those seeking a "sensuous" beauty, Ives imagines Emerson as a composer, his lectures and writings as music. This passage culminates in a description of the dramatic endings that punctuate many of Emerson's essays and poems: "Of a truth, his codas often seem to crystallize in a dramatic though serene and sustained way the truths of his subject—they become more active and intense but quieter and deeper" (25). Here, as frequently is the case, Ives's characterization of Emerson doubles as a characterization of himself. The statement applies well to the conclusions of many of Ives's pieces, including the "Emerson" movement and "Grantchester." These codas, like many others, are serene, sustained, quiet, and, both in terms of register and metaphysical connotations, deep.

Given the prominence of dualistic thinking in the *Essays,* Ives could hardly hold up Emerson's work as a model of artistic beauty without identifying its antithesis. This distinction goes to the music of Debussy, whose harmonic practice Ives compared, undeterred by the difference of medium, to that of Emerson the "composer." Debussy's music is weak and effeminate, its attractions only surface-deep:

A microscope might show that he [Emerson] uses chords of the ninth, eleventh, or the ninety-ninth, but a lens far different tells us they are used with different aims from those of Debussy.... If he uses a sensuous chord, it is not for sensual ears. His harmonies may float, if the wind blows in that direction, through a voluptuous atmosphere, but he has not Debussy's fondness for trying to blow a sensuous atmosphere from his own voluptuous cheeks.... There is a distance between jowl and soul—and it is not measured by the fraction of an inch between Concord and Paris. (24-25)

Ives seems to have taken Brooke's poem as an opportunity to illustrate this distance. This passage from the *Essays* refers slyly to Debussy's *Prélude à l'après-midi d'un faune*, evoking the faun and his pipe,[8] and in "Grantchester," the reference is explicit. Ives accompanied the line "a Faun a-peeping through the green" with a quotation of the opening flute melody of the *Prélude* in the upper register of the piano. In the *Prélude*, this melody gives way to a lush harmonic and orchestrational world, as though the faun's music were generating the erotic environment, his vision of nymphs. Ives's quip about Debussy's cheeks suggests that he understood the music in a similar way; the *Prélude*'s opening melody is the source of empty sensuality and its symbol.

In summarizing Ives's mature borrowing practices, Burkholder has stressed that "[Ives] is speaking for himself, in a language that is his own, one that assimilates all the musical tongues he had learned" (1995: 425). In his incorporation of the *Prélude* in "Grantchester," however, Ives was looking not to assimilate but to differentiate. In an apparent attempt to distance himself from music he regarded as decadent and effete, Ives took unusual steps to assure that the quotation would be recognized. He subtitled the song "with a quotation from Debussy" and identified the melodic reference itself with a footnote on the score. The message is clear enough: the quotation has been imported from the outside and is not part of the essence of the song. The stigma is reinforced by Brooke's text, as interpreted by Ives. The "clever modern men" are attracted to the world of fauns and naiads that Ives associates with the *Prélude* and, perhaps, the larger milieu of French symbolism. But the vocal persona does not engage in such frivolities ("these are things I do not know"); all he knows of Grantchester is the spiritual experience of nature evoked musically by the coda, solitary contemplation of one's natural environment as encouraged by Emerson and Thoreau.

This coda emerges as a counterweight to the middle section of the song, in which Ives's borrowing from Debussy is considerably more extensive than the quotation he identifies. The derivative passage draws upon the entire first five measures of Debussy's *Prélude*—not merely the initial sound of the flute, but the "sensuous atmosphere" that it brings into being as well. Example 3.6 illustrates, using the E-major orientation of the *Prélude* as a tonal reference point.[9] Some of the connections with the *Prélude* are easily apparent. The quotation of the flute melody in the piano, for instance, is anticipated in the vocal line. Debussy repeats the flute melody in mm. 1-2 of the *Prélude*, and thus Ives's consecutive statements of the melody can be heard as a single, modified quotation of these measures, as suggested in the example. These statements are dissociated from one another, however, by a change of instrumentation, register, and, most conspicuously, key. Each of these three disruptive elements continues to obscure the connection to Debussy's *Prélude*. The second quotation of the familiar chromatic portion of the flute melody is followed by the diatonic portion of the melody, beginning in the piano's right hand at the word "green." Here, the tonality shifts up-

Example 3.6. "Grantchester," p. 37/3–p. 38/2, connections with Debussy's *Prélude* and Wagner's Prelude to *Tristan und Isolde*.

ward by a semitone from A♭ to A. At the word "dead," the melody is transferred back to the voice, by which time it has descended two octaves relative to its model in the *Prélude*. The paraphrase concludes with mm. 4–5 of the *Prélude*: after the piano simulates the harp arpeggio, the tonality shifts back down by a semitone, restoring the earlier pitch level.

In sum, Ives recasts the opening of the *Prélude* as a tonally warped version of the original. Ives's manipulation of his source is perhaps most striking when it involves the full harmonies of mm. 4–5. The harmonic progression from a half-diminished seventh chord to a dominant seventh that characterizes this portion of the *Prélude* takes on a very different flavor as a result of the semitonal shift in Ives's song. In the *Prélude,* these two chords share the same bass (A♯/B♭), which strips the progression of any clear functionality and thereby lends it a mystical aura. In "Grantchester," where the bass descends a semitone from one chord to the next, there is likewise no firm tonal context in which the progression can be heard. But on a local level, it suggests a predominant-to-dominant motion supported by a ♭$\hat{6}$–$\hat{5}$ bass line. More specifically, the half-diminished seventh chord functions like an augmented-sixth chord resolving to the dominant.

The *locus classicus* of this progression was also likely an important musical reference point for Ives when he was composing "Grantchester": the opening of Wagner's Prelude to *Tristan und Isolde*. Ives's progression, a D♯ half-diminished seventh chord resolving to a D dominant seventh, both chords in root position, transposes the famous first two chords from Wagner's Prelude, the *Tristan* chord and its resolution, down a whole step from A minor (the implied key at the opening of the Prelude) to G minor (see Example 3.6). Clearly, Ives wished to undermine the fluidity of the music borrowed from Debussy's *Prélude* using a series of tonal shifts, but the last of these may have been motivated primarily by a desire to refer more literally to the composer whose presence is already felt so strongly in the *Prélude*. Enhancing the reference, Ives's vocal line incorporates the ascending chromatic melody that accompanies the opening pair of chords in Wagner's Prelude, also transposed down a whole step (see the vocal setting of "Naiad's reedy," highlighted on the example). Although the melodic figure is displaced rhythmically in relation to the chords, the basic metrical pattern remains the same—most significantly the treatment of the third note, G♯, as an accented passing tone.

Ives seems to have made veiled references to the opening of the *Tristan* Prelude in other pieces, probably more extensively than has been acknowledged. The musical entwining of Wagner and Debussy in "Grantchester" reflects Ives's commentary on the composers in the *Essays*. His negative assessments of the composers share basic characteristics: their music is effeminate, lacks substance, and evidences moral deficiencies. In describing his own disillusionment with Wagner's music in the "Epilogue," he likens Wagner's "sensual" harmonic vocabulary to Debussy's: "Those once transcendent progressions, luxuriant suggestions of Debussy chords of the ninth, eleventh, etc., were becoming slimy" (73). It is perhaps no coincidence that Ives added an eleventh, G♯, above Debussy's/Wagner's half-

diminished seventh chord in "Grantchester" (p. 38/2) and continued to emphasize this pitch class above the following dominant seventh.

After drawing this comparison with Debussy in the "Epilogue," Ives continued with his critique of Wagner:

> An unearned exultation—a sentimentality deadening something within—hides
> around in the music. Wagner seems less and less to measure up to the substance and
> reality of César Franck, Brahms, d'Indy, or even Elgar (with all his tiresomeness);
> the wholesomeness, manliness, humility, and deep spiritual, possibly religious, feel-
> ing of these men seem missing and not made up for by his (Wagner's) manner and
> eloquence, even if greater than theirs (which is very doubtful). (73)

Here, Ives is using Wagner to set up the substance/manner dualism, which he
introduces for the first time two pages later. As history progresses, he suggests,
the absence of substance beneath the showy manner of Wagner's music will be
exposed. Ives dramatizes the gradual and inevitable exposure of the relative emptiness of Wagner's music with an anecdotal account of his own changing attitude
toward it, from enthusiasm in his twenties to annoyance and cynicism in middle
age. He came to hear the "deadened" core of this music and could no longer
go back. Just as Ives coordinates precisely the Debussy quotation with the word
"Faun," the coordination of "dead" with the half-diminished seventh chord that
marks the point of overlap between Debussy's *Prélude* and Wagner's Prelude can
be understood as a commentary on the substance of this music.

The *Essays* provide additional clues to the interpretation of this portion of the
song. In the opening pages of the "Epilogue," Ives relies heavily on the metaphor
of time as a stream, eventually coming to the conclusion that it "flows past" fad-
dish composers such as Wagner but has no effect on the value of universal figures such as Bach and Beethoven (71–75). Water is a recurring theme in Brooke's
poem, and one with similar connotations. In the first stanza, the persona describes Grantchester from his bed in Berlin:

> Oh! there the chestnuts, summer through,
> Beside the river make for you
> A tunnel of green gloom, and sleep
> Deeply above; and green and deep
> The stream mysterious glides beneath,
> Green as a dream and deep as death.

Later, in the lines immediately following the passage Ives borrowed, the persona
names some of the literary figures whose ghosts linger near these waters, drawing inspiration:

> Still in the dawnlit waters cool
> His ghostly Lordship swims his pool,
> And tries the strokes, essays the tricks,
> Long learnt on Hellespont, or Styx.

Dan Chaucer hears his river still
Chatter beneath a phantom mill.
Tennyson notes, with studious eye,
How Cambridge waters hurry by . . .

Again, it is easy to imagine how Ives might have been drawn toward these lines, seeing in them a shared image of time's passing and genius's immunity to it.

Given the autobiographical perspective of Brooke's poem, the persona's desire to return to the splashing grounds of Lord Byron et al. is easy to understand. As a writer, to be in Grantchester is to draw upon a deep reservoir of creativity. For Ives, this source was the Emersonian Over-Soul; as he explained near the end of his "Epilogue," the artist is "nourished . . . in the soil of its literature" (1961: 100). Elaborating further, he wrote:

> If an interest in and a sympathy for the thought-visions of men like Charles King-sley, Marcus Aurelius, Whittier, Montaigne, Paul of Tarsus, Robert Browning, Pythagoras, Channing, Milton, Sophocles, Swedenborg, Thoreau, Francis of Assisi, Wordsworth, Voltaire, Garrison, Plutarch, Ruskin, Ariosto, and all kindred spirits and souls of great measures from David down to Rupert Brooke—if a study of the thought of such men creates a sympathy, even a love for them and their ideal-part, it is certain that this, however inadequately expressed, is nearer to what music was given man for than a devotion to "Tristan's Sensual Love of Isolde," to the "Tragic Murder of a Drunken Duke," or the sad thoughts of a bathtub when the water is being let out. (100–101)

Brooke, who died in 1915 while fighting in the war, is featured here as a recent inductee into Ives's pantheon; music should aspire to the spiritual and intellectual content of his work and that of his artistic and philosophical brethren. The passage treats *Tristan und Isolde,* on the other hand, as an object of disdain, associated not with the eternal chain of genius but the discharge of dirty bathwater. Brooke and Wagner are representatives of the substance/manner divide, and this duality lies just beneath the surface of "Grantchester." The song does not merely set Brooke's poem but emulates its substance; it does not merely quote Wagner and Debussy as a whimsical response to the word "faun," but critiques the superficiality of their music.

The presence in the song of these European composers, particularly Wagner, points to an element of the source poem that remains on the outskirts of Ives's setting. Brooke's persona is an Englishman on the Continent, a castaway in Berlin longing for his homeland. His contempt for his immediate surroundings is obvious; he complains, for instance, about the beer-drinking "*Temperamentvoll* German Jews" who surround him. Ives's choice of excerpt highlights the basic idea of separation, allowing him to establish the persona's absence from Grantchester with the opening lyric. The sound of alienation is suggested at the very onset of the song, by an angular *forte* sonority built from minor sevenths stacked over an A in the bass, a silence-breaking musical shock on par with the culture shock endured by Brooke's persona, transplanted from his pastoral home into the company of rowdy Berliners. This opening dissonance soon relaxes into an F-major triad, approached via the descending bass line A-G-F, each note supporting a broadly spaced chord. Above the second of these, a dotted motive in the upper voice outlines a descending third, introducing the dactylic meter of the word "Grantchester" that will soon be heard in the voice. After the bass descends to F, a similar motive emerges, diatonic in F major and marked "slower" and *pianissimo*. The blurred texture of this passage, as in the openings of so many of Ives's songs, invokes the realm of memory. And indeed, the serenity of the latter portion of the introduction and its F tonality offer a preview of the coda—a memory animated in the present—and provide a glimpse of the transcendent experience that will later be revealed more completely. The introduction also previews the musical path by which the coda will be approached: the transition to the coda in p. 38/3/2–p. 39/1/1 is a transposed and stretched-out reprise of the opening of the song.

The introduction not only gestures ahead to the coda, however, but it suggests the persona's longing for the experience embodied there. The echoing figures marked *slower* fail to resolve in concordance with the underlying F-major harmony: the lower and upper voices approach, but stop just short of F4 and C5, respectively, eschewing the perfect fifth that would have matched the lowest voices in the left hand. The first line of text, "Would I were in Grantchester," moors the affect of these hanging gestures to the temporal and geographical dislocation of the persona. Ives's setting of these words clarifies the connection. Similar to the introduction, the piano's entrance features an unprepared dissonant harmony (an E half-diminished seventh chord), which initiates a stepwise descent of a third in the bass (E-D-C). This bass line and the voice together outline a C dominant seventh, a chord that arrives vertically, with added dissonances, at the word "Grantchester." But rather than affirming F-major tonality, the music turns away. At the repetition of the words "in Grantchester," the bass negates its preceding motion to the dominant, retracing its steps and abruptly changing register: see the C-D-E bass motion in p. 37/2/1, which reverses the E-D-C descent of p. 37/1/2. The bass's arrival on E supports a sustained, open-fifths sonority whose relative hollowness is a sonic symbol for the distance between the persona and his desired location at this moment. A return of F major, and thus a return to Grantchester, will have to wait.

The following passage, up to the first *Prélude* reference, struggles to recapture the near resolution onto F. Harmonically, this music is the most complex and dissonant of the song. It includes two variants of the E half-diminished seventh chord that initially led to the C dominant seventh in p. 37/1/2. Each of these is fleeting, however, and neither chord steers the music back toward a functional progression that would confirm F major. The first variant, voiced as a stack of minor sevenths and thus recalling the opening sonority, accompanies the word "Some." Like its predecessor in p. 37/1/2, this chord follows a pause in the vocal line, supports E4 in voice, and initiates the descending bass line E-D. Thus it seems to reboot the vocal entrance, attempting once again to reclaim the lost F-major tonality of the piano introduction. But the bass overshoots C, landing instead on B while generating no sense of F tonality. Soon thereafter, at the word

"Earth," the second variant arrives, and now the phrase proceeds to a closed-position F-major triad on the word "such." But this cadence is tonally nonfunctional, a harmonic *non sequitur* following the series of complex and expansive harmonies that precedes it. It comes across as glib and unearned, a reflection of the shallow experiences of those who, "it may-be, get in touch with Nature there, or Earth, or such," as the persona patronizingly characterizes some visitors to Grantchester.

These casual visitors, in Ives's reading, are of a type with the "clever modern men," and Ives uses Debussy's skin-deep music to associate these constituencies musically. The vocal setting of "Nature there, or Earth, or such" is a partial transposition of Debussy's flute melody, transformed via rhythmic modifications. Thus, it anticipates the overt quotation that immediately follows, providing a bridge from the first section of the song, and its perfunctory close on F major, to the second, which puts on hold the pursuit of F tonality and the transcendent experience of Grantchester it signifies. This objective returns only after a full rejection of frivolous reveries, signaled by the words "But these are things I do not know," which set off the amalgamation of the two Preludes from the coda that follows. These words are spoken and notated with invisible note heads, as though this passage into another realm of experience is ineffable and imperceptible through the senses. Sonically, the rejection is rendered via a partial reprise of the piano introduction. This return is sudden and disruptive. It begins with a transposed variant of the opening sonority, now over a B♭ bass, which disrupts the D♯–D–C♯ descending bass line initiated by the *Tristan* progression in p. 38/2–3, leaping upward (C♯2 to B♭2); a double barline emphasizes the disconnect visually. A nearly exact transposition of the second chord from the introduction follows over A in the bass, again topped by the dactylic motive, recalling the rhythm of "Grantchester" earlier in the song. Unlike the introduction, however, here the chord is sustained while the motive spawns a long chain of descending thirds; these are joined by the voice ("I only know that") and eventually fade into the coda. Whereas the introduction had ended with a wistful glimpse of a past experience, the coda now reveals this experience in all its fullness. F does not emerge as a stable bass note until the very end, but the emphasis of the seventh C–B♭ in the piano ostinato and the organization of the vocal line around C4, F4, and A4 keep this tonal target ever-present. Thus, when F finally arrives in the bass, despite the continued presence of dissonant layers above it, the sense of resolution is strong.

I have now outlined a chronological hearing of the song in which the persona, by reflecting upon a place from his past, is ultimately able to transport himself there, in the present moment, or perhaps outside of time altogether. This hearing follows a simple narrative of departure and return implied by the text. The introduction provides a glimpse of Grantchester; the main portion conveys the persona's geographical estrangement, with Debussy and Wagner symbolizing the Continent; and the coda provides the return the persona had longed for in the opening line. Prominent musical returns—the opening sonority (transposed in p. 38/3/2), the words "in Grantchester" and their associated rhythmic figure (p.

Example 3.7. "Grantchester," dominant-tonic relationship between p. 37/1/2 and end of song.

39/3)—contribute to this sense of cyclic form. The three-stage scenario hinges on the musical depiction of the persona's separation from his homeland as sudden and traumatic, as implied by the opening sonority. When the initial vocal entrance leads to a C dominant, the stage is set for an affirmation of the concluding, F-major portion of the introduction. A harmonic and registral dislocation follows instead, and the repeated text "in Grantchester" leads not to F major but to an empty sonority built on E. This failed resolution not only motivates the passage that follows, as I have suggested, but hangs over the remainder of the song, a lingering symbol of geographical estrangement.

The reconciliation of this separation is achieved in the coda. The F tonality that emerges at the end is a return to the tonality of the opening; these locations provide the only regions of stable tonality in the song. Several additional features amplify the sense of cyclical return. The trichord in the piano's upper register, F♯4–E5–G5, that chimes at the end of the song reprises the upper portion of the C dominant from the opening vocal phrase. The left-hand portion of the C dominant had outlined the seventh C–B♭ (spelled A♯), and this interval recurs at the end of the song as well, in the left-hand ostinato. In addition to these harmonic connections, the opening and closing vocal lines are closely associated: in each case the text "in Grantchester" is set with descending seconds and similar dactylic rhythms (compare p. 37/1/2 and p. 39/3). Whereas the opening vocal line had ascended by step to B♭4, however, the final setting of "in Grantchester" leaps over this pitch to C5. As this relationship implies, the connection between these framing passages is not merely associative; we are also encouraged to hear a *directed* relationship between the unfulfilled C dominant of p. 37/1/2 and the concluding F-centered "tonic" sonority of the coda, with the latter providing the sense of resolution that earlier had been denied. Example 3.7 illustrates, juxtaposing these two passages. This linear connection suggests that the coda be heard as more than an aural representation of memory, or a vivid recollection of the past experience implied by the song's opening lyric. The leap in musical time instead suggests a leap in lived time, as though the persona has been transported, across space and outside of time, to the hills of Grantchester. The possibility of navigating the song in the nonchronological manner shown in Example 3.7 models the persona's ability to navigate time in this way.

The linear connection between these framing moments brackets off most of the song, highlighting the antithetical relationship between the music of the introduction and coda—stable, sustained, static—and the relatively disjointed music in between. These musical contrasts model experiential ones, spiritual communion with nature versus fractured urban existence. Even though the city/ country duality of Brooke's poem is not explicit in the portion Ives chose to set, the theme is still evident in Ives's song, particularly in his symbolic deployment of Debussy the composer. In the *Essays,* Ives identified Debussy's cosmopolitan lifestyle as precisely the cause of his deficient connection to nature, characterizing him as a "city man with his week-end flights into country aesthetics," and suggesting that the substance of his music might have been better had he "hoed corn . . . for a living" (82). Thus, the Debussy quotation, associated with "modern" men whose relationship to nature is superficial and intellectual, serves as an emblem of urban modernity. Likewise, the harshly dissonant and loud opening sonority—a verticalized whole-tone segment based on the same whole-tone scale as the Debussy quotation Ives identified—can be understood as an ultra-concise representation of the city clamor suffered by Brooke's protagonist. It is a means of setting up the narrative situation in the song's introduction, which outlines the persona's journey from where he is to where he desires to be.

The high F (F6) that begins the *Prélude* quotation Ives identified, along with the supporting harmony in the piano, recalls the opening sonority and creates a related effect: another shocking arrival. This F is unprepared by the smooth melodic approach before it (G♯5–A♯5–B5–C6); it arrives instead as a registrally displaced continuation of the piano's "alto" voice D4–E4. The harmonization of this F by a G♯-minor triad alludes to the characteristic harmonization of C♯ by an E-major triad in the *Prélude,* but this harmony is a non sequitur here: the preceding harmonization of "clever modern men," the most strongly directed progression of the song, sets up a resolution onto an A tonic via the progression V/V–V$^4_3$.

The G♯-minor triad, in other words, is one semitone too low; transposing it upward would create a reasonably satisfying resolution of the strongly articulated E dominant seventh that precedes it. Ives often uses sudden semitonal shifts such as this one to suggest portals in time—pathways between the present and remembered past, for instance. Here, the fissure in the musical fabric, perhaps intentionally coordinated with a page break, points toward just such a portal. Specifically, the tonal progression that accompanies "clever modern men" points backward, to the beginning of the introduction. Example 3.8 illustrates, showing how the opening sonority can provide a point of arrival for the tonicization of A initiated in p. 37/3. The opening sonority fulfills the voice-leading tendencies of all four voices in the piano while functioning plausibly in the tonal

Example 3.8. "Grantchester," directed relationship between the end of p. 37/3 and the opening sonority.

context established by the preceding dominants, primarily because of the evocation of A major by the sonority's outer voices, A and C♯. C♯ recurs again and again in the *Prélude* as the head tone of the main thematic idea; this association, along with the similar spacing of the initial sonority of the song and the G♯-minor triad of p. 38/1, allows the former to be heard as a compelling substitute for the latter.

By connecting the *Prélude* quotation to the introduction, this hypothetical progression strengthens the sense that the introduction contrasts insincere, urbanized experience with spiritual connection to nature, modeling a pathway between these experiences, a way back to Grantchester for the displaced persona. Extended through the entire introduction, the bass line of the progression shown in Example 3.8 would outline a descending whole-tone segment from B to F. This segment is thematically linked to the *Prélude* quotation. The first allusion to Debussy's melody, the vocal setting of the words "Nature there, or Earth, or such," elaborates the same whole-tone descent. The harsh opening chord can thus be understood as part of a larger trajectory: the chromaticized whole-tone vocal descent B-A-G-F at p. 37/3 ("Nature there . . .") is directly followed by a pure version in the bass (from p. 37/3 to p. 37/1/1), with the same whole-tone collection serving as basis of the first chord of the song.

Ives's coda, in its opening moments, returns to these particular incarnations of the whole-tone collection. The top four pitch classes of the song's opening chord are linearized as the upper layer of the piano ostinati at p. 39/1/2 (C♯-D♯-F-G). Similarly, the initial references to the *Prélude* melody are linearized in the lowest layer of ostinati; B-B♭-A♭-G-G♭-F is an amalgam of the two descending vocal lines in p. 37/3, including the chromatic line A♭-G-G♭-F shared by both. The countermelody in the upper voice of the piano at "clever modern . . . ," G♯-A♯-B-C, can be heard in the bass line of p. 39/1/2 as well, but in reverse, beginning with the simultaneous articulation of C and B on the downbeat. These two ostinato layers function as a pair. All the pitch classes that comprise the ascending scale in the right hand of p. 39/1/2 are also part of the bass line throughout the coda (which is more chromatic); the two lines plod along in contrary motion, with staggered half notes creating a composite quarter-note rhythm.

Intuition/Expression 97

In sum, the coda revisits and transforms the essential harmonic and melodic material from early in the song—the opening sonority and the Debussy quotation, as well as the unresolved C dominant evoked by the middle ostinato layer in the piano. And thus, to the extent "Grantchester" is "music about music," the coda is significant not merely as Ives's alternative to the music of Debussy and Wagner, but as his recuperation of certain aspects of this music. Specifically, the coda recasts the sensual materials of these composers—the slinky *Prélude* melody and the related whole-tone material—within a distinctly Ivesian environment of tonal and rhythmic stasis, claiming them as Ives's own. The eleventh chord that Ives singles out in the *Essays* figures in the coda as well. The source is not the modified *Tristan* chord in p. 38/2, however, but its precursor in p. 37/1/2: the prominent E half-diminished seventh chord that expands outward to a C dominant at the end of the measure, forming a complete eleventh chord (with raised eleventh). As mentioned, the C dominant is renewed in skeletal form in the piano's left hand during the coda; virtually the complete eleventh chord (missing only the ninth) is then reconstituted at the end of the song with the edition of the bell-like trichords.

In "Grantchester," then, Ives seems to have sought to distinguish his use of certain compositional materials from their treatment in *fin de siècle* French music and the landscape of Wagnerian and post-Wagnerian harmony. Ives was proving, perhaps primarily to himself, that his use of these materials was substantial and masculine, just like the parallel strategies in Emerson's writings he refers to in the quotation from *Essays* above. Whereas Wagner's extended harmonies were fundamental to his "slimy progressions," Ives's function differently; he strips his harmonies of any melodramatic tension, and leaves the upper extensions unresolved, as at the very end of the song. Brooke's poem offered Ives an opportunity to draw this musical contrast; its juxtaposition of a profound existential experience with an effete Greek pastoral fantasy no doubt captured Ives's attention as an apt analogue for the dichotomy between his music and that of Debussy and Wagner, with Brooke's reference to a faun providing an enticing hook.

Ives attributed the limitations of Debussy's music to his lack of connection to nature, and in this arena, the benchmark was not Emerson but another of Ives's spiritual role models, Thoreau. It is tempting in "Grantchester" to hear an implicit comparison between Debussy and Thoreau: Ives imagined Thoreau's own flute in the optional melody near the end of the *Concord* Sonata, a "transcendental tune of Concord" wafting over Walden Pond (Ives 1961: 69). And Ives compared the two directly in the "Epilogue" of the *Essays:*

We might say that [Debussy's] substance would have been worthier if his adoration or contemplation of Nature—which is often a part of it, and which rises to great heights, as is felt, for example, in *La Mer*—had been more the quality of Thoreau's. Debussy's attitude toward Nature seems to have a kind of sensual sensuousness underlying it, while Thoreau's is a kind of spiritual sensuousness. It is rare to find a farmer or peasant whose enthusiasm for the beauty in Nature finds outward expression to compare with that of the city man who comes out for a Sunday in the country, but Thoreau is that rare country man and Debussy the city man with his week-end flights into country aesthetics. We would be inclined to say that Thoreau leaned towards substance and Debussy towards manner. (82)

Ives's "Grantchester" is best understood as an illustration of this idea about the source of artistic substance. Ives grafts a musical duality, Ives vs. Debussy and Wagner, onto the country/city duality of Brooke's poem; by associating his own distinctive musical idiom with Brooke's idealized notion of meditative communion with Nature, and Debussy's/Wagner's music with the artificial experience of the "clever modern men" (the inspiration for the "city man" in the quote above?), Ives uses the song to make a case for the proper source of musical expression. The obviousness of the Debussy quotation helps to establish a direct connection between the associated category of experience and mode of artistic expression. And the same is true for Ives's coda; its transfixing ostinato texture not only represents a transcendent experience, but it presents itself as a product of this experience. Using Debussy as a negative example, Ives's song asserts its own artistic value.

Part II: Contexts and Methodologies

4   Elements of Narrative:
The Unanswered Question

In the broadest sense of the term, there can be little argument that Ives's music is very often narrative in character, its meanings linked to explicit or implicit stories. As I hope to have established, the reconfiguration of hypothetical, *a priori* linear successions is an important means by which these stories are conveyed. To choose one of many examples from the preceding chapters: in Ives's Piano Sonata no. 1, the B-major interpolation near the end of Movement IVb can be understood as a moment of remembrance inserted within an ongoing story suggested by Ives's programmatic commentary. This is a narrative conception, one that can be refined with the help of simple narrative concepts and terminology.

Until recently, however, studies of musical narrative have rarely considered how post-1900 compositional techniques might contribute to narrative effects in music. Since narratives concern linear event-sequences, and because linearity is in general more easily perceived in music of the eighteenth and nineteenth centuries than in music of the twentieth, scholars interested in narrative have often steered clear of this more recent music.[1] But this situation is changing. Recent years have seen a resurgence of narrative approaches, including Byron Almén's wide-ranging *A Theory of Musical Narrative* (2008) and two books dedicated exclusively to music after 1900, Vincent Meelberg's *New Sounds, New Stories: Narrativity in Contemporary Music* (2006) and the collection *Music and Narrative since 1900* (Klein and Reyland 2012). Meelberg goes so far as go argue that a narrative orientation is an indispensable means by which listeners can make sense of difficult contemporary music.

Ives's music is ripe for narrative analysis, not despite but because of compositional techniques particular to the twentieth century—reordered chronologies and the layering of independent material chief among them. In this chapter, I examine these features in *The Unanswered Question*, a piece whose foundational narrative impulse is clear. As I illustrate, this impulse derives from the work's suggestive title, its program, and the program's evident relationship to the characteristically Ivesian features of the music. In addition to offering a distinct perspective on one of Ives's most familiar works, I hope to suggest that narratological treatments need not be confined to Ives's explicitly programmatic works, abundant as they are. More broadly, I suggest ways of considering narrative and musical "voice" in music after 1900, and how modern techniques engendered new intersections with narrative forms.

Elements of Narrative Structure

The Unanswered Question is undeniably programmatic, as we know from Ives's own comments. To reach this conclusion, however, one hardly need go further than the music itself. The unusual formal and textural procedures defy explanation in terms of established compositional practice or any newly invented, purely systematic approach; any effort to understand these procedures will almost certainly draw on potential programmatic meanings. But, of course, we are not meant to apprehend the music "in the abstract": Ives composed a short note, to be published with the score, outlining performance indications and a narrative program. The program establishes the identity of the three instrumental groups, providing a rationale for the musical character of each, and describes how their disposition in the piece corresponds to a narrative sequence of events:

> [The strings] are to represent "The Silences of the Druids—who Know, See and Hear Nothing." The trumpet intones "The Perennial Question of Existence," and states it in the same tone of voice each time. But the hunt for "The Invisible Answer" undertaken by the flutes and other human beings becomes gradually more active, faster and louder through an *animando* to a *con fuoco*.... "The Fighting Answerers," as the time goes on, and after a "secret conference," seem to realize a futility, and begin to mock "The Question"—the strife is over for the moment. After they disappear, "The Question" is asked for the last time, and the "Silences" are heard beyond in "Undisturbed Solitude." (Ives 1985: 10)

The overall effect is of music generated by a preformulated, *ad hoc* narrative idea, "verbalized" as an explanatory aid; the program is not grafted onto the music as an afterthought but revealed as a basic component of "the work itself." As its apparent motivating factor, the program is the *raison d'être* of everything that we hear. To listen to the piece apart from an awareness of that which it seeks to represent would be to miss its point altogether.

Evaluating the status of the program, however, is not as straightforward as it might appear. Ives had devised his title upon composing the piece in 1908; "The unanswered Q??" appears atop his original sketch (Example 4.1). Yet he did not write down the program until he returned to the piece over two decades later, around 1930–1935, making revisions and arranging for a professional copy.[2] Thus, it is not easily established to what extent the program was part of Ives's conception of the piece—the essence of a larger programmatic idea indicated by the title—in 1908.

Untangling this issue is difficult. Some clues are provided by two different texts whose language and ideas intersect with those of Ives's 1930s program. First, as Wayne Shirley pointed out in a brief 1989 essay, Ives's title was almost certainly inspired by a line from Ralph Waldo Emerson's poem *The Sphinx* (first

Example 4.1. *The Unanswered Question*, pencil sketch (f2514) (Charles Ives, *The Unanswered Question*, used by Permission of Peer International Corporation).

Example 4.2. *The Unanswered Question*, "The Silences of the Druids," mm. 1–15.

published in 1847), "Thou art the unanswered question" (1989: 8–9, 13). Ives was acquainted with Emerson's writings by 1908: he wrote his senior essay on Emerson at Yale in 1897–98. Furthermore, he turned to Emerson as a musical subject not long after composing *The Unanswered Question*; he began composing his *Emerson Overture*, which ultimately provided material for the "Emerson" movement of the *Concord* Sonata, around 1910–14 and possibly earlier (Sinclair 1999: 111). Most important, Ives's later program for *The Unanswered Question*, as expressed through its text and amplified by the music, intersects with Emerson's *The Sphinx* in its imagery, its structure, and its worldview—even though it intro-

Adagio

Example 4.3. *The Unanswered Question,* "The Question."

duces several new features. If Ives's title all but confirms his engagement with the poem in 1908, and his 1930s program suggests the poem's influence as well, then the case for projecting the program back upon the 1908 version of the piece becomes stronger. Second, the 1930s program seems to grow out of Ives's writings about Emerson in the *Essays,* first published in 1920. This strong connection to the "Emerson" essay associates the program with Ives's thinking at least as early as 1920 and strengthens the notion that both it and the music were creative reactions to Emerson's writings.

One salient feature of *The Unanswered Question* is the layering of its instrumental forces into three distinct groups: strings, flute quartet, and trumpet.[3] These groups maintain a high degree of independence, often proceeding as though unaware of one another. In addition to instrumentation, they are distinguished by pitch material, tempo, register, dynamics, degree of metric regularity, degree of continuity, and Ives's performance indications.[4] Ives suggested that the strings actually perform from offstage, separated from the other instruments. From this spatially and sonically distant position, they sustain soft, diatonic harmonies throughout the piece, establishing G major with occasional intimations of C major (Example 4.2). These harmonies are widely spaced and change slowly, providing a serene setting for the sporadic activity of the other instruments. In front of this almost exclusively diatonic backdrop, the trumpet poses its unchanging, atonal question seven times. The Question (Example 4.3) becomes progressively louder over the course of its first six statements, each one followed by a brief response from the flutes. The responses, too, become gradually louder over the course of the piece, as well as faster, more rhythmically square, and more agitated in character (Examples 4.4a–f). The primarily chromatic motion of the individual flutes creates sonorities that are not tonal, but at times suggestive of tonal harmony. The exchange between trumpet and flutes ends with a final statement of the Question by the trumpet that returns to the triple-*piano* of the first statement.

Ives's program provides a clear motivation for the unusual insularity of the instrumental groups. That the Druids "Know, See and Hear Nothing" and are characterized as silent—that is, nonresponsive—provides a rationale for why the strings neither influence nor are influenced by the other instruments in any immediately apparent ways. These "Druids" would seem to be representatives of the unfathomable cosmos beyond. Such grand proportions are obvious enough from the program, and Ives reinforced them by subtitling the piece "A Cosmic Landscape" in one worklist.[5] The only obvious interactions among instrumen-

Example 4.4a–f. *The Unanswered Question,* "The Answers."

(d)

Allegro moderato

(e)

Allegro

(f)

Allegro (faster and faster)

Example 4.5. *The Unanswered Question,* (a) chromatic wedge formed by first three Answers; (b) comparison of opening sonorities of Answers 3 and 4.

tal groups are the flutes' "Answers" to the trumpet's periodic Question. Thus, the flute music is unique in that it *reacts* to the music of another instrumental group. Coupled with the relatively static nature of both the string and trumpet music, this circumstance helps to direct attention to the flute music as the most active of the three layers. The trumpet repeats the same short motive again and again, while the tones of the strings change so slowly that it is difficult to hear any harmonic directionality once the other instruments have added themselves to the texture. In the flutes, however, one is aware of progression. In addition to the gradual *crescendo, accelerando,* and other factors noted above, the relatively nondescript and amorphous quality of Answers 1–3 gives way to the more distinctively motivic character of Answers 4–6, in which the flutes incorporate the Question as a way of mocking it. Especially when coupled with knowledge of the programmatic note and the work's provocative title, these features invite one to hear the six Answers as an ordered, linear succession rather than as a set of unrelated, autonomous moments, despite the lengthy pauses that separate them. Again, Ives's program calls for this linear hearing of the flute part, grafting onto it the teleology of a basic narrative: the flutes' "hunt for 'The Invisible Answer' ... becomes gradually more active," leads to a "secret conference," and ends with frustrated mocking. In contrast, the program depicts the other parts as constant: the Question is *perennial,* the Silences are *undisturbed.*

Not only do these features establish the Answers as related events in an ordered succession, but numerous voice-leading connections suggest that certain Answers pick up where others have left off. In this sense the Answers may be understood as connected across the intervening space. The first Answer (Example

Example 4.6. *The Unanswered Question,* voice-leading connections from end of sixth Answer to beginning of first.

4.4a) is characterized by a chromaticized voice exchange between the pitches D and F in Flutes 1 and 4. These two flutes continue to move chromatically and in contrary motion to one another in the second and third Answers (Examples 4.4b, c), beginning each Answer where they left off in the previous one. Example 4.5a places the first three Answers in continuous succession, outlining how Flutes 1 and 4 each traverse once through the chromatic aggregate while moving in contrary motion to one another, resulting in a "wedge" (this one fanning inward, in contrast to those at the beginnings of "Majority," "Nov. 2, 1920," and the "Emerson" movement of the *Concord* Sonata). Of particular interest is how each flute comes full circle by the end of the third Answer, as if about to loop back seamlessly to the beginning of the first; this potential is suggested in Example 4.5a and is discussed further below.

Similar voice-leading connections involve the fourth, fifth, and sixth Answers (Examples 4.4d, e, f). As shown in Example 4.5b, the opening sonorities of the third and fourth Answers share three of four pitches. Thus the fourth Answer can be regarded as an alternate continuation of the second. An anomalous sustained chromatic cluster in the flutes fills the space between the fifth and sixth Answers. Low in register and soft in dynamic (the revised version specifies *pianissimo*), it apparently constitutes the "silent conference" Ives referred to in his programmatic note. Finally, as Example 4.6 shows, the descending octatonic tetrachords and the high, shrill sonority that constitute the final gesture of the sixth Answer (see the second half of Example 4.4f) provide strong voice-leading connections back to the very first flute sonority. Thus the sixth and final Answer, like the third, could lead back smoothly to the beginning of the first, suggesting that the flute material has the potential of continually looping back on itself. Just as the trumpet returns to the original dynamic of triple-*piano* at the end of the piece, the flutes, were their responses to continue beyond their sixth Answer, would presumably return to the opening as well. Unlike the connections among the first four Answers, expressed through many parameters and supported by chronological succession, the pitch connections shown in Example 4.6 are not reinforced by dynamics or textural features or by the order in which we hear musical events. Whereas the former connections come across as necessary and defining elements of the musical coherence among the early Answers, the latter connections seem to be more symbolic, further removed from a concrete musical reality.

‖: 1   2   3 :‖ 4   5   6 ‖

* hypothetical repeat (ad libitum)
** hypothetical repeat (ad infinitum)

Example 4.7. *The Unanswered Question,* summary of connections among Answers.

Example 4.7 summarizes the various connections among the Answers and shows the potential for directed motion than arises from them, using traditional musical notation and performance indications to emphasize the circular paths described above. As these examples imply, the six Answers could be conceived as fragments originating from a continuous linear succession that has been split into segments by the interpolations of The Question and silence. After hearing the piece, a listener can retrospectively reconfigure and connect the Answers to create a coherent linear chain of events. Moreover, as also suggested in the example, the first three Answers are capable of generating *ad libitum* loops of self-repetition on their own, while all six Answers, similarly, could be looped *ad infinitum.* If the Perennial Question of Existence persists beyond its necessarily limited set of appearances in the work proper and recycles continually through time (as we are invited to imagine), the Answerers rehearse their Answers along with it.

The notion of retrospective reconfiguration recalls the familiar structuralist account of how we infer a chronological "story" from the often more disruptive "discourse" presented by a novel or a film.[6] Despite certain limitations and potential misapplications as a means of describing narrative structure, the story/discourse model has basic utility as a comparative and interpretational tool. As the narratologist Ken Ireland has noted, "Whichever the labels and couplings we prefer, the justification for applying the concepts of *fabula/syuzhet,* even after more than seventy years, remains strong. . . . In specific cases, reconstitution of a *fabula* genuinely illuminates a work" (2001: 45). In the case of *The Unanswered Question,* the concepts call attention to organizational features shared with other narrative media—features that pertain to sequences of events linked with explicit narrative content. Specifically, the succession shown in Example 4.7 is analogous to a story, while the actual fragmented disposition of the flute music is analogous to a discursive representation of that story, in which the chronology and continuity of musical events are altered. A simple (if anachronistic) analogue can be found in almost any mainstream television program in a narrative format, including sitcoms, dramas, and reality shows. Such programs are generally structured around multiple story lines, none of which is presented continuously: instead, each story line unfolds in isolated segments, interrupted regularly by other story lines (as well as commercials). Despite this presentation, viewers easily draw connections between segments that are separated in time, ultimately perceiving a network of multiple continuous stories. In the same way, despite the regular interruptions of the Question, a listener might perceive directed motion, in addition to the recurring timbre within a broad pattern of intensification, among the flute segments in the manner represented by Example 4.7. Another analogue, more historically relevant, is a technique from film: parallel editing, the cutting back and forth between two zones of activity. As recounted by Tom Gunning, the procedure originated in 1906–08—that is, the same time Ives was composing *The Unanswered Question*—and was assimilated by D. W. Griffith two years later, assuring its posterity (1991: 76–77).

Scholars have occasionally applied the concepts of story and discourse to music, most notably Anthony Newcomb in his discussions of "archetypal plots" (1984, 1987; see also Berger 1992: 425, Burke 1999, Grey 1992, and Treitler 1989: 186–91). But few have used these concepts to characterize reconfigured sequences of linear musical events, let alone discuss such phenomena at all. In fact, Carolyn Abbate has insisted that such reorderings should *not* be understood in terms of story and discourse. Surfacing briefly in her book *Unsung Voices,* this argument glanced at Jonathan Kramer's analysis of Beethoven's String Quartet, Op. 135, in which Kramer had sought to demonstrate how instances of discontinuity in the first movement might be a symptom of "strands of continuity" that are "scrambled" and "intertwined" (1973: 126). In keeping with her insistence that musical narrativity requires more than structural isomorphisms with narrative forms, Abbate denied this analysis any suggestion of narrativity: "Is such a reformation a discursive narrating of the plot of the elusive, illusory story? Obviously not: there is more to narrating than mere reordering." Elsewhere in the book, she states her position more clearly: story is a "projection . . . a reader's or writer's assumption, a construction," and thus, "'story' and 'discourse' are in no way sufficient as signs of *narrativity*" (1991: 49, 48). In other words, as a "projection," the presence of a story explains more about the approach of the reader/listener than about the text itself.

The linear "story" suggested in Example 4.7 might well be a projection, but it is one that the music and its programmatic backdrop surely invite us to make. To overlook it—or worse, to deny the legitimacy of the invitation—is to miss something important. It arises because of musical connections that, once noticed, point toward it as a reconstructed conceptual source of the flute music—much as in narrative visual media, various features instruct us to recreate coherent stories out of the slices of life we see. The chromatic wedge that can be formed by the first three Answers, for instance, is a self-contained, symmetrical construct, a touchstone example of Ives's systematic composition that one could easily imagine appearing unadulterated in another piece.[7] The flute music can be understood as an outgrowth of this coherent musical structure. In fact, much of the "story" of Example 4.7 makes sense in relation to traditional contrapuntal and voice-leading procedures. The particular way that the Answers relate to this story, however, is not easily accounted for in reference to common compositional practice. Other applications of the story/discourse model to music—comparing a piece to its generic formal archetype (Newcomb) or comparing a passage to its progenitor within the same piece (Treitler)—graft the narratological model onto familiar compositional strategies that are easily described in purely musical terms. Yet in the case of the flute Answers, traditional musical models are insufficient: one is compelled to look elsewhere for a precedent. Literature is an obvious place to start. As Burkholder has explained, Ives wrote "literary music," music "that is avowedly 'about' something, as indicated by title, marginalia, or program notes, and that corresponds in its structure and meaning to literary forms, whether narratives, poems, jokes, essays, or plays" (1985: 17). Notwithstanding Abbate's peremptory declaration that music's resemblance to story and discourse alone cannot establish narrativity, it seems shortsighted to insist that such musical effects as those described above—or in Beethoven's op. 135 à la Kramer—are "obviously not" narrative. And the structural analogy can only gain strength when considered in tandem with other aspects of Ives's music.

Elements of Narration

Conceptualizing *The Unanswered Question* as a discursive representation of the flutes' story as outlined in Example 4.7 helps us better to perceive the music through the lens of Ives's program, one articulation of the story's "content." The Fighting Answerers begin their search for the Invisible Answer by engaging in civilized discussion, building on hypotheses in an orderly fashion (hence, the continuity and stability of the first three Answers when placed in continuous succession). Since the Answer is ultimately unobtainable, this discussion is futile, circular (hence, the potential connection from the third Answer back to the first, as though the Answerers could rehearse the same reasoning again and again). At some point, the Answerers lose patience, abandon their discussions, and begin to mock the Question (hence, the chromatic meandering of the earlier Answers gives way to pointed elaborations on the trumpet's motive). As the flutes begin to give up on their quest, they no longer follow a logical argumentative thread; instead, the Answers become disassociated from one another, as the flutes become preoccupied with ridiculing the Question (hence, the absence of the same degree of linear coherence we saw among the initial three Answers). The mocking proves just as futile as the more genuine attempts made before it, likewise going nowhere (hence, the final Answer loops back to the first, implying that the struggle to find an answer continues eternally).

No doubt, we are meant to interpret this story as an allegorical representation of the existential struggles of human beings. One can imagine varying degrees of specificity with which this allegory could be related to "real life." For instance, we might understand the temporal component of the story as no more than a practical convenience, an illustrative device—human beings, living in "real time," could hardly be thought to follow this simple trajectory in their metaphysical pursuits. Or, we might assign it greater significance, imagining, say, a historical narrative, in which the sincere humanistic concerns of the past devolve into the alienation and cynicism of the modern era. Yet this layer of meaning would be logically posterior to the more basic story expressed through music and program, whose identity must be perceived before more nuanced interpretation is possible.

If we take the conjunction of the Answers to be the story that *The Unanswered Question* is about, however, we have supplanted a sequence of events that seems a more obvious choice for the piece's narrative content: the alternating Questions and Answers. If the piece is indeed about a single, *uninterrupted* sequence of events in the lives of the Answerers, what exactly is the status of this alternation that clearly forms the essence of the work? To answer this question, we must consider further how and why the flutes' story is modified within the piece itself. In terms of their effects on the story's chronology, the modifications are of two basic types. First, the piece omits events from the story: the flutes' potential circular returns to the opening Answer never actually occur. Second, the piece inserts music between story events: the flute part is divided into Answers that are separated by statements of the Question and space filled by the ever-present strings. If we were dealing here with a bona fide narrative, we could refer to these modifications in terms of the common discursive techniques "ellipsis" and "pause" (Genette 1980: 99–109). The notion of "ellipsis" transfers with relative ease to the segmentation of the flutes' Answers, a commonsensical way of referring to the circular returns that, for obvious practical reasons, are only suggested. We cannot invoke the term "pause" so easily, however, for a narrative pause is filled by something that has a narrative function. Specifically, in literature, discursive pauses allow the narrator to describe, explain, and otherwise comment on story events. Do the spaces between flute Answers, each filled by the constant backdrop of the strings and one statement of the Question, have a comparable function?

Here we arrive at a central problem of studies of narrative in music. Much debate has arisen from the apparent fact that the *narrator*, a fundamental component of literary narratives, has no obvious equivalent in music. The same problem is faced by theorists of film: film obviously is in most cases a narrative medium, at least in the more general sense of the term, but its narratives tend not to derive from an explicit or implicit speaker, as in literature. Almost all studies of musical narrative make the implicit assumption that a causal succession of events is far and away the most essential component of narrative. In these studies, the ordered event-sequences of music are the basis for claims of its narrativity, and no narrating presence is necessary: music is regarded as a sort of "non-narrated narrative." Many film theorists, on the other hand, guided by Christian Metz, have dealt with this problem by identifying filmic devices that function *like* a narrator or imply a narrating presence. As Metz put it in 1974: "The spectator perceives images which have obviously been selected (they could have been other images) and arranged (their order could have been different). In a sense, he is leafing through an album of predetermined pictures, and it is not he who is turning the pages but some 'master of ceremonies,' some 'grand image-maker'" (1974: 21).[8]

According to André Gaudreault, it is the presence of reordered events in film that points unequivocally to the presence of a narrator: "Only the narrator is capable of taking us along on his flying carpet through time. . . . It is he who re-makes [*re-met*], in front of me, in the order that suits him, these events that already occurred. And . . . it is the montage-activity of the filmic narrator that allows the inscription of a true narrative past" (1988: 111; translation mine).[9] In 1990, Seymour Chatman posited an implicit filmic narrator comprised of a combination of visual means (editing, cinematography, choice of images) and auditory means (the quality and source of sounds) (1990: 134–35). Jakob Lothe, whose work I draw upon below, reinforced this view a decade later (2000: 27–31). For each of these authors, the presence of *editing,* as it effects chronology (among other things), necessarily points to the presence of some consciousness that has organized the film's various shots and sequences, whether or not we can locate that consciousness and its voice.

For pieces that involve reordered successions akin to event-sequences restructured via editing in film, the existence of these structural characteristics of narrative might generate the perception that they have been brought about by some presence interior to the work and thereby evoke the quality of narration. Thus, if the flute music in *The Unanswered Question* is understood analogously to a narrative sequence of events (as is encouraged by Ives's program—itself a narrative), and this sequence is understood to derive from such a model as that proposed in Example 4.7, then we might seek the existence of some presence, however it would ultimately be construed, that has done the deriving.

Certainly, one might question the value of establishing the existence of a narrator, or some entity functioning like a narrator, if it cannot be concretely identified but only inferred via our perception of its traces. Indeed, to justify the existence of a narrator theoretically requires dubious logic if this narrator cannot be located as an actual presence. More fundamentally, one might question the absolute need for a narrator in a theory of narrative. The concept seems for the most part both forced and unnecessary in film theory, where it serves mainly a practical function, making possible general theories that can apply to both film and literature. Yet in *The Unanswered Question*—and much of Ives's other music as well—the logic of film theory can sensitize us to the potential projection of an actual narrating presence, a presence that functions analogously to a narrator.

Here it is helpful to return to the notion of "pause." The spaces between Answers are filled most conspicuously by statements of the Question; less prominently, the strings continue with their nonresponsive music. This music might seem to bear no relation to the developing sequence of questions and responses, yet there are subtle connections that bind the string music closely to the music of the flutes. These are most obvious with regard to Answers 1–3. Each of these Answers participates in a close harmonic and melodic relationship with the underlying string music. In each case, the strings sustain a diatonic harmony while the flutes waft around that harmony, with two or three of the flutes ultimately coming to rest on pitch classes that are semitonal displacements of those sustained by the strings. Voice leading gives the impression that the flutes approach, but stop just short of, a resolution onto the supporting string harmony. Example 4.8 illustrates this circumstance. For each Answer, the lower staff shows the basic harmony sustained by the strings, whereas the upper staff provides an arhythmic reduction of the Answer, with brackets showing how the final sonority might

Example 4.8. *The Unanswered Question*, harmonic relationships between flute Answers and underlying string sonorities.

resolve onto pitch classes from the underlying string harmony via smooth and logical voice leading. In some cases, chromatic motion leads directly toward the implied resolution; see, for instance, how the outer voices of Answer 2 move toward the pitches shown in brackets. In others, harmonic function suggests the implied resolution—the combination of F-B-D at the conclusion of Answer 1, for instance, sustained over a C-major triad suggests a resolution onto the same. In Answer 3, the presence of C and E in the final sonority, heard in the context of the underlying C-major triad, implies the resolution of the offending dissonances F and C♯ in Flutes 1 and 4 onto E and C, respectively (the resolution onto E is strongly implied by the chromatic descent in Flute 1 as well).

In addition to these harmonic connections, the strings anticipate the melodic material of many of the Answers, as illustrated in Examples 4.9a and 4.9b. The lower staff of Example 4.9a provides an arhythmic reduction of Flute 1's melodic line in the first, second, and third Answers. The upper staff shows the primary melodic material of the strings that immediately precedes each Answer. Note that in all cases, a descending diatonic line in the strings is followed by a descending chromatic line in Flute 1 of comparable length; the flute line always approaches, but falls just short of, the final pitch class of the descending string line.

After the fifth Answer, as the flutes enter their "secret conference," we hear a short, distinctive melodic line in the first violins. Here is a rare moment when a bona fide motive emerges in the strings—the rest of the string part is dominated by scalar lines that move too slowly to be heard as motivic and lack any sort of distinctive profile. Example 4.9b reproduces the first violins' short melody and shows how immediately it is followed by the Question and subsequent mocking by the flutes, with each instrumental group using shorter rhythmic values than the last. The first violins' melody is five notes long and shares the basic contour of the Question: both descend initially, leap to their highpoint on the pen-

Example 4.9. *The Unanswered Question,* (a) melodic relationship between Flute 1 and prominent string lines; (b) mocking of Question; Invisible Answer (?).

ultimate note, and then descend to the final note, arriving on either the same or nearly the same pitch on which they began. The juxtaposition of the motives in all three groups invites comparison, encouraging us to understand the first violins' motive in relation to the Question. But this motive is not questioning—purely and simply, it outlines a cadential gesture in C major, strongly reinforced by its harmonization in the lower strings and ending with a definitive $\hat{2}$–$\hat{1}$ motion rather than a disorienting dissonance. Could this be the Invisible Answer the flutes are seeking, inscribed in C major, Ives's symbol of God, truth, and celestial harmony? We might well look for this Answer in the tonally grounded music of the strings, positioned antithetically to the trumpet's dissonant motive. This invocation of what may be the Invisible Answer at the same moment that the flutes abandon their search is tinged with irony. From our perspective, the Answer is there for the Answerers to behold; yet, to them, it is invisible.

In sum, diatonic material from the string part—be it melodic lines or sustained harmonies—often appears, either subsequently or concurrently, in chromatically altered form in the flutes.[10] The diatonic/chromatic dichotomy differentiates the strings from the other groups. The strings' pure diatonicism, the backdrop of this "Cosmic Landscape," evokes the equilibrium of the universe, the "harmony of the spheres."[11] This elemental Harmony establishes itself from the outset, as the strings play alone. The first entry of the trumpet, with its tonally nebulous Question, disrupts the Harmony, taking us to the relatively troubled and confused state of affairs on Earth. The flutes subsequently adopt the chromaticism of the Question in their confounded replies, a connection that grows more apparent with the later Answers. Because the strings often set up the harmonies and melodic lines of the flutes, it might seem, from a purely musical standpoint, that the chromatic lines of the flutes respond to the diatonic material of the strings. But such an interpretation makes little sense in relation to Ives's program: the Fighting Answerers are not privy to the knowledge of the Druids and thus would not be capable of reacting to them. Might, on the other hand, the Druids be anticipating the activities of the Answerers? Again, Ives's program would seem to deny the possibility, characterizing the Druids as insentient. Indeed, there is a strong association between the string music and the "impassive, harmonious existence of a cosmos radically indifferent to our desires, our plans, our questions" (Marcotte 1997: 184; translation mine). Indifferent, perhaps—but oblivious? Druids are known for their abilities as seers, and, as we have already seen, Ives's designations "silent" and "invisible" require qualification. Thus we might wonder if Ives's Druids know, see, and hear more than he chose to specify in his later program.

Taking these factors into consideration, along with the melodic and harmonic connections shown above, we might conclude that these metaphorical Druids, aware on some level of the Answerers' question-and-response struggles occurring in the world beneath them, provide a context in which to understand these struggles. They suggest knowledge the Answerers cannot gain, including an "Invisible Answer" that casts into relief the failure of the Answerers' search. Unaware of the Question, they write the real Answer into the cosmos, although it is unseen by merely human Answerers. Returning to the original question of whether the flute pauses—the moments in which the flutes are not heard—can be understood in terms of narration, I would suggest that the strings fill these pauses with what can be characterized as *commentary:* the Druids prepare us for what the Answerers will say, their musical courses tracing around what the Answerers want to know but cannot learn.[12]

Commentary is a hallmark of narration, a basic purpose of the discursive pause. As Chatman put it, commentary "conveys the overt narrator's voice more distinctly than any feature" (1978: 228). We do not simply hear the activities of the Fighting Answerers as they occur, but we hear them as they are contextualized by the strings, reconfigured and periodically remarked upon. As commentators, the strings remain detached from the human activity on which they comment: they do not participate in it, nor are they affected by it—a condition powerfully reinforced by their position offstage. A crucial and oft-noted aspect of diegetic mediation is *distance*—distance, that is, between the narrator and the characters and events of a story; narrators tend to be far removed from the events they present and comment upon. Incorporating the work of Genette (1980) and Wayne Booth (1983), as well as Edward Bullough's notion of "psychical distance" (1957), Lothe proposed a tripartite model of how narrative "constitutes itself" by distancing the narrator from the characters and events of the story. Such distance could be accomplished in any of three different realms: "temporal," "spatial," or "attitudinal." Lothe treated temporal distance as the primary form: narration is "normally retrospective" and "temporal distance is often [its] motivating factor." The narrator frequently occupies a different location than the characters of the story, establishing spatial distance as well. Finally, Lothe defined attitudinal distance as the relationship between "the narrator's level of insight, judgements, and values" and those of the characters, a relationship that points toward the narrator's position within the text's overall "value system" (2000: 35–36).

In *The Unanswered Question*, the strings maintain temporal, spatial, and attitudinal distance from the action of the flutes—both musically and in terms of their extramusical associations. The string music is static, whereas the flute music drives forward in various ways; thus, the temporal natures of the two musical layers are qualitatively different. The strings are physically, or *spatially* distant from the flutes; they perform from offstage. Extramusical factors contribute further to each type of distance. The Druids are eternal, existing outside of the confines of time, whereas the Fighting Answerers, as humans, are mortal; the strings' anticipations of the Answers, viewed in conjunction with the program, reinforce this temporal disjunction. The Druids are celestial, whereas the Answerers dwell on Earth. Finally, the Druids are pure and in possession of a higher truth, whereas the lives of the Answerers are tainted by ignorance—clearly, the strings' "insight, judgements, and values" are each on a higher level than those of the flutes.

All these aspects of distance between the strings and flutes combine to create a plausible context for narrative. With the string part positioned in a conceptual space that *could* be occupied by a narrator and also taking on potential functions of a narrator, the music conforms to some of the more closely circumscribed views of musical narrative.[13] Thus, in addition to being structured like a narrative, *The Unanswered Question* could be construed as exhibiting some important characteristics of *narration* itself—including possession of an identifiable voice (albeit a metaphorical one) doing the narrating. Along these lines of argument, the notion of a "non-narrated narrative" becomes unnecessary. The narrative of the Fighting Answerers is not simply there, but has its source in the strings. That it appears to us in fragments, alternating with a repeated "Question," is a discursive convenience, a practical way of showing the constant presence of the Question and how it nags at the Answerers. On this reading, the alternation does not exist in the "real world" of the story, but is part of its narrated representation. Ever present; removed yet somehow aware of all; framing our experience of the Questions and Answers, bringing them forth, and constantly influencing our perception of them: to the extent that *The Unanswered Question* can be conceptualized as a narrative, the narrator is found to be most plausibly represented in the strings.

The Unanswered Question and Emerson's The Sphinx

This narrative conception of *The Unanswered Question* relies on musical analysis. Yet the analysis alone would not have led as forcefully to the narrative reading had I not considered the music through the lens of the short program that Ives appended to the work in the early 1930s. Beyond this local significance, though—that within the confines of the piece itself—the program surely also reflects crucial aspects of the personal philosophy that so thoroughly informs Ives's music. This larger context can refine our understanding of the program and at the same time offer new possibilities for extending the work's potential narrative implications.

As we have seen, Ives's philosophical view, especially by 1920, drew heavily on the Transcendentalist, "Concord" philosophers, Emerson foremost among them. The Emersonian aspect of Ives's thought is evident in his 1930s program for *The Unanswered Question*.[14] Its presence in this text is brought out via comparison with the two sources mentioned above: the "Emerson" essay from the *Essays*, a passionate explication of the special nature of Emerson's thought and the particular value of his writings; and Emerson's *The Sphinx*, likely one of the many writings from which Ives derived his verbal portrait of the author. As mentioned above, we can almost certainly conclude that Emerson's work played some role in Ives's composition of the original version of *The Unanswered Question* in 1908, given the correspondence between the piece's title and a line from *The Sphinx*. In and of itself, this connection does not establish that Ives had any clear thoughts concerning Emerson's writings when first composing the piece. Yet a consideration of the rest of the poem suggests connections between it and Ives's 1930s program. In turn, this makes a strong case that the poem was also a source of inspiration for Ives in 1908.

A thorough explication of Emerson's poem would be superfluous; there is little evidence to suggest that Ives drew upon it in anything approaching a comprehensive way. Moreover, numerous other poems and essays by Emerson put forth similar ideas to those in *The Sphinx* that are most relevant here; it would be a mistake to overemphasize the importance of this particular poem because of a single textual correlation. Yet this correlation is provocative just the same, and the poem is representative of some of the key ideas of Emerson's that interested the mature Ives the most. Thus, it is helpful to take a brief survey of elements of the poem that intersect with aspects of Ives's program, elements that might be understood to have had an impact on Ives as he composed the music itself in 1908—and then, a quarter of a century later, its "official" program.

The poem begins with the voice of the Sphinx herself. Her words establish the focus of the poem, an ancient "secret":

> Who'll tell me my secret,
> The ages have kept?—
> I awaited the seer,
> While they slumbered and slept;—

The second stanza specifies the nature of this secret (we might well call it "The Question of Existence"):

> The fate of the man-child;
> The meaning of man;

After this introduction, the Sphinx explains the secret in greater detail, illustrating man's singularly flawed existence via comparison with the rest of the world. In stanzas 3–6, she describes the harmonious, unified state of affairs enjoyed by all other earthly phenomena. In stanza 5, for instance:

> Sea, earth, air, sound, silence,
> Plant, quadruped, bird,
> By one music enchanted,
> One deity stirred,—

"Silence" comes up one other time in these four stanzas; we hear, in stanza 3, of how

> In beautiful motion
> The thrush plies his wings;
> Kind leaves of his covert,
> Your silence he sings.

This "silence" is "sung," and we might well surmise that the song belongs to that "one music" uniting all plants, animals, and elements.

Missing from Earth's roll call, of course, is man. He emerges in stanza 7, his corrupt existence in stark juxtaposition with the preceding depiction of earthly harmony:

> But man crouches and blushes,
> Absconds and conceals;
> He creepeth and peepeth,
> He palters and steals;

In stanza 8, as told by the Sphinx, "the great mother" interrogates the reason for man's plight through a series of questions asked in "accents," and in stanzas 9–14 "a poet" replies, providing "answers." We learn that man's "soul sees the perfect, / Which his eyes seek in vain" (stanza 10). The poet also tells us that man will never answer the secret (stanza 11):

> Profounder, profounder,
> Man's spirit must dive;
> To his aye-rolling orbit
> No goal will arrive;

Instead, he is destined to suffer through "Eterne alternation" (stanza 13). Finally, in the fifteenth of the seventeen stanzas, the Sphinx addresses the poet, although she seems to speak to all of humankind:

Thou art the unanswered question;
Couldst see thy proper eye,
Always it asketh, asketh;
And each answer is a lie.
So take thy quest through nature,
It through thousand natures ply;
Ask on, thou clothed eternity;
Time is the false reply. (Emerson 1994: 5–8)[15]

Here, she both indicates the perenniality of the question and the doomed nature of man's replies.

First of all, we can see that *The Unanswered Question,* as characterized by Ives's 1930s program, shares the general worldview of *The Sphinx.* Each work divides the universe into three distinct entities: (1) a harmonious, unified element; (2) "man," whose existence is fundamentally flawed and who experiences a profound existential crisis; and (3) a higher entity that poses the existential dilemma to man. And each work introduces these three entities in a similar pattern. Early on, a large section is devoted to the depiction of the harmonious, unified state on Earth, and perhaps the cosmos as well. The conclusion of this section is followed by both the introduction of humans, their troubles in stark contrast with the peaceful accord of the rest of the world, and a series of alternating questions and answers between humans and the universal questioner. Finally, a statement from the questioner concludes the work (in *The Sphinx,* the Sphinx proclaims: "Who telleth one of my meanings, / Is master of all I am").[16]

In addition, a basic trope seems fundamental to the imagery of both Emerson's poem and Ives's program; each text refers to a level of experience or knowledge that is available not through the senses but only through some sort of extrasensory perception. Emerson invited his readers to imagine "sung silence," part of nature's underlying "music." Ives also explored this possibility of "hearing silence," realizing the "Silences of the Druids" as string music. Ives's piece creates a world where we can also "see the invisible": the "Invisible Answer" resides in the Silences above, barely audible through the din of the flutes, available only via "unexplained consciousness."[17] Might these Silences be Ives's version of Emerson's "Over-soul," the realm of the "perfect," known to man's soul but "sought in vain" by his eyes? Consider this excerpt from Emerson's essay "The Over-soul," originally published in the same year as *The Sphinx,* in relation to Ives's "Answerers" and "Silences": "We live in succession, in division, in parts, in particles. Meantime within man is the soul of the whole; the wise silence; the universal beauty, to which every part and particle is equally related; the eternal ONE" (Emerson 1990: 153).[18]

These various connections bring out a strong Emersonian component in Ives's program. They suggest that, far from having "forgotten all about Emerson by the time he revised the piece" (Shirley 1989: 9), Ives drew heavily—perhaps by this time automatically—on Emerson's writings when composing the program in the 1930s. This conclusion should not be surprising, given Ives's intense engagement with Emerson's ideas by 1920; indeed, his assimilation of Emerson's thought was thorough enough by this time that he might not have been conscious of the degree to which his program was indebted to it. What is significant here is the possibility that the main lines of engagement were already present as early as 1908. The derivation of Ives's 1908 title, and the extent to which the "Sphinxian" aspects of the program are tied to features of the music—all features that were present in the 1908 version—lead to this conclusion. And if the 1930s program is heavily indebted to Emerson—and to *The Sphinx* in particular—it follows that, since Ives most likely was already responding to *The Sphinx* in 1908, some proto-version of the 1930s program probably existed in his mind upon composing the original version of the piece.

To see the presence of Emerson behind Ives's original conception of the music and program of *The Unanswered Question* might help us to understand the origins of the distinctly narrative aspects of the work. Ives's inquisitiveness regarding the nature of human existence and his desire to explore the topic musically cannot be traced solely, or even primarily, to Emerson's influence. They would instead seem to be the products of a variety of interrelated factors. But the idea to explore these philosophical issues through a *narrative* involving a series of responses to an existential question might well have come from Emerson's writings—most likely, from *The Sphinx*. That Ives happened upon this idea independently seems unlikely, especially given the influence of Emerson's work on Ives. If we can speculate that the repeating musical "Question" was the core element of Ives's initial conception of his piece, then we can even isolate a line from *The Sphinx*—"always it asketh, it asketh"—as quite possibly the source of inspiration.

The Unanswered Question, From Without and Within

The ideas from *The Sphinx* that seem to have made the greatest impression on Ives in 1908 are some of the same ideas that he chose to bring out in the "Emerson" essay from his *Essays,* our most complete document of Ives's mature philosophical and musical views (at least as crystallized by 1920). To be sure, it would be a procedural error unreflectively to map the fully formatted philosophy of 1920 onto a work from 1908.[19] Still, it seems an even larger error to ignore it altogether. Nor can we ignore that the language of *The Unanswered Question* program of the 1930s is reminiscent of the 1920 Emerson essay at many points. Tracing the trajectory of *The Unanswered Question* from its original composition in 1908 to the codification of an appended program in the 1930s situates the *Essays* in the middle of a history of Ives's ongoing engagement with Emerson's thought. Within any broader conception of the work extended through historical time, the *Essays* can hardly be declared irrelevant.

Of the four "impressionistic pictures" of the "Concord" philosophers that make up the *Essays,* the "Emerson" essay is by far the longest, reflecting Ives's especially high esteem for Emerson's thought. Ives's Emerson searches for and gains uncommon exposure to the "eternal" and the "infinite"—the realm of Truth, known in *The Unanswered Question* as the Invisible Answer: he is an "invader of the unknown" who seeks "the divine truth, underlying all life." Emerson "stand[s] on a summit at the door of the infinite . . . peering into the mysteries of Life, contemplating the eternities, hurling back whatever he discovers there." Yet his inquiries not only extend outward into the universe, but also turn inward into the human soul: he is "a recorder freely describing the inevitable struggle in the soul's uprise." Thus, Emerson connects those strata of life so starkly disconnected in *The Unanswered Question*: with discoveries "cosmic, religious, human, even sensuous," he "would discover . . . that 'wondrous chain which links the heavens with earth'" (Ives 1961: 11, 14, 12, 11).

The original version of *The Unanswered Question* thus foreshadows Ives's many descriptions, twelve years later, of the quintessential Emersonian vision. In this sense, Emerson—along with us, and Ives himself—lies outside of the music, listening in. Yet, at least when considering the piece along with the 1930s program, we appear to be invited to project an Emerson *inside* the music as well. The music not only seeks to suggest what Emerson intuits, but it models his transmission of knowledge to the world, showing him in relation to what he studies. Like the Druids, Ives's Emerson possesses special powers of perception: he is "a prophet," "a seer"; his eyes possess "the strength of distance"; "[a] kind of higher sensitiveness seems to culminate in him." He does not convey his knowledge in direct or obvious ways, however. Emerson is "more a discoverer of beauty than an imparter of it" and he is "more interested in what he perceives than in his expressing of it"; "so close a relation exists between his content and expression, his substance and manner, that if he were more direct in the latter he would lose power in the former" (Ives 1961: 11, 13, 15–16, 21, 29–30).

Considered in the light of Ives's later program, specific musical procedures bring to life passages from the Emerson essay, likewise identifying Emerson inside the music, embodied by the Silences. Ives wrote that we "incline to go with [Emerson] but halfway" on his existential journeys, a statement that applies curiously well to the Fighting Answerers: after beginning the piece engaged in earnest inquiry, their first three Answers closely connected to the music of the Silences, they abandon their search in the second three Answers, with their music no longer bearing much relation to that of the strings. Another example is the strings' five-note "Invisible Answer" motive, an apt musical analogue of how "[Emerson] must struggle if he would hurl back anything [of the infinite]—even a broken fragment for men to examine and perchance in it find a germ of some part of truth" (Ives 1961: 14). In *The Unanswered Question* we may catch a glimpse of the presence—transfigured into musical representation—that Ives in 1920 would come to identify with Emerson, the human surrogate for the Silences, who, imparting his silent knowledge, narrates the story of existence to us.

There is still one other figure whose presence might be felt in the music of the strings: Ives himself. Ives's musical representation of the Silences of the Druids belongs to the elusive realm of what he would later call "substance," its inherent indescribability reflected in the near-imperceptibility of the string music and the flutes' inability to hear it. In the tradition of blind soothsayers in literature (recall Tiresias in *Oedipus Rex*), the Druids' awareness of the Answerers is not direct, via the senses, but indirect, via some indefinable process, impossible to express (hence, the Druids' silence). In giving us access to substance via the strings' silent music, Ives placed himself in the role of Emerson. Presenting to us the "wondrous chain," Ives was staking a claim of becoming Emerson's composer-equivalent, seeking to achieve in music what Emerson had achieved in prose. Or, perhaps the priority is reversed: perhaps Ives, in the Emerson essay, attributed to Emerson qualities he had associated first with himself as a composer, praising Emerson for the degree to which his philosophical program coincided with his own. Once again, we might well wonder whether Ives, in describing Emerson in 1920, was more fundamentally describing himself.[20]

From this perspective, it might even be possible to liberate ourselves from the literal meaning of Ives's 1930s "Druid" program. Viewed through a different lens, *The Unanswered Question* responds remarkably well to a "hypothetical" program concerning Ives's own personal musical mission and the persistently surprised or shocked response that it received. Thus, within a diatonic and settled institution (string background), Ives presents his nonconforming musical challenge or "question" (trumpet), which remains "unanswered" by the public (flutes) in varying degrees of puzzlement and/or aggression.[21] Ives in fact recalled how *The Unanswered Question* was one of several pieces that was "played—or better tried out—usually ending in a fight or hiss . . ." while he was living at the "Poverty Flat" apartments (1972: 61). It is possible, from this vantage point, to associate the Answerers with Ives's public, initially confused by, and ultimately dismissing and mocking, his music. ("It is awful. It is not music, it makes no sense," we hear them say.)[22] The atonal melody—an emblem for everything progressive in Ives's music—persists beyond its negative reception, however, in keeping with Ives's prognostication for his musical style. We might also conceive of *The Unanswered Question*, then, as thickly veiled autobiography, in which Ives elevated the trope of the misunderstood artist to the loftiest heights imaginable, a struggle of cosmic proportions.[23]

5 Ives and the Now:
"The Things Our Fathers Loved"

At the conclusion of his 1927 essay "Photography," a critique of the photographic medium and its claims on fidelity and truthfulness, Siegfried Kracauer asserted the potential of film to invest photographic images with a contextual meaning they lack: "If the disarray of the illustrated newspapers is simply confusion, the game that film plays with the pieces of disjointed nature is reminiscent of *dreams* in which the fragments of daily life become jumbled. This game indicates that the valid organization of things is not known" (Kracauer 1993: 436). According to Kracauer, isolated photographs lack context and hence significance. Film can remedy the situation, not simply by setting photographic images in motion (that is, by restoring their temporal context), but by "fragmenting" and "jumbling" the moving images—in other words, through editing. The model for film editing, Kracauer implies, is memory, where images are retained and arranged according to their significance and meaning. That the "valid organization" of these images is indeterminate should be regarded positively: truth is found not via faithful technological reconstructions of events from the past but by representing the past as we make sense of it in our minds. Kracauer's essay dates from the end of the silent-film era, when many of the now-familiar conventions of narrative cinema had already been codified. These conventions generally support the illusion that films represent real life. Kracauer seems to suggest, however, that at a fundamental level films represent not life itself so much as our *recollections* of life, and that the organization of shots in a film is best understood in terms of indeterminate psychological processes or cognitive structures.

The notion of memory and film as sites where "the fragments of daily life become jumbled" is useful for conceptualizing Ives's music, another such site. Ives was composing his music about memory using techniques such as fragmentation and collage during the same years that film was emerging as an artistic medium. For these reasons as well as those outlined in my discussion of narrative in chapter 4, the cinema provides one of the most useful models for understanding the organization of Ives's fragmented musical textures and their meanings. In the first section of this chapter, I offer a two-part interpretive analysis of "The Things Our Fathers Loved," a familiar song and a concise and provocative example of how Ives used fragmentation and multidirectional motion to represent memory.

43
The Things Our Fathers Loved
(1917)
(and the greatest of these was Liberty)

Slowly and sustained

Example 5.1. "The Things Our Fathers Loved," complete score.

ff
all Red, White and Blue
Now! Hear the
più accel.
l.h.
ff
ff
songs! I know not what are the
l.h.
l.h.
l.h.
poco rall.
words But they sing in my
r.h.
l.h.
rit.
p much slower
soul of the things our Fath-ers loved.
very slowly and sustained
pp
pp
rit.
ppp
ppp

Ives's song is fundamentally about bringing the past to life in the present moment, an imperative that is inherently modernist and is shared with the cinema, where the dead images of photography are animated in front of the spectator. Thus, in the second section of the chapter, I consider my analysis in the context of modernist ideas about time and temporality, particularly as these ideas were shaped and reflected by the cinema. In so doing, I hope to shed additional light on the oft-cited problem of how to reconcile Ives's decidedly modernist compositional techniques with his defiantly anti-modernist worldview.

"The Things Our Fathers Loved": Two Analyses

"The Things Our Fathers Loved," completed in 1917, has been frequently discussed in scholarly literature on Ives (see Burkholder 1995: 306–11; Feder 1990: 249–66; Hepokoski 1994; Metzer 2003: 25–27; Morgan 1997; and Starr 1992: 57–67). Often cited as an exemplar of the composer's style, it highlights numerous definitive characteristics, all in a mere twenty-two measures: borrowing, attenuated tonality, fragmentation, open-endedness, and the subject of memory. Ives himself (perhaps with some help from his wife, Harmony) wrote the text, further distinguishing the song as quintessentially Ivesian. The vocal persona begins with a reflection:

I think there must be a place in the soul all made of tunes, of tunes of long ago;

A string of four memory fragments follows, each but the third identified as an *aural* memory and distinguished as such by the presence of at least one borrowed tune. The text and music together give a sense of "being there," of the past materializing before us:

I hear the organ on the Main Street corner,
Aunt Sarah humming Gospels;
Summer evenings,
The village cornet band, playing in the square. The town's Red, White and Blue,
    all Red, White and Blue

Finally, amidst a whirlwind of musical activity, the persona returns from these daydreams to the reflective mode of the song's opening, her fervent words undermined somewhat by a musical ending that is distinctly subdued and questioning:

Now! Hear the songs! I know not what are the words
But they sing in my soul of the things our Fathers loved.

As in many of Ives's works, the text clearly refers to a real-world situation, a person engaged in recollection and contemplation. But the temporal status of the situation is fundamentally ambiguous: does the text simply refer to a chronological series of events—a reflection followed by a series of memories followed by another reflection—or does it jump back and forth in time between the present of the persona's reflections and the past to which they refer? Any attempt to resolve this ambiguity would diminish rather than enhance our understanding of the song; instead, I point to musical features that support each interpretation, offering first a linear hearing of the music and the events it represents and then a nonlinear hearing. In semiotic terms, each hearing weaves together accounts of the "temporality of the signifier" and the "temporality of the signified" (Monelle 2000: 83). A "temporally polyphonic" hearing, as Steven Rings has recently dubbed it, will ultimately emerge, where the linear and nonlinear hearings are allowed to coexist (2008: 202). Whereas the linear hearing will have some conceptual similarities with previous studies of this song, the nonlinear hearing will offer an entirely new analytical entry point and interpretive perspective on the song's potential meanings.

Linear Hearing

Ives's musical setting depicts the persona's shift into memory with a high degree of subtlety. C major is often an emblem of truth in Ives's music, as we have seen, and the bald C-major triad of m. 1 prepares the opening lyric as a statement of utmost sincerity, while additionally providing an initial glimpse of "the soul" and the idealized images of the past within it. This clarity is maintained in the vocal line and the accompaniment of the piano's left hand in mm. 2–3 (I–IV in C major) but is slightly eroded by the melodic echoes of the piano's right hand, whose transpositions of the vocal line up a major third gesture toward the whole-tone collection and its characteristic lack of tonal focus: the daydream is beginning. The C♯ of m. 3 instigates a more decisive tonal shift, as the underlying F-major triad proceeds to F♯ major in m. 4. The effect is of a harmonic slide, with parallel semitonal voice leading in the piano's left hand and motion from A to B♭ (A♯) in the voice; furthermore, the vocal line of mm. 3–4 paraphrases Stephen Foster's "My Old Kentucky Home" in F major, but with the final two pitches (D♯–C♯) shifted one semitone too high (Burkholder 1995: 307).[1] The F♯ chord (functioning as its enharmonic equivalent, G♭) leads to an E♭ dominant ninth chord in mm. 4–5, the latter poised to progress to A♭ as an applied dominant, and thereby to chromaticize a stepwise ascent from the F♯ harmony of m. 4. But rather than an A♭ chord, an A-minor eleventh chord arrives in m. 6, a second disorienting harmonic event.

In sum, mm. 1–6 feature two upward, semitonal harmonic shifts: the F-major triad of m. 3 slides to F♯ in m. 4, and the normative resolution of the E♭ dominant to A♭ is displaced to A♮ in m. 6. The overall effect is of a gradual shifting of consciousness, from reflection in the present to reflection on the past: the persona is drifting into a dream.[2] This effect is enhanced by an ongoing sense of harmonic blurriness, generated first by the countermelodies of mm. 2–3 and then by the overlap between the F♯ and E♭ harmonies beginning at m. 4.2.[3] The semitonal shifts of mm. 4 and 6 can be understood to disrupt the normative progression C–F–D⁷–G: F and D⁷ are displaced by one semitone (mm. 4–5) and G by two (m. 6). This progression would have confirmed C major as a tonal center, a key that evaporates completely from the song after the opening measures. The second half of this progression (D^7–G) is obscured by the harmonic shifts in mm. 4–6, and the subsequent measures are fixated on this loss and all it represents—namely, the tonal path back to C major and the "place in the soul" it signifies. This fixation takes the form of the melodic motive G–D which dominates mm. 6–9, grafted onto the A-minor and F-major harmonies of these measures—another example of harmonic blurriness that contributes to the dreamlike quality of this portion of the song. The motive appears first in the piano's right hand in m. 6, an anticipation of the vocal cadence in m. 7, which completes a borrowed fragment of the tune "On the Banks of the Wabash" (see Burkholder 1995: 307–10 for a convenient overview of borrowed tunes in the song). The motive lingers in mm. 8–9, modifying the voice's brief reference to the tune *Nettleton*, which properly would end with a repeated G, not with the descending fourth G–D. The attempt to regain the tonal motion D^7–G, as we shall see, is greatly intensified later in the song.

The upward harmonic shifts of mm. 4 and 6 are balanced by reciprocal semitonal shifts *downward,* corresponding to the vocal persona's emergence out of memory in mm. 14–15. First, the F-major tonality of mm. 11–13 abruptly gives way to an E dominant on the downbeat of m. 14. The proper resolution of this dominant to A major is delayed until m. 14.3. In turn, this A-major triad progresses to the D dominant of m. 15; thus, a "middleground" descending-fifths progression, E^7–A–D^7, lends coherence to the relatively chaotic harmonic activity of mm. 14–15 and provides momentum toward the desired, but ultimately unrealized, resolution of the D dominant to G major. Yet coexisting with these elements of harmonic continuity is an unmistakable harmonic breach at the downbeat of m. 15. The A-major triad of m. 14.3 does not lead directly to the D^7 of m. 15 but first initiates an octatonic sequence, consisting of a descending octatonic bass (A–G–G♭–F♭), with the first and third notes functioning as the roots of major triads (A major, G♭ major; these triads ascend in the right hand). The next chord in the sequence would be an E♭-major triad in root position, as opposed to the D^7 that arrives on the downbeat of m. 15. The sense of disjunction here is compounded by the vocal line, which, after a stepwise ascent spanning a minor sixth in m. 14, jumps from B♭ to D, the vocal apex of the song (aside from ornamental D♯s in mm. 4 and 5).

Thus, the shift into memory at the beginning of the song, evoked by two upward semitonal shifts, is reversed later in the song by two downward semitonal shifts. The return to the here-and-now in m. 15 is marked by a return to the overriding pitch level of mm. 1–3, while the D dominant lost in m. 5 is regained. This mirroring of departure and return is enhanced by the nature of the two pairs of semitonal shifts. Just as the first pair features a harmonic slide (F to F♯) followed by a harmonic substitution (A for A♭), the second pair likewise features a slide (F to E) followed by a substitution (D for E♭). Tellingly, each pair of shifts commences from F and traverses a diatonic third within F major (F to A, F to D). The overall result is a symmetrical design spanning the song's memory section (mm. 3–15.1). The reciprocal pairs of semitonal shifts frame seven measures that are quasi-symmetrical with respect to tonality, enhancing the overall symmetry: mm. 7–9 and 11–13 are firmly anchored in F major, whereas m. 10 ("Sum-

Example 5.2. "The Things Our Fathers Loved," displaced connection from m. 5 to m. 15.

mer evenings") sits ambiguously in the center. Thus, F is not only the point of departure for each pair of harmonic shifts but the central tonal area of the memory section as well.

Nonlinear Hearing

The critical moments of entering and leaving the realm of memory, as explained above, are the downbeats of m. 6, where the first memory commences ("I hear the organ on the Main Street corner"), and m. 15, the return to the present, the "Now." Each moment features a semitonal harmonic substitution that arrives with a jolt, as though the tonal surface has shifted. An alternative hearing, however, is that the music's *temporal* surface shifts at these moments; that in each case a musical succession has been fractured and its component parts separated from one another. Examples 5.2 and 5.3 propose these temporally displaced successions. In Example 5.2, m. 5 is juxtaposed with m. 15, showing how the E♭ dominant can be interpreted as a German-sixth chord leading to the D dominant of m. 15. Highlighted in the example is the standard resolution of the augmented sixth to an octave, articulated by the bass and vocal line; C♯ is the focus of the vocal line in mm. 4–5, intensifying its need to resolve. The example also highlights the G–F dyad of the piano's right hand in m. 5 echoed by F♯–E in m. 15, a registrally displaced semitonal descent above the bass's descending semitone. These associated dyads form part of a larger textural correspondence that helps bind mm. 5 and 15 together across the intervening music: in each measure the piano part features a sustained bass, an arpeggiated texture in the mid-register, and a shared rhythmic motive in the upper register, as highlighted on the example.

Example 5.3. "The Things Our Fathers Loved," displaced connection from m. 14 to m. 5.

In Example 5.3, m. 14 is juxtaposed with m. 5, demonstrating how the E♭ harmony of m. 5 might continue the octatonic sequence initiated at m. 14.3. As shown in the example, my proposed realignment of these measures is supported by the retention of common tones between the G♭ triad of m. 14 and the E♭ harmony of m. 5, and quasi-symmetrical octatonic motions in the bass and vocal lines within the ambitus A to E♭/D♯, together comprising a complete octatonic collection. The A to E♭ motion in the bass can be understood as a reversal of the E♭ to A bass motion in mm. 5–6, one which supplies a harmonic logic missing in these measures. Thus, whereas in mm. 14–15 an actual progression from A (m. 14.3) to D displaces a motion to E♭, in mm. 5–6 an actual motion from E♭ to A displaces a motion to D; both moments revolve around the same constellation of three chordal roots.

The initiation of another displaced harmonic progression appears in m. 10 ("Summer evenings"). Although the essential harmonic succession in this measure, A^7–C^4_2, forms part of a chromaticized progression in F major (I–III^7–V$^4_2$–I), it is isolated in many ways from the measures that precede and follow; see, for instance, the awkward voice leading into A^7 and away from C^4_2. The succession itself has a similar flavor to the jarring semitonal shifts on the downbeats of mm. 4 and 14. This quality stems from the semitonal bass motion (A to B♭), the non-normative resolution of the A dominant, the vocal leap, B to F♯, within an otherwise stepwise line, and the A appoggiatura in the upper melody of the piano, which disrupts an otherwise chromatic ascent. In all these respects, a smoother and more logical continuation is provided once again by m. 15 (Example 5.4). In this recomposition, the A dominant resolves to a D dominant, with strong root motion in the bass and a characteristic resolution of the tritone C♯–G to C♮–F♯ (see the lower portion of the piano's right hand). The C♯ octave in m. 10 actually splits, resolving downward to C♮ in the piano (the seventh of D^7) and upward to D in the

Example 5.4. "The Things Our Fathers Loved," displaced connection from m. 10.2 to m. 15.

voice (the root); this dual motion forms a counterpart to the German-sixth resolution shown in Example 5.2, which features chromatic contrary motion *toward* an octave and the identical C♯–D motion in the voice. Finally, the piano's G♯ in m. 15 can be heard as the goal of the ascending upper piano line of m. 10, concluding an elaborated E–F♯–G♯ motion, a reversal of the countermelody in m. 2: note that in both m. 2 and m. 15, the presence of G♯ alludes strongly to the "even" whole-tone collection (WT_c).[4]

Thus, the two dominants of m. 10, A^7 and C^4_2, rather than merely functioning within the F-major context of mm. 7–13, are oriented toward two different tonal areas: A^7 pushes toward D^7, and thus ultimately toward G major, the unattainable goal of the song's final measures, whereas C^4_2 leads back to F major, the tonal core of the dream sequence. In other words, the two dominants initiate opposite trajectories in tonal space, with C major, the point of departure in mm. 1–2, as the point of equilibrium. G major is one step on the circle of fifths to the sharp side of C major, whereas F major is one step to the flat side, and the crucial A and E♭ harmonies are extensions of these steps: A is three steps to the sharp side, E♭ three steps to the flat side. The tonal motion A^7–D^7–(G) pushes back toward C, whereas the motion C^4_2–F pushes away from it. These opposite motions in tonal space suggest opposite motions in time: A^7 pushes away from the past and toward the present, ultimately approaching the imagined future of G major, whereas C^4_2 pulls the persona back into the past.

These trajectories between past and present provide an interpretive context in which to understand the displaced connections proposed in Examples 5.2–5.4. The E♭ "German sixth" of m. 5, like the A^7 of m. 10, finds its harmonic fulfillment in the D^7 of m. 15. And thus, whereas in the linear hearing m. 5 is fully subsumed within the drift into memory, in the nonlinear hearing it fights against this drift, striving forward in the opposite direction, toward the "Now." The octatonic sequence initiated in m. 14, on the other hand, like the C_2^4 of m. 10, is harmonically oriented toward the memory section, pushing back to the E♭ harmony of m. 5. Once again, my linear and nonlinear hearings of m. 14 suggest opposite temporal trajectories: whereas in the linear hearing this measure initiates a decisive return to the present, in the nonlinear hearing it pulls the persona back toward psychological absorption in the past. Viewed in tandem, my nonlinear hearings of the framing moments of the memory sequence (as modeled in Examples 5.2 and 5.3) effectively bracket off the entire section as a self-enclosed unit that might exist entirely outside the flow of "real time" experienced by the persona in the present. In one interpretation, the persona's reflections in the present (mm. 1–5 and 15–22) proceed uninterrupted, as implied by the linear connection between mm. 5 and 15, whereas the memories of mm. 6–14 cycle in an endless loop within the persona's soul, as implied by the potential of m. 14 to circle back to m. 5 (cf. the flute "Answers" in *The Unanswered Question*). The A dominants of mm. 10 and 14, as alternative paths of return to m. 15, are portals linking past and present.

The "Now" of m. 15 in this interpretation is a loaded moment. It not only emerges climactically from the crescendo and accelerando of m. 14, set up harmonically by the A dominant, but it also satisfies the harmonic urges of mm. 5 and 10; each of these measures (mm. 5, 10, and 14) is associated with a different memory or stage in the process of remembering. With all of this musical motion and corresponding psychological activity directed in one place, it is no wonder that the persona seems overwhelmed by memory in mm. 15–20, as the dynamic reaches *fortissimo* and the piano figuration becomes hyperactive. Meanwhile, the recollections of mm. 5–14 spill over into the present moment and pile upon one another: the upper layer of the piano part in mm. 15–18 and 20 recalls the piano's reference to "The Battle Cry of Freedom" in mm. 11–13; the rapid figuration in the piano's mid-register emerges as an accelerated variant of the left-hand arpeggios in mm. 5–6; and in m. 18, the voicing of the A-minor ninth chord recalls the harmony of m. 6, which provided a backdrop for the first distinct memory (the organ on the Main Street corner). Simultaneous with all these memory traces or recollections of recollections, the refrain from "In the Sweet Bye and Bye" emerges in the vocal line—yet another tune of long ago, but one that is no longer consigned to the realm of memory. This tune from the past is brought to life, surfacing in m. 15 as a port within the emotional storm represented by the piano, much as it supplied a rallying point at the climax of "From Hanover Square North." The song is an artifact from the past, one of those very songs of which the persona sings ("Now! Hear the songs . . ."), but it is now fully *present*. Indeed, to bring the past to life in the present may have been the fundamental project of Ives's music, and the persona seems on the verge of success at this moment.

But this is a project that Ives repeatedly exposed as not fully realizable. In "The Things Our Fathers Loved" a negative judgment is rendered by the end of the song, when the voice's quotation of "In the Sweet Bye and Bye," sung in G major and largely faithful to the original, disintegrates just as it should cadence on G (see mm. 21–22). Instead of the hoped-for G major triad, the song ends on a sustained *pianissimo* chord anchored on D♯, apparently an unconsummated chromatic move back to D initiated by the E-minor harmony of m. 20. The lower dyad of this chord, D♯–A♯, gestures back to the E♭–B♭ dyad of m. 5, whereas the upper three pitch classes, F♯–B♯–G♯, reactivate the whole-tone tinged dominant of mm. 15–17, with B♯ (C) and G♯ occurring in the same register. In other words, the final chord references the primary portals through which the persona passes between the past and present. But whereas the dominants of mm. 5 and 15–17 are dynamic and forward-directed, the final chord of the song is completely inert, devoid of tonal tension, and therefore devoid of direction or possibility. This final harmony contains exclusively sharped notes, which provide the best indication of how far the music has strayed from the C-major triad of m. 1: the voicing of the lower D♯-minor triad mimics that of the opening C-major triad, inviting the comparison, but the root of D♯ suggests an insurmountable distance on the sharp side of the circle of fifths—specifically, nine steps on the circle, as opposed to the two steps required to travel from the D dominant back to C. The gulf between past and present, nearly overcome in the preceding measures, is ultimately reopened. This regression is reinforced by Ives's invocation of the song's title as its final lyric, the only instance of the past tense in the song. Whereas each memory is sung in the present tense, as though the past has been transported into the present, and the climactic, imperative "Now!" reinforces this effect dramatically, all this is undermined by the final chord and the final word.

Modernism and the Present Moment

Whereas the ending is unmistakably Ivesian, the representation of memory in "The Things Our Fathers Loved," and the song's apparent desire to bridge the gap between past and present, is best understood as more than an Ivesian concoction: it is a quintessentially modernist formulation that has numerous points of contact with contemporaneous ideas about time, memory, and their representation. For example, the idea that memories are unaffected by our lived experience of time evokes Freud's notion of the unconscious as atemporal, a site of permanent storage where memories, rather than fading, retain their original fullness over time (see Freud 1955a: 577–78, and 1955b: 187).[5] Or, the experience of Ives's persona might bring to mind the narrator of Proust's *Remembrance of Things Past* and his *"moments bienheureux,"* in which memories flood the narrator in extended moments triggered by specific nonvisual senses.[6] Proust represented such an experience most famously in the madeleine episode from the first volume of *Remembrance* (1913), where the taste of a small cake ultimately unlocks for the narrator numerous visions of his childhood (Proust 2006: 63–64), memories similar to those of Ives's persona in "The Things Our Fathers Loved," where recollections are linked to a particular sense (hearing) and experienced as a single instant of great intensity.[7] Proust's novel is frequently linked to the philosophy of Bergson, and indeed Bergson's notion of *durée* provides a related means of conceptualizing the intermingling of past and present in Ives's song. As Bergson described the concept, using an often-quoted musical metaphor: "[The ego] forms both the past and the present states into an organic whole, as happens when we recall the notes of a tune, melting, so to speak, into one another" (1910: 100).

Such conceptions of memory and time are relevant to an understanding of Ives's music, part of a much larger constellation of ideas and strategies for making sense of the modern world. An especially enlightening point of contact, however, is the emerging medium of film. The beginning of Ives's compositional career roughly coincided with the arrival of the cinema: he was a student at Yale when the Lumière brothers debuted their films in 1895–96. And Ives was maturing as a composer during the first decade of the twentieth century, when film was evolving from a "cinema of attractions," whose primary aim was to "show" images rather than to "tell" stories, into a predominantly narrative medium (see Gunning 1990), one that an increasingly large number of Americans were experiencing in Nickelodeon theaters. The primary technical development that made this evolution possible was the cut: the editing of film strips gave filmmakers access to narrative techniques previously unavailable and largely unimagined in the context of cinema. In my analysis of "The Things Our Fathers Loved," displaced musical successions function in a similar way, signifying jumps forward and backward in time in the manner of filmic montage. And thus, as with *The Unanswered Question*, it is useful to conceptualize this song in relation to narrative models.

The cinematic qualities of Ives's music are not demonstrably the result of any direct influence of narrative cinema on Ives, as is the case with Debussy (see Leydon 2001), but rather evidence of how early narrative cinema and Ives's music are mutual artistic responses to certain key questions and problems posed by modernity. In her book *The Emergence of Cinematic Time,* the film theorist and historian Mary Ann Doane has argued persuasively that the cinema provides the best means of understanding modernist ideas about temporality. Prominent among these ideas is an obsession with defining and capturing the present moment: "The present . . . acts as a zero or placeholder for something outside of what is perceived as a more and more rigorously ordered social system, organized by technological, industrial, economic, and political determinants—the intricate web of commodity capitalism. . . . The present . . . marks the promise of something other, something outside of systematicity" (2002: 106). This fixation on the present moment is a feature of the work of Freud, Proust, and Bergson, and Doane demonstrates its centrality in the thought of a wide range of artists and intellectuals, including Charles Baudelaire, Charles Sanders Peirce, Paul Souriau, and many others. Most importantly, Doane traces this modernist preoccupation as it was reflected and shaped by technology, beginning with its roots in photography, continuing through the exercises in chronophotography by Etienne-Jules Marey and related attempts to depict movement via photography, and culminating with the invention and early development of the cinema. In this historical narrative the arrival of cinema signals a crucial shift in thinking about the present moment. A photograph captures the moment; however, when we view the photograph, this moment seems to be frozen in the past. The cinema, on the other hand, offers a fundamentally different experience: it takes a series of photographic images and creates from them the illusion of motion and presence; it takes events from the past and brings them to life in the here and now. This point of view was rendered concisely by Roland Barthes, who theorized that photographs are perceived as being in the past, the "having-been-there," whereas film is perceived as being in the present, the "being-there" (1977: 44–45; see also Doane 2002: 103).

Implicit in Barthes's categorizations, *motion* is the feature that distinguishes cinema from photography. For Kracauer, as indicated at the beginning of this chapter, the key element that differentiates the temporality of these two mediums was not simply the illusion of movement manufactured by film, however, but film's ability to create narratives via editing, to combine "parts and segments to create strange constructs" (1993: 436; see also Doane 2002: 102–3, and Gaudreault 2009: 81–89). For Doane, it was the cinema's very basis in the succession of still images—that is, its basis in photography—that determined the central importance of editing: "The cut is the most exemplary cinematic operation. For the cut is the haunting echo of the frameline—its reiteration at a different level" (217). And thus, like Kracauer, Doane emphasized the importance of cinematic editing in establishing a distinct temporality: "[Time] becomes something that can be held or possessed in a metaphorical sense. This is why the cut as ellipsis is a crucial figure. Time becomes delimitable, commodifiable, objectlike" (217–18).

This packaging of time into discrete units via editing, as discussed in the previous chapter, is a defining feature of narrative cinema, the most important means by which films achieve narrative status. Among the earliest editing conventions to gain currency was parallel editing, what Gunning identified as "the key figure of the narrative system" (1991: 110). Parallel editing emerged as a means of representing actions that are separated in space but simultaneous in time; to cite a cliché, think of the hero rushing to rescue the heroine tied to the train tracks. Today's film viewer understands the temporal signification of such sequences effortlessly, and thus it is easy to miss the inherent contradiction of the convention: as Doane noted, for parallel editing to function effectively, "succession must be accepted as the signifier of its opposite, simultaneity" (2002: 189). This apparent incongruity no doubt initially confused filmgoers, and indeed the widespread adoption of this and similar editing strategies by filmmakers appears to elude rational explanation. However, parallel editing is best understood not as an awkward practical solution to a representational problem but as an artistic strategy shaped by modernist ideas about temporality. The question of "sequence versus simultaneity," as the cultural historian Stephen Kern has shown (citing parallel editing as one of many examples), was a defining problem of modernity (2003: 68, 70–72).[8] Just as important, parallel editing was a means of entertainment. As characterized by Doane, "Parallel editing successfully eroticizes time, injects it with desire, expectation, anticipation, and displaces the spectatorial time of viewing by contributing to the construction of a 'lived,' imaginary temporality" (2002: 193).

All this provides a helpful context for conceptualizing Ives's treatment of temporal relations in "The Things Our Fathers Loved." As I have suggested, at many points in the song, succession signifies simultaneity: the images of the memory sequence, although they may be understood as part of an ongoing chronological representation of events (as in my linear hearing), may also be understood as occurring in a timeless instant, as though the dotted barline of Example 5.2 had been pulled open to reveal an infinite space (as in my nonlinear hearing). Pushing the analogy further, we might identify two cross-cut stories around which the song is organized, one characterized by descending fifths (the "middleground" progression E^7–A–D^7 of mm. 14–15, and the displaced progression A^7–D^7 shown in Example 5.4) and one by descending semitones (the $E\flat^7$–D^7 progression shown in Example 5.2, extended to include the E–D♯ bass motion in mm. 20–22).[9] Borrowing Doane's words, Ives's splicing of these tonal motions "injects [time] with desire, expectation, anticipation": A^7 and $E\flat^7$ strive toward D^7 but in each case the dominant arrival is delayed; when it does arrive in m. 15, the climactic energy is unmistakable.

But this analogy is limited. The two tonal motions (descending fifths and descending semitones) are not clearly differentiated nor do they "parallel" one another, and while they may come together at the D dominant of m. 15—hero and heroine united in the same frame—this union is undermined as the G-major resolution slips away in the final measures. More than the relentless linear logic and goal-achievement that define parallel editing, Ives's musical montage is founded on the free-associational logic of memory or dreaming, a quality Kracauer associated with the cinema and attributed to the possibilities of editing, as we have seen. But whereas parallel editing is too orderly to serve as a conceptual model for Ives's song, Kracauer's notion of "jumbled fragments" is too chaotic: behind Ives's fragments is the suggestion of something continuous, evoked by the sustained "Now!" of the song's climax and more subtly by the displaced connection that frames the entire memory sequence ($E\flat^7$–D^7). In the *Essays,* Ives wrote of an "ever-flowing stream, partly biological, partly cosmic, ever going on in ourselves, in nature, in all life," in which "many things are constantly coming into being, while others are constantly going out—one part of the same thing is coming in while another part is going out of existence" (1961: 71). It is this experience of the present moment as continuous flow that Ives sought to evoke in "The Things Our Fathers Loved," the commingling of past and future in the present—in this case, over a prolonged dominant that never resolves.

Ives's song seeks desperately to hold onto the present moment, and so, as I have suggested, did many modernists. According to Doane, the primary impetus was the desire to escape the industrialized world: "The subject is no longer immersed in time, no longer experiences it as an enveloping medium. Through its rationalization and abstraction, its externalization and reification in the form of pocket watches, standardized schedules, the organization of the work day, and industrialization in general, time becomes other, alienated" (2002: 221). Ives's anti-technological sentiments are well established, and the notion that Ives's music and its various experiments with musical time register his alienation from time in the industrialized world is compelling, borne out by the relationship between his music and the ideas expressed in his prose writings, texts, and programs.

More concretely, the modernist fixation on the present can be understood as a confrontation with mortality. Industrialization created for many the sensation of time's acceleration; the duration of one's life felt increasingly calculable and hence the specter of death more palpable. The unprecedented bloodshed of World War I and the unfathomable number of premature deaths it claimed fed into these feelings, and certainly it was at the forefront of Ives's mind when he composed another song from 1917, "Tom Sails Away," which is explicitly about America's youth going to war. At one stage, Ives conceived of these two songs as a miniature collection called "Two Songs" (Sinclair 1999: 657), and the same basic narrative structure that defines "The Things Our Fathers Loved"—reflections in the present framing a central memory section—characterizes "Tom Sails Away" as well. In a passage that closely parallels the return to "Now!" in "The Things Our Fathers Loved," the persona of "Tom Sails Away," after recalling Tom's idyllic childhood, sings: "But Today! In freedom's cause Tom sailed away for over there . . ." As the final two words are repeated, the vocal line evokes the melody of "Taps," and the implications for Tom are clear. The connection between these two songs sheds light on Ives's quotation of the refrain from "In the Sweet Bye and Bye" in mm. 15–22 of "The Things Our Father Loved," a tune about eternal rest ("we shall meet on that beautiful shore"). Ives's persona, though apparently immersed in the present, has an eye toward a future reunion with her "fathers"; but although the tune she paraphrases looks forward to a peaceful reunion, the ending of Ives's song belies a profound unrest.

Gayle Sherwood Magee interpreted the quotation of "In the Sweet Bye and Bye" as a reflection of Ives's anxiety about the war: "[Ives's] placement of a unified, complete American melody in opposition to a European-styled accompaniment that threatens to overwhelm it embodies the contemporary reality of national unity in the face of a foreign war" (2008: 127). Alongside Magee's reading, I would suggest a parallel metaphor in which the persona sings one of her (our) fathers' tunes, pulling it into the present, in an attempt to brace herself from the onrush of anxiety that threatens to overwhelm her as she emerges from memory to face present realities. Kracauer's explanation of the impulse to preserve the past in photographs and on film is a helpful point of comparison: "That the world devours [photographs] is a sign of the *fear of death*. What the photographs by their sheer accumulation attempt to banish is the recollection of death, which is part and parcel of every memory-image" (1993: 433). Ives's use of memory fragments might be understood, similarly, as palliatives against mortality—his fellow citizens', and perhaps his own.[10]

In 1933, Ives made the first of a series of recordings in which he played and sang his own music (these have since been made available on the disc *Ives Plays Ives*, which surely contains one of the most essential and entertaining performances of Ives's music on record, the composer's own rendition of his song "They Are There!"; see Ives 1999). After his initial sessions at Abbey Road studios, Ives jotted down his reactions in a rant whose manic energy makes it well worth quoting in full:

Machinery!—and what everything else is, and the other side of life as machinery, or as a result of its influence and fixtures—all of this, whatever the above means, I saw this A M. I wanted to record (for my own observation) certain passages of piano things of mine. In the first place you have to be there at a certain time—so does Paderewski when he gives an 8:31 concert. How do you know at 8:31 that you are going to feel like playing note #92? Then you have to play what you have to play, which may not be exactly what you have to play. A bell rings—two bells—and a nice red light starts—and you start. You get going, going good maybe the first time, as I did this A M. Then the nice engineer comes back and says you took over four minutes, and the last part was not recorded. As I remember, the last part was the only part of the above "going good" part. Then he played it over—it happened to be one of the best [times] that I've played it—so I told him that was just O.K., and I'd play some of the other passages. Then he says—"What?—that recording is all gone—we didn't keep [it]—it was only to get the time"—!! So I had to play it again—and it was awful this time—sweaty fingers, short of breath, everything going wrong, wrong notes, rhythm dying, mad inside, cussing under your breath. Then the man comes in and says "This is all recorded"—even the cuss words. Then just as I was going good again, the red light [goes out] and the buzzer sounds, and the time is up. The next record has to start in the beginning of the last measure—but how can you dive off a rock when you're in the middle of the pool? So I told him I'd start all over again, and this time I got started going wrong and kept it up perfectly, and it was recorded perfectly! Now what has all this got to do with music?—this is the business of music as it is today! It's all just music to make business, rather than the business to make music. A man may play to himself and his music starts to live—then he tries to put it under a machine, and it's dead! (1972: 80–81)

In this remarkable tirade, Ives provides us with a vivid image of the modern artist virtually debilitated by anxiety about technology and its control over time. He went so far, in the final sentence, as to equate audio recording with death, and he perhaps hinted at this association metaphorically as well: "The red light goes out and the buzzer sounds, and the time is up." Ironically, whereas mechanical reproduction was heralded by many as a means of immortality, a way of preserving sounds and images for eternity, it was also saddled with opposite connotations. For Ives, to record music was to take the life from it. In the early cinema, the absence of a character in the frame brought connotations of death, a key element in generating suspense via parallel editing: when the film cuts away from the heroine, it implies her impending demise.[11]

Ives produced very few new compositions after 1918, and this lack of productivity over the last thirty-five or so years of his life has been the subject of much speculation. As mentioned in the introduction, the most convincing explanation has been provided by Magee, who claimed that Ives suffered from neurasthenia. As Magee concluded, "When viewed through the lens of neurasthenia, Ives's relationship to the modern world is redefined as one of anxiety, a fear of change and upheaval" (Sherwood 2001: 577)—a conclusion powerfully supported by Ives's account of his experiences at Abbey Road. But even years before these sessions, when composing "The Things Our Fathers Loved," Ives was on the verge of what, according to Magee, was his second neurasthenic breakdown in the fall of 1918. And thus this song and its troubled ending can be heard as the work of a composer with profound and pressing concerns about the status of his music, his life, and humanity in the modern world.

6   Cumulative Composition: Ives's Emerson Music

The *Concord* Sonata is an exceptional work of Ives's in many respects. Its composition dates from the tail end of Ives's most active period as a composer, the years leading up to his debilitating health problems in the fall of 1918, when Ives composed many of his most enduring works. The sonata was the most important piece in establishing Ives's stature as a composer, beginning with Ives's publication of the score, along with the *Essays,* in 1920, and culminating in John Kirkpatrick's performance of the sonata at Town Hall in New York in 1939 and Lawrence Gilman's glowing review that famously heralded the *Concord* as "the greatest music composed by an American" (1939: 9). The *Essays* demonstrate Ives's special regard for the sonata and his intense desire for its underlying ideas to be understood; they also provide an extensive interpretive context for the music that has played an important role in the sonata's enduring attractiveness to listeners, performers, and scholars.

Ives was particularly invested in the music of the "Emerson" movement. It is the longest of the four movements, just as the "Emerson" chapter from the *Essays* is the longest of the four corresponding chapters. As the *Essays* make clear, Ives held Emerson in special esteem, and his writings had a singular influence on Ives's music. And Ives devoted unusual time and energy to the music, as is evident not only from the multiple drafts and revisions of the movement, but from the complex compositional history in which it is embedded, a history spanning four decades and including a series of interrelated compositions, many of which exist in multiple and/or fragmentary versions. Aspects of this evolution have been studied extensively by several scholars (Clark 1972, 1974; Brodhead 1994; Block 1996, 1997; Porter 1998). Despite this body of work, however, the interrelationships among the various sketches, completed scores, and recordings that constitute Ives's "Emerson music"[1] are so complex and rich in the questions they pose that a study of the evolution of this music is not doomed to redundancy. On the contrary, the existing scholarship facilitates continued consideration of fundamental questions regarding Ives's compositional process and views about his own music that have not been adequately addressed.

Drawing upon this work as well as my own comparison of the relevant sources, I present in this chapter a new outline of the interrelationships among the various components of Ives's Emerson music. This comparison differs from previous studies in two important ways. First, it is more comprehensive, taking as its starting point Ives's *Emerson Overture* and incorporating all subsequent pieces that derive material from this seminal work. Rather than proceeding from the assumption that the "Emerson" movement of the 1947 edition of the *Concord* Sonata is a "definitive text"—a typical view held by scholars and performers alike— I regard the revised sonata movement as but one especially prominent stage in an ongoing compositional history. This perspective allows for the elevation in status of certain other stages, most importantly the alternate versions of the *Four Transcriptions from "Emerson"* that Ives recorded in the 1930s and 1940s; these recordings, although they have received little more than passing mention in the scholarly literature, represent a critical juncture in Ives's development of the Emerson material. Second, I focus not on the minute details of specific passages and how they differ from one incarnation of the Emerson material to another, but rather on the basic material that links these sketches, scores, and recordings as seen from a global perspective. This broad view of the Emerson music leads to new ways of understanding Ives's creative process: his trademark tinkering with material over the course of his career can be understood as a natural extension of the networks of multiple fragmented chronologies he fashioned within individual pieces. This final chapter thus extends the scope of my study, illustrating how multidirectional motion provides an apt conceptual model for Ives's obsessive revisions and reformulations of his Emerson music, and suggesting how this model might be applied to similar constellations of pieces as well.

The *Emerson Overture* and Its Progeny

The history of Ives's Emerson music begins with the *Emerson Overture for Piano and Orchestra* (also known as the *Emerson Concerto*), a composition that Ives worked on around 1910–14 and never finished. Ives originally planned to include this work in a set of overtures devoted to "Men of Literature," including Robert Browning, Matthew Arnold, Bronson Alcott, and apparently several others (Sinclair 1999); he ultimately completed only one of these, the *Robert Browning Overture* (c. 1912–14). Ives's initial work on the *Emerson Overture* survives in nine pages of sketches, five of which pertain to the opening section. Much of the basic material of the *Concord* movement is present in this initial sketch, including the opening melodic wedge; components of the "human-faith-melody"; the allusions to Beethoven's Fifth Symphony; and, less obviously, references to Wagner's Prelude to *Tristan und Isolde*. The other four pages of sketches for the overture correspond to isolated passages from later in the *Concord* movement, including much of the final two pages (pp. 18–19). Aside from these sketches, the remainder of the overture—approximately two-thirds of the work—must be reconstructed primarily from annotations Ives made years later when working on various versions of the *Concord* movement and the *Four Transcriptions,* in which he linked passages from these works to the original overture (Porter 1998: 7–18).

The clearest and most reliable indication of Ives's original conception of the overture is provided by his sketches for the opening section. His composition of the overture most likely began with this opening, and it constitutes the overture's most fully realized musical material. Furthermore, Ives distributed into other pieces material from this section of the overture numerous times beginning around 1910 and continuing into the 1920s; he does not appear to have reworked material from any other portion of the overture to anywhere near this extent. For these reasons, the music of the opening section of the *Emerson Overture* provides the best means of studying the evolution of the Emerson music over its nearly four-decade history.

The various incarnations of this material from the overture include the following sketches, scores, and recordings (see the endnotes for details regarding dates of composition):[2]

- The **Emerson Overture** itself (c. 1910–14).[3] Ives drafted the opening section on six pages of pencil sketches; one page is lost.[4] The opening section contains several piano cadenzas that Ives referred to as "Centrifugal Cadenzas." In drafts of a 1935 letter to John Kirkpatrick, he explained, "The Overture . . . seems more like a Piano Concerto with sort of cadenzas," or "a concerto with an overdose of cadenzas" (Ives 1972: 203). David G. Porter completed a reconstruction of the overture, which remains unpublished but was performed in 1998 by pianist Alan Feinberg and the Cleveland Orchestra under the direction of Christoph von Dohnányi; Feinberg recorded the work in 2002 with James Sinclair and the National Symphony Orchestra of Ireland (Ives 2003).[5] Given the far greater accessibility of the recording as compared to Ives's sketches, I use it as a reference point throughout the discussion that follows—with some qualifications, as addressed below. Table 6.1 outlines the manuscript sources for the opening section of the overture, identifying each page based on Ives's informal numbering, Sinclair's microfilm numbers, and the corresponding passages from the Sinclair/Feinberg recording. The gap from 1:30 to 1:40 in the Sinclair/Feinberg timings corresponds to a speculative portion of the reconstruction with no direct connection to Ives's original sketches.

- Three piano studies, **Study no. 1** (c. 1910–11), **Study no. 2** (c. 1910–11), and **The Anti-Abolitionist Riots in the 1830's and 1840's** (c. 1912–13), also known as Study no. 9.[6] Of these studies, only *The Anti-Abolitionist Riots* has been published; the sketches for Study no. 1 are incomplete. The printed edition of *The Anti-Abolitionist Riots* was edited by Henry Cowell (Ives 1949); all references to the score below refer to this edition. Each of these studies is composed mainly of material from the overture. Sinclair has speculated that all three of these studies predate the *Emerson Overture* (Sinclair 1999), whereas Porter concluded that Ives derived these works from the overture after deciding not to finish it (Porter 1998). Ives recorded Study no. 2 and *The Anti-Abolitionist Riots* several times in 1938 and 1943 (see Ives 1999, tracks 18–21, 35, and 37).

- The "Emerson" movement of Sonata no. 2 for Piano: *Concord, Mass., 1840–60*—or, as it is commonly known, the **Concord Sonata** (c. 1916–19).[7] The sonata movement is essentially a greatly condensed version of the overture, arranged for piano. The original version of the sonata is little known today, having been displaced in the repertoire by the second, revised edition published in 1947. The second edition of "Emerson" does not, for the most part, insert or delete passages; rather, it differs from the first edition in its frequently thicker texture, notational details, and added

Ives's numbering	Microfilm number	Sinclair/Feinberg recording
p. 1	f0565	0:00–0:23
p. 2	f2212	0:23–0:26; 0:41–1:10
(patch; inserted later)	f2213	0:26–0:41
p. 3	f2214	1:10–1:30; 1:40–1:55
p. 4	(missing)	1:55–2:18
p. 5	f2215	2:18–2:56
p. 6	f2216	2:56–4:06

Table 6.1. Sketches for the opening section of the *Emerson Overture*

performance indications.[8] The most substantial revisions involve the incorporation of elements from the *Four Transcriptions from "Emerson"* of the mid-1920s (discussed below); as Geoffrey Block has explained, "the completion of the *Four Transcriptions from 'Emerson'* also completes the main compositional work on the second edition of the *Concord Sonata*" (1996: 28).[9]

- The **Four Transcriptions from "Emerson"** (c. 1923–24, c. 1926–27).[10] The 1920s version of the score survives in an ink copy by Emil Hanke, the primary source of Thomas M. Brodhead's critical edition (Ives 2002a); all references to the score refer to this edition unless otherwise noted. The *Transcriptions* divide the *Concord* movement into four shorter ones, eliminating several long passages, while restoring some of the orchestral textures excised in the sonata movement. The first transcription also reinstates a significant amount of material from the overture that had been omitted from the sonata. Ives recorded the first transcription several times from 1933 to 1938, first at Abbey Road studios in London (1933) and subsequently at locations in New York City; he recorded the third transcription several times as well. These recordings are now easily accessible on the disc *Ives Plays Ives;* Ives's recordings of the first transcription occupy tracks 1–2, 5–6, 11–12, and 23–24.[11] Ives's recordings of the first transcription differ from the Hanke score in substantial ways, most notably by restoring even more material from the original overture. These emendations are recorded in chaotic and only partially legible form in a photostat reproduction of Hanke's score with annotations by Ives and George F. Roberts. This annotated reproduction is known as "Copy C" (f4938–51), and it is accompanied by an additional thirteen pages of inserts (outlined in Sinclair 1999). Because of the difficulty in deciphering Ives's annotations on Copy C, Ives's recordings of the first transcription are the most useful source for understanding his conception of this music in the 1930s.

Figure 6.1 summarizes the chronology outlined above.

Despite the substantial body of scholarship devoted to close, detailed comparison of many of the sources, no concise summary exists of the interrelationships among these sketches, scores, and recordings. On the contrary, existing scholarship tends to replicate the almost overwhelming complexity of these interrelationships.[12] A broader point of view requires a privileging of similarity over difference, an emphasis on what pieces have in common rather than on all

c. 1910–14	Ives composes the *Emerson Overture*, Studies nos. 1 and 2, and *The Anti-Abolitionist Riots*
c. 1916–1920	Ives composes and publishes the "Emerson" movement of the *Concord Sonata*
c. 1923–27	Ives composes the *Four Transcriptions from "Emerson"*
1933–43	Ives records portions of the *Four Transcriptions*, Study no. 2 and *The Anti-Abolitionist Riots*, and the "Emerson" movement of the *Concord Sonata*
1939–1947	Following Kirkpatrick's successful premiere of the *Concord*, Ives creates and publishes a second edition

Figure 6.1. Approximate chronology of the *Emerson Overture* and derivative pieces and recordings.

the details that distinguish them. I do not wish to undermine the significance of such details—indeed, I often focus on them myself in what follows. But an examination of these minutiae is most meaningful if it sheds light upon global relationships. Informed by this perspective, in the comparative analysis that follows, I attempt to strike a balance between micro- and macro-level analysis, focusing on only the most significant features that distinguish among the sketches, scores, and recordings under consideration. The goal is to generate a bird's-eye view of how these incarnations of the "Emerson" music share material with one another, and ultimately to assess the meaning and significance of how this music evolved over time.

The Evolution of the Emerson Music

The opening of the *Emerson Overture* is laid out on six pages of pencil sketches, as summarized in Table 6.1. The fourth and final "Centrifugal Cadenza" was to directly follow the music on p. 6. As Ives explained in a partially illegible note on the lower right corner of the page: "to [sign] slip back of . . . [illegible] marked as . . . [illegible] cadenza #4 Em. Concerto."[13] Ives likely added this note several years after completing the sketch, when he wrote out the cadenza as one of many inserts to be added to the *Four Transcriptions* as sketched in Copy C.[14] Ives had no plans to resume composition of the overture at this time; he seems simply to have wanted to note that one of the inserts derived from his original plans for the fourth cadenza. Although this insert cannot be tied to any extant sketches for the overture itself, it obviously derives from sketches for Study no. 2, which Ives composed around the same time that he worked on the overture. The sketches for Study no. 2 correspond to the bottom portion of p. 6 of the overture sketches followed by the transcription insert labeled as Cadenza 4. Thus, it seems safe to speculate that when Ives sketched the opening section of the overture, he intended that the music on p. 6 be followed by Cadenza 4, and that this cadenza would closely correspond to a portion of his sketches for Study no. 2

Emerson Overture (Sinclair recording)			"Emerson" movement (2nd ed.)
Section A	Introduction	0:00–0:13	—
Section B	(orch)	0:13–0:22	p. 1/1 (beg.)
Section C	Cadenza 1	0:22–0:26	p. 1/1 (end)– 1/2 (beg.)
Section D	(orch)	0:26–0:54	p. 1/2 (end)
Section E	Cadenza 2	0:54–1:50	—
Section F	(orch)	1:50–2:34	—
		2:34–2:36	p. 1/3/2
Section G	Cadenza 3	2:36–2:41	p. 1/3/3
		2:41–3:03	—
		3:03–3:16	p. 1/4–1/5/1
Section H	(orch)	3:16–3:39	p. 1/5/2– p. 2/1 (beg.)
		3:39–4:06	—
Section I	Cadenza 4	4:06–5:05	—
		5:05–5:13	p. 2/1 (end)
		5:13–5:45	—

Table 6.2. Material shared between first sections of the *Emerson Overture* (0:00–5:45) and the "Emerson" movement of the *Concord* Sonata (p. 1/1–p. 2/1).

(Porter arrived at the same conclusion in his reconstruction). For this reason, I include the fourth cadenza as part of the first section of the overture, despite its absence in the extant sketches. Demarcated in this way, the first section corresponds to 0:00–5:45 of the Sinclair/Feinberg recording, the music that Ives would later condense into the first "Emerson" transcription.

This opening section is essentially a longer treatment of the material best known from p. 1–p. 2/1 of the "Emerson" movement, whose relative familiarity—the 1947 version in particular—serves as a helpful means of introducing the overture's musical content. Table 6.2 illustrates the material shared between the two. The left column outlines Porter's reconstruction of the opening section of the overture, divided into subsections (all timings are taken from the Sinclair/Feinberg recording). Each is designated with a letter, A-I, to assist with the comparative analysis. The right column shows the corresponding portions of the "Emerson" movement, including all the music of p. 1–p. 2/1 save for p. 1/3/1 (more on this measure below). As is evident from the table, the "Emerson" movement maps onto the overture, but with several substantial passages from the overture omitted. Most of this unused music is from Cadenzas 2–4, little of whose material Ives maintained in the *Concord*.

Despite the relative self-sufficiency of Ives's sketches for the opening section, some aspects of Porter's reconstruction are speculative, in addition to his treatment of Cadenza 4 (which is strongly defensible, as discussed). As shown in Table 6.1, p. 4 of Ives's original sketch is missing; Porter's reconstruction inserts material from the first transcription, mm. 13–18. There is no way of knowing just how closely Ives's p. 4 corresponded with this portion of the transcription, but the original sketch was likely very similar. The last two measures of Ives's p. 3 correspond to mm. 11–12 of the transcription, and the first seven measures of Ives's p. 5 correspond to mm. 19–26; thus the music from mm. 13–18 of the transcription can be logically substituted for the missing p. 4. This passage from the transcription does not constitute a discrete section, so it is unlikely that Ives's original conception of the music was radically different. Furthermore, much of the same material (mm. 13–16 of the transcription) is present in *The Anti-Abolitionist Riots*, where it also follows the music found on the last two measures of p. 3 in Ives's overture sketch (see p. 4/2–4/4 of *The Anti-Abolitionist Riots*).

Two of Porter's speculative decisions are more problematic, however. First, near the end of Cadenza 2 (1:30–1:40), Porter included a short passage that Ives did not sketch. Cadenza 2 corresponds closely with a large portion of *The Anti-Abolitionist Riots*, and Porter seems to have borrowed additional material from this study: see the passage beginning midway through p. 3/4 and continuing to the *fff* chord near the beginning of p. 4/1. Porter may have been motivated by a desire for conformance between the overture and study here, rather than the reconciliation of any problem presented by the overture sketches. Second, and of greater significance, Porter's reconstruction incorporates after Cadenza 1 (0:26–0:41 of the recording) music from a patch (f2213), one system long, that Ives seems to have created for insertion in p. 2 of his sketches, as well as a measure on p. 2 that would immediately follow this patch but that Ives crossed out (0:41–0:42). The patch corresponds to mm. 6–10 of the first transcription, and most of this material (mm. 6–9) is included in the *Concord* movement as well; see p. 1/2, from the first D♯ in the bass near the beginning of the system to the low A-sharp octave near the end.[15] It is unclear when Ives sketched this patch, and its precise placement within the overture is unclear as well. Furthermore, Porter's inclusion of the patch is unnecessary, because Ives's sketch on p. 2 is coherent without it. Excluding the crossed-out measure, the music on this page of sketches corresponds to a portion of *The Anti-Abolitionist Riots*—the last system on p. 1 followed by the first three systems on p. 2.[16] Thus, it would seem that Ives's original plan for this portion of the overture corresponded to *The Anti-Abolitionist Riots*, and that he later revised the same portion in a manner anticipating the *Concord* movement and the first transcription. In this original plan, the material of Cadenza 1 proceeds almost directly to Cadenza 2, with only a small orchestral passage mediating between the two—0:42–0:54 of the recording, the rough equivalent of the end of p. 1/3 from *The Anti-Abolitionist Riots*. The impression is of a single cadenza, which may explain Ives's occasional confusion about whether the overture contained three or four cadenzas.[17]

These last two problems suggest the incorporation of slight emendations to Porter's reconstruction. An outline of the emended version of the opening section is shown atop Figure 6.2, which represents the subsections A–I, each constructed to approximate scale. Piano cadenzas are designated by white, orchestral passages by gray; some intermingling of piano and orchestra in sections A, E, and F is not shown in the interest of clarity. The two problematic portions of Porter's reconstruction are omitted, as indicated by gaps in sections D and E. The

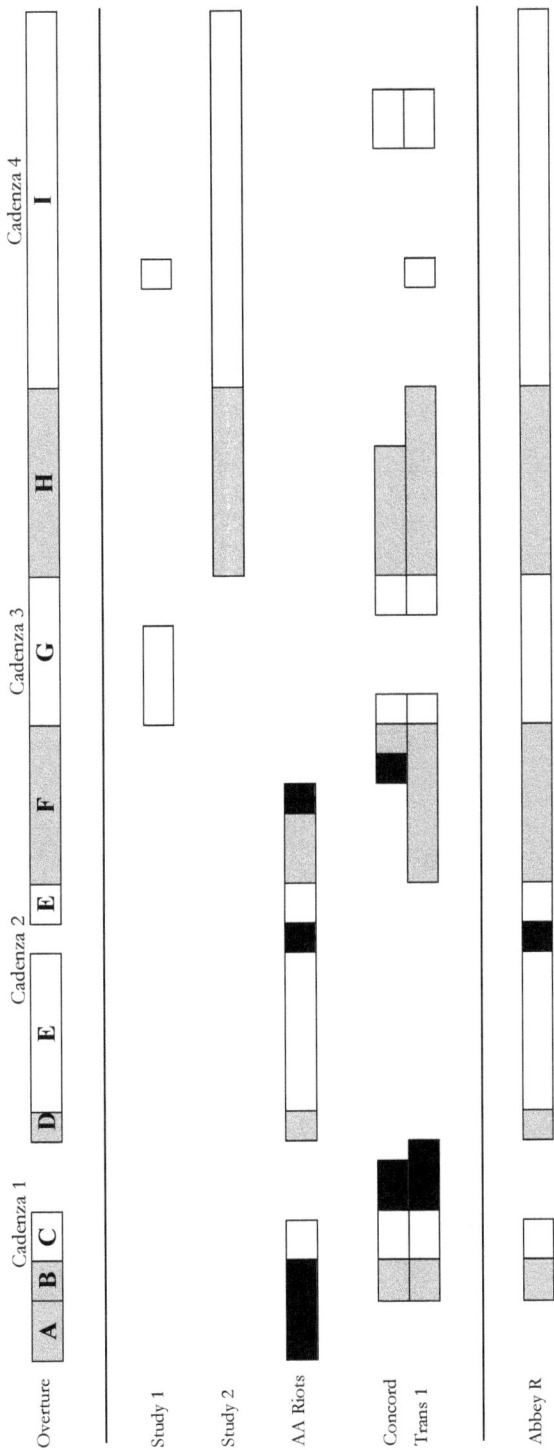

Figure 6.2. Comparison of the opening section of the *Emerson Overture* and derivative pieces and recordings.

THE ANTI-ABOLITIONIST RIOTS
IN THE 1830's AND 1840's

Example 6.1. Study no. 9, *The Anti-Abolitionist Riots in the 1830's and 1840's*, p. 1.

I. "Emerson"

Note:— As a general rule, the notes are natural, unless otherwise marked, except those immediately following a note with an accidental,— natural signs are thus used more as a convenience than of necessity.

Example 6.2 Sonata no. 2 for Piano: *Concord, Mass., 1840–60* (first edition), "Emerson," p. 1.

Example 6.3. *Four Transcriptions from "Emerson,"* Movement I, p. 1.

remainder of the figure summarizes the correspondences between the overture and each of the piano pieces derived from it or composed in consort. (The score excerpts reproduced in Examples 6.1–6.3 provide a partial frame of reference.) Aligned below the outline of the overture are comparable outlines for each subsequent incarnation of the overture material. The system of color-coding used for the overture is maintained throughout the figure to facilitate comparison of each piece with the overture and as a visual reminder of which sections derive from cadenzas and which from orchestral passages. For each individual piece, gaps indicate the omission of material from the overture, not incompleteness or lack of continuity; black is used to indicate passages that do not correspond to material from the overture. For example, *The Anti-Abolitionist Riots* (Study no. 9) begins and ends with original material; in between is music derived from sections C–F of the overture, as well as a small portion of material inserted within section E that is not present in Ives's overture sketches (although it is included in Porter's reconstruction, as discussed above). The black boxes following section C in the *Concord* movement and first transcription correspond to the patch included by Porter but omitted from my outline of the overture atop the figure. The figure is not concerned with perfect, note-for-note correspondences among pieces, an approach that would be extremely limiting, given Ives's propensity for relentless revision. But the relationships and derivations it models are mostly straightforward; those that are less exact I address below.

It will be helpful to survey Figure 6.2 in more detail, moving chronologically (from top to bottom). Studies nos. 1 and 2 and *The Anti-Abolitionist Riots,* all of which Ives seems to have worked on at roughly the same time as the overture, feature the music of the four cadenzas. While it is possible, as Sinclair has speculated (1999), that Ives derived the overture's cadenzas from these studies, a more likely scenario is that the studies were spin-offs of the cadenzas, or workshops in which he would develop material from the overture, perhaps planning to reinsert it later. Following this line of reasoning, each of the studies can be viewed as a workshop for one of the three primary cadenzas: Study no. 1 for Cadenza 3, Study no. 2 for Cadenza 4, and *The Anti-Abolitionist Riots* for Cadenza 2. Unlike all the other pieces shown in Figure 6.2, Study no. 1 modifies the chronological ordering of material from the overture; the fragment of section I shown in the figure is actually interpolated within the longer fragment of section G that appears to precede it, a situation I have not attempted to show. The details of Study no. 2 and *The Anti-Abolitionist Riots* vary among the manuscript and printed sources and Ives's recordings, but the broad correspondences with the overture outlined in the figure are clear and consistent across these multiple versions.

The two editions of the "Emerson" movement from the *Concord* Sonata are conflated in the figure, as the sections under consideration differ not in their basic material but in texture and notational details. The only exception involves the end of the second system in each edition, represented by the black box following section C in the figure; the second edition corresponds more closely to the first transcription here, adapting the music of m. 9. P. 1/3/1 of the "Emerson" movement, an apparent reference to the Prelude to *Tristan und Isolde,* is unique to the sonata and appears in both editions; it is represented in the figure by a black box near the end of section F. This passage incorporates a melodic line, transposed, from about midway through section F of the overture—1:55–1:59, the equivalent of m. 13 in the first transcription.

The first transcription maintains all the material from the "Emerson" movement, save for the *Tristan* measure, but expands upon it by reinserting material from the overture. The figure focuses on two versions of the transcriptions: Ives's original version, as rendered in the critical edition, and Ives's first recording of the transcription in 1933 at Abbey Road studios (Ives 1999: tracks 1–2). As can be seen, in his 1933 recording, Ives greatly expanded the original version of the transcription, restoring additional material from the overture. His treatment of section C on the recording is based on a variant that he first introduced in *The Anti-Abolitionist Riots,* consisting of a two-measure interpolation (p. 1/2/3–4) followed by a varied repetition of the measure preceding the interpolation (see the beginning of p. 1/3). Ives's 1933 recording preserves these features of the earlier study, but changes the content of the interpolation (0:10–0:16), borrowing instead from the study's introduction in what seems to be a moment of free association. Ives made two other recordings of the complete transcription in the mid-1930s (Ives 1999: tracks 5–6 and 11–12). Each of these corresponds closely to the earlier 1933 version aside from some shortening of the material derived from Cadenzas 2–4 and one instance of backtracking in each recording.[18] These recordings from the mid-1930s establish that the initial recording of 1933 was not merely an improvised take on the transcription but rather a version that he had settled on and played in more or less the same way on multiple occasions over a substantial stretch of time.

The interrelationships I have just summarized have never been outlined in a concise format, nor have all these incarnations of the Emerson music been considered together in any detail; most studies have ignored the recordings entirely. But this synoptic view of these scores, sketches, and recordings reveals a clear, basic narrative of how the opening music of the overture evolved from its inception to Ives's recordings of the 1930s:

- Ives sketched the opening section of the *Emerson Overture,* which he envisioned as part of a set of overtures devoted to "Men of Literature."

- Ives isolated the three main cadenzas, including some of the adjacent orchestral music, and developed each in a separate piano study; one of these, *The Anti-Abolitionist Riots,* became a complete piece with distinct character and programmatic connotations of its own. Virtually no music is shared among these studies.

- Ives later returned to the overture material, but now with a much different goal: to incorporate this music into one of his most ambitious compositional projects, the *Concord* Sonata, a return to his earlier "Men of Literature" idea, but with a somewhat different cast of authors. For the beginning of the "Emerson" movement, Ives drew upon his sketches for the overture, incorporating the orchestral music but now mostly passing over the cadenza material that he had developed in the three studies.

- After publishing the *Concord*, Ives returned to the "Emerson" movement, using it as the primary source for his *Four Transcriptions*. The first transcription preserves virtually all of the music from p. 1–p. 2/1 of the "Emerson" movement, while restoring a substantial amount of additional material from the first section of the overture. This material is drawn almost exclusively from the orchestral passages omitted from "Emerson," including most of the portions of sections F and H that had been included in *The Anti-Abolitionist Riots* and Study no. 2, respectively. As a result, the transcription incorporates all orchestral material from the opening section of the overture save for the two-measure orchestral introduction (0:00–0:13) and the brief passage that separates Cadenzas 1 and 2 (0:42–0:54).

- Several years later, Ives recorded the first transcription, preserving all material from the printed version while restoring the missing cadenza material from the overture. This recording adhered very closely to the entire first section of the overture, omitting only the music of the two-measure orchestral introduction and incorporating a short insertion near the end of the music from Cadenza 2, as in *The Anti-Abolitionist Riots*.

- Finally, a few years after Ives's final recording session in 1943, Arrow Music Press published Ives's revised edition of the *Concord*. The revised "Emerson" movement incorporated many features from the *Four Transcriptions,* but restored none of the passages from the overture that were absent in the first *Concord* edition. In their basic material the two editions are the same, and thus the second is essentially regressive in terms of the evolution of the overture material.

Thus, the history of Ives's Emerson music, as it evolved from the first musical sketches for the *Emerson Overture,* is essentially a three-stage process by which the music was composed, broken down into its component parts, and then gradually reconstructed—or, to put it in the simplest of terms, a process of creation, analysis, and re-synthesis. In 1934, John Kirkpatrick, by this time intimately familiar with the "Emerson" movement of the *Concord* but having only recently seen the transcriptions, wrote in a letter to Ives: "I hadn't realized the extent to which your music may be considered in a state of flux, so to speak. . . . It was rather a shock to find [the 'Emerson' movement] could so readily be dismembered and reassembled by its own maker" (Owens 2007: 215). These words suggest an apt analogy for the evolution of Ives's Emerson music: the creation and assembly of a jigsaw puzzle. Again, the process is best understood in three stages. (1) The overture section is the original, uncut image. Many of the cuts are implied, however, suggesting that Ives may have already conceived of this music as fragmentable. The two-measure introduction is easily separable, for instance. See also the central portion of Cadenza 3 (2:41–3:03): if inserted into the *Concord* movement, this passage would fall precisely between the end of p. 1/3 and the beginning of p. 1/4, suggesting that in the overture it functions as an interpolation. In p. 5 of his sketches, Ives labeled the beginning of this passage "as cadenza," despite the fact that the solo piano entrance occurs two measures earlier, an anomaly that affirms the idea that he conceived of a musical division at this moment.

Example 6.4. *Four Transcriptions from "Emerson,"* ink score (f4873).

(2) The three studies are the puzzle pieces, cut by the jigsaw and awaiting assembly. They comprise almost all of the music of the overture, and, as with puzzle pieces, there is virtually no overlap among them. (3) The first edition of the *Concord* movement and the score of the first transcription are two different stages of the partially assembled puzzle, with the transcription adding portions of each of the three studies that the *Concord* movement had not incorporated. Finally, the

1933 recording is the fully assembled puzzle, with one small piece missing (the two-measure introduction).

The jigsaw puzzle analogy is especially appealing because, in addition to providing a temporal metaphor (the creation and assembly of the puzzle), it provides a spatial one (the puzzle and its pieces). As Robert P. Morgan has convincingly argued, Ives's music is distinguished by its many spatial qualities. But whereas Morgan was primarily concerned with how the music is heard, spatial relationships are fundamental to an understanding of the compositional process. Ives's manuscripts comprise countless instances of the composer's puzzle-like treatment of sketches and scores. A single page might contain fragmentary sketches for more than one piece, and these sketches might have been made at radically different times. Ives frequently revisited old scores again and again, and he often returned to his original sketches, adding annotations, indicating insertions, cutting out portions with scissors, or overlaying new music over the old, sometimes merely scribbling over old sketches with pen or pencil, and other times using more unusual means, such as attaching new scraps of staff paper over the music he wished to edit. The patch for p. 2 of Ives's overture sketches, for instance, is a straightforward instance in which Ives returned to a sketch, composed a few bars of new material on a scrap of staff paper, and simply indicated the insertion of this patch on the original sketch. Inserting patches in this manner was common practice for Ives. He created numerous such patches for insertion in the overture score and the closely related Copy C of the *Four Transcriptions;* the fourteen pages of Copy C are in fact accompanied by nearly as many pages of inserts.

A particularly interesting use of inserts is shown in Example 6.4, which reproduces the first page of Ives's ink score of the first transcription (f4873), created in preparation for the Hanke copy at some point in the early to mid-1920s. Recall that the first transcription retains virtually all the music from the opening section of the *Concord* movement (p. 1–p. 2/1) while reinstating music from the overture. In this ink score, rather than writing out the entire transcription, Ives borrowed two different segments from the printed score of the *Concord* movement (p. 1/1 and p. 1/4–5). The first of these visible is in the example. Ives cut out each score segment and attached it to staff paper with sewing pins (perhaps borrowed from his wife, Harmony), like a newspaper clipping added to a scrapbook.

It might seem that Ives was merely interested in saving himself time here; he wished to make only minor changes to the first system of the "Emerson" movement, as indicated by his pencil emendations. But the first two quarter-note beats of the second system of the transcription conform precisely to the "Emerson" movement as well—why didn't Ives include this portion of the "Emerson" score in his cutout? Perhaps it was simply too cumbersome, given the small size of this portion of the second system. But Ives frequently cut out various non-rectangular shapes in other instances, raising the possibility that he had a particular reason for not doing so here. Recall that in both *The Anti-Abolitionist Riots* and in Ives's 1933 recording of the first transcription, precisely when the music reaches the equivalent of the end of the first system of the "Emerson" movement, it proceeds in a completely different manner, a short transition followed by music derived from Cadenza 2 of the overture (compare the continuations of section C as represented in Figure 6.2). This means of approaching the music of Cadenza 2 seems to have been part of Ives's original plan for the overture, as explained above. Thus, the precise fragment of the "Emerson" movement that Ives pinned into his score for the first transcription is a musical fragment for which he had conceived two radically different continuations. Even though his continuation of this fragment in his ink score for the first transcription adhered to that of the "Emerson" movement, the work of Ives's scissors suggests that his conception of the fragment was still shaped by its alternative continuation in the overture and *The Anti-Abolitionist Riots.*

Thus, the orientation of the music on the printed page in the "Emerson" movement—its organization into discrete systems—points to aspects of Ives's conception of the music's structure. There are other instances in Ives's works where this seems to be the case, including the page turn in "Grantchester" and p. 1/4–5 of the "Emerson" movement, which Ives cut-and-pinned into his score for the first transcription as well.[19] Ives's creation and treatment of inserts such as these in the various manuscript sources for the concerto and transcriptions suggest that he conceived of the Emerson music as a collection of musical fragments, passages, or entire sections that are separable and can be assembled in multiple ways. And the same is true for other similar constellations of interrelated pieces as well—one need look no farther than the second movement of the *Concord,* "Hawthorne," than to find oneself in the middle of an equally dense thicket of cross-relationships. Indeed, as William Brooks has convincingly argued, "Ives's entire output, in fact, is unique for the way in which it forms a great web of interrelated compositions" (1974: 48).

Whereas the jigsaw puzzle analogy is perhaps the best way of conceptualizing Ives's treatment of his manuscript materials, as a temporal analogue for the evolution of the Emerson music its significance is secondary. In this regard, the best analogue is to be found in Ives's music itself. The compositional history of Ives's Emerson music closely resembles a conceptual model for many of Ives's individual pieces, correlating with the three-stage process characterized above: (1) the overture is analogous to a tune or other musical succession that Ives would frequently use as a compositional starting point; (2) the three Studies are the fragments of this tune as they are heard in the actual piece, frequently in isolation and without regard for their original ordering; and (3) the *Concord* movement, the first transcription, and the 1933 recording are stages in the ultimate emergence of the complete tune, achieved near the end of a piece or strived for but never fully realized. In sum, the history of Ives's Emerson music is one of Ives gradually coming back to and attempting to recapture an earlier musical idea, a pursuit of the past that is modeled by thematic processes in individual pieces.[20] More specifically, the three-stage process through which I have characterized this pursuit resembles nothing more than cumulative form: the evolution of Ives's Emerson music is best conceptualized as an example of cumulative form writ large, with the 1933 recording representing the culmination of this music's lengthy compositional history.

Nevertheless, it is the "Emerson" movement from the revised *Concord* Sonata that seems to be universally regarded as the definitive version of Ives's Emerson music. But Ives was highly ambivalent about traditional notions of "the work" as a stable entity, represented by the printed score and enjoying privileged status. Almost immediately after the initial publication of the *Concord*, Ives began to question whether the effort required to learn and perform the sonata was justified, and he began to promote alternatives to complete performances of the printed score. In a 1921 letter to his friend Clifton Furness, Ives wrote: "I hesitate to encourage anyone to play [the 'Emerson'] movement. . . . The reception it will get from most audiences (or auditors for that matter) will not balance the time & effort in preparation. The Thoreau is more practicable & can be made more readily acceptable" (Owens 2007: 89–90). Many years later, as Ives was beginning to consider recording the transcriptions, his feelings do not seem to have changed. In a 1932 letter to the composer and conductor Lehman Engel, who had proposed a series of lecture-recitals on the *Concord* with the pianist Hortense Monath, Ives responded:

> To play the whole second sonata is a long & rather hard job for any pianist—& for most listeners, it seems. If Miss Monath thought best I might suggest one or two of the Transcriptions of the first movement with the last movement in the printed book "Thoreau." The first two movements of this Sonata, as they stand in the printed book, are for the most part a reduction for piano from a Piano-Concerto score. The transcriptions are nearer and more practicable to play. (Owens 2007: 183)

Thus the transcriptions—particularly the first and third, which seem to be the "one or two" transcriptions Ives referred to here, the same pieces he chose to record multiple times during his 1930s sessions, while neglecting the *Concord* entirely—emerged for Ives as perfectly valid and perhaps even preferred substitutes for the "Emerson" movement, with this demotion of the latter enacted symbolically, we might imagine, by the work of Ives's scissors. His return to the "Emerson" movement in 1939, as he began planning the *Concord*'s second edition, seems to have been driven by external demand more than any internal motivations (Block 1997: 28–30, 48).[21] There is a compelling case, then, to be made for elevating the importance of Ives's 1933 recording as the culmination of a long-term compositional process. To adequately interpret this process, however, requires a more careful consideration of its relationship to cumulative form—specifically, to an instance of cumulative form in the *Concord* Sonata itself.

Cumulative Form and the Human-Faith-Melody

Melodically, much of the *Concord* Sonata is organized around what Ives referred to as the "human-faith-melody" in his short essay on the third movement, "The Alcotts": "All around you, under the Concord sky, there still floats the

"Emerson" (1920),
p. 1/1-2

Slowly (♩ = about 76-72)

"The Alcotts"
(end)

A   B

Example 6.5. *Concord* Sonata, cumulative setting of "human-faith-melody" (1).

influence of that human-faith-melody—transcendent and sentimental enough for the enthusiast or the cynic, respectively—reflecting an innate hope, a common interest in common things and common men—a tune the Concord bards are ever playing while they pound away at the immensities with a Beethoven-like sublimity, and with, may we say, a vehemence and perseverance, for that part of greatness is not so difficult to emulate" (Ives 1961: 47–48). The "Alcotts" essay helps to identify the melody in the sonata. One paragraph earlier, Ives imagines Elizabeth Alcott playing "the old Scotch airs" and Beethoven's Fifth Symphony on the piano at the Orchard House, the Alcott family residence (47); these musical references seem to correspond, respectively, to the melody in E♭ that begins at the end of p. 55/3, and the numerous overt references to the Beethoven's Fifth motive. These correlations invite us to listen for the human-faith-melody as well, and it would seem to emerge, "pounding away with a Beethoven-like sublimity," near the end of the movement (the final two systems on p. 57), just as Ives mentions it near the end of his "Alcotts" essay.

Fragments of the melody are featured prominently in each of the first three movements, leading up to the definitive statement at the end of "The Alcotts."[22] The tune is reprised in the added flute line near the end of the final movement, "Thoreau" (p. 67/1 and p. 67/3–p. 68/1). The "Alcotts" version, transposed down an octave and with Ives's thick harmonization omitted, is shown at the bottom of Example 6.5. Some of the melodic elements of this melody were present in the original *Emerson Overture*, but it appears that Ives did not conceive of the complete melody until composing the *Concord*. The melody is structured in two balanced halves, labeled A and B in the example.[23] Each half has a similar rhythmic

Example 6.6. *Concord* Sonata, cumulative setting of "human-faith-melody" (2).

profile and can be divided into three segments accordingly, as shown (A1, A2, A3, etc.; these are shown more clearly in Example 6.6).

The presence of these melodic segments early in the "Emerson" movement is not difficult to identify and has been noted in the scholarly literature (see in particular Burkholder 1995: 350–54). The segments are first heard in isolation, but then begin to coalesce, moving toward the eventual apotheosis of the melody at the end of "The Alcotts." Ives first develops the two halves of the melody separately, gradually divulging more of each half. The process is orderly and its pacing deliberate. The incipits of each half of the melody are initially juxtaposed, as shown in Example 6.5, indicated by gray boxes for the first half and unshaded boxes drawn with dashed lines for the second. (A few additional statements of A1 are omitted from the example; see p. 1/5 and p. 2/1.) Next, each half of the melody is stated in full, with some rhythmic variation. Example 6.6 illustrates. Part A is stated in C major, and part B in G-sharp major with some unusual enharmonic spellings. Several aspects of these complete statements of parts A and B close off any sense of melodic fulfillment, however, allowing the thematic revelation of "The Alcotts" to achieve its full impact. Each statement competes for our attention with contrasting musical material, and portions of the two melodic halves are even stated simultaneously on p. 2/2. The two melodic halves are not pre-

Example 6.7. Schubert's Symphony no. 9 (Movement I, mm. 1–8) vs. Ives's "human-faith-melody" (end of "The Alcotts").

sented in proper sequence, and they are stated in different keys, although they are bound together by a melodic emphasis on C. Perhaps most importantly, each melodic half is interrupted, part A by a short interpolation (see the solid arrow) and part B by about a minute's worth of music, most of which I have omitted from the example (see the dotted arrow). Because of the duration of the latter interpolation, the resumption of part B of the melody is unlikely to be heard as such, and in fact has not been noted in the Ives literature.

Although the human-faith-melody is an Ives original, it does borrow melodic elements from several sources: the "fate motive" of Beethoven's Fifth Symphony (B1) and the opening fanfare of the *Hammerklavier* Sonata (B2), as well the Baptist hymns "Martyn" and "Missionary Chant," and possibly one of Ives's usual suspects, the patriotic song "Columbia, the Gem of the Ocean" (the last was proposed by Block 1996: 34, 36).[24] Block has also identified the first four notes of the melody (A1) as a "questionable borrowing" from the opening horn theme of Schubert's Ninth Symphony, the *"Great"* C major (1996: 58–61, 84); both melodies begin with the pitch succession C–D–E–A. Block was deeply uncertain about the status of this possible borrowing and did not pursue the connection.[25] But there is substantial evidence to suggest that it is meaningful and worth considering further.

As shown in Example 6.7, the connection between the two melodies is more substantial than the four-note connection Block cited. Almost every note in Ives's melody can be derived from Schubert's, as I have indicated with annotations on the example. There are some striking rhythmic correspondences as well: for example, Schubert's last three notes, D–E–C, can serve as a rhythmic reduction of Ives's. Clearly, several important aspects of these melodies are quite different— the metrical treatments of corresponding motivic cells, the overall rhythmic profiles, and the melodic contours in particular—making the connection difficult to hear relative to many of Ives's borrowings. But concealed borrowings can be just as meaningful as obvious ones, and the pitch relationships here are thorough enough to invite consideration of what this potential borrowing might mean.

Ives modeled several songs after Schubert's, and he made many references to Schubert in his writings, including references to how his father, George, a professional musician, played horn arrangements of Schubert songs (Ives 1972: 127, 246–47). As Ives reminisced in *Memos:*

Example 6.8. Canon from "Remembrance" (1921); main motive compared with Schubert's Symphony no. 9 (mm. 1–2).

> [There was] something about the way Father played hymns. . . . He had the gift of putting something in the music which meant more sometimes than when some people sang the words. He once gave a concert in Danbury on the basset horn, playing songs of Schubert and Franz. He had the words printed on a sheet and passed them through the audience, who were expected to read the words and sing silently with him. Somebody heard him play the *Erlking* (Schubert) and felt that he sang it (through the basset horn or trombone, I forget which it was) and carried him away with it, without the words, as Bispham did singing it. Hearing him play these songs got me, to a certain extent, writing songs for the horn or some instrument, with the words underneath, which should be sung. Some of the songs in the book of *114 Songs* were first written in this way. (1972: 46)

The best example of such "Songs with-out Voice," as Ives called them, is Ives's short piece for chamber ensemble "The Pond" (c. 1912–13), which features a canon for flute or violin in counterpoint with horn or trumpet. Ives included a text under the horn or trumpet part: "A sound of a distant horn, O'er shadowed lake is borne, my father's song." Ives later arranged this piece and its text as a song called "Remembrance" (1921). The upper two systems of Example 6.8 reproduce the complete vocal part of "Remembrance" and a portion of the piano's right hand, which joins with the voice to form the canon. The song ends with the opening melody of "Taps" in the piano, as I have highlighted with brackets, clarifying the song's status as a miniature memorial to George, who himself played cornet, as well as the horn and many other instruments.

As shown in the example, the canon between voice and piano in "Remembrance" is based on the same notes as the opening of Schubert's Great C major, but heard in exact retrograde (or tonal inversion about the axis C); Ives's melody borrows the rhythm of Schubert's first measure as well. A wealth of evidence, then, suggests that in the song "Remembrance," Ives memorialized his father by invoking George's performances of Schubert. It is a small step to interpret the human-faith-melody in a similar way; it also seems to borrow from Schubert, a melody scored by Schubert for horn, the very instrument Ives associated with his father in the song "Remembrance." That Schubert's melody is diatonic within C major would have appealed to Ives: C major's power for Ives as a symbol of purity and the elemental made it the perfect key to express the simplicity and unassailable truth-content of his human-faith-melody.

The human-faith-melody is reprised by the flute near the end of the "Thoreau" movement, transposed to B♭ and stopping a few notes short of completion. Ives referred explicitly to this flute melody near the end of his "Thoreau" essay: "It is darker—the poet's flute is heard out over the pond and Walden hears the swan song of that 'Day'—and faintly echoes. . . . Is it the transcendental tune of Concord?" (Ives 1961: 69; the ellipses are Ives's). These words suggest a close connection between Thoreau's Walden Pond and Ives's father's pond as imagined in Ives's piece "The Pond," which he also referred to as "Echo Piece." Both ponds are characterized sonically by the flute and by echoes, and thematically by death. At the end of Ives's "Thoreau" essay, Thoreau submits to his own mortality; as Ives wrote, partially quoting from *Walden,* Thoreau "blend[s] . . . with the harmony of [Nature's] solitude," becoming "a part of herself" (68–69). Ives's conflation of his biological father and Thoreau, his spiritual one, is suggested further by another passage from the "Thoreau" essay, where Ives wrote of how Thoreau's work provided him comfort at the time of George's death: "my Thoreau—that reassuring and true friend, who stood by me one 'low' day, when the sun had gone down, long, long before sunset. . . . You may know something of the great human passions which stirred that soul . . . but you know him not—unless you love him!" The "one low day" Ives refers to here, as many scholars have noted, almost certainly refers to the day of George's death. The presence of this passage in the "Thoreau" essay suggests that death, an explicit subject in the song "Remembrance," is an implicit one in the "Thoreau" movement as well.

This interpretation of the "Thoreau" movement sheds light on the meaning and significance of Ives's cumulative treatment of the human-faith-melody in the *Concord.* This movement revives the music of Ives's father, now mingled with the bells of Concord and Thoreau's flute at Walden Pond, a place where time blends and blurs. To bring the music of the past to life in the present was the primary goal of Ives's cumulative settings of borrowed tunes as well. In these settings, the old tunes would sound new, *of* the present, because Ives would seem to be creating them himself, from scratch, beginning with fragmentary ideas, grappling for something more substantial, and eventually stitching these fragments together into complete melodies. Ives often seems not to borrow his tunes but to construct them, arriving at a final version only through extensive labor and searching, and celebrating his achievement through an ecstatic statement of his musical creation. In this way, cumulative form can be understood to model the creative act itself. But the human-faith-melody is unusual in that it is primarily a tune of Ives's own composition, one that seems to have emerged from difficult labor over the course of many years and through many interrelated sketches and scores. Thus, the cumulative treatment of this melody in the *Concord* Sonata not only models creativity but, more importantly, reenacts a real compositional act, Ives's gradual assembly of the human-faith-melody from its component parts. And this process was part of a much larger one, the evolution of Ives's Emerson music as a whole. As we have seen, this evolution shares the structure of cumulative setting, suggesting that for Ives, the process of composition and the formal processes within compositions were inseparable. Or, to put it more simply: Ives's compositional life imitated his art, and vice versa.

* * *

Ives, as I imagine it, stepped into the recording studio at Abbey Road in 1933 hoping to recapture the intuitive force of his original overture. This was to be the apotheosis of his Emerson music, a culmination of his compositional efforts that would elevate the music toward the divine by granting it technological immortality. But he left sorely disappointed, frustrated, and confused. Recall the diary entry quoted in the previous chapter, written shortly after Ives's session: "A man may play to himself and his music starts to live—then he tries to put it under a machine, and it's dead!" For Ives, the phonograph, an apparent means of preserving music, quickly proved to have the opposite effect. He did not give up on the project, but his subsequent recordings of the first transcription became more labored, with starts and stops, and did not achieve the coherence of the first. Often, in these and other recordings, he would end a piece suddenly and prematurely, out of apparent frustration. Listen, for example, to his 1943 recording of a fragment from the third "Emerson" transcription. This was his last attempted recording of any movements from this work (Ives 1999: track 36). Ives simply abandons the take after a minute, exclaiming, "Oh no, I can't!"

The fragmentary nature of these recordings is a direct product of Ives's struggles with technology, just as the fragments that characterize so much of Ives's music are very often the product and expression of his struggles with modern life. The continuous whole from which these fragments derive is the idealized past, always complete in Ives's imagination. And the attempted assembly of musical fragments around which Ives's pieces are so often structured is an outgrowth of his preoccupation with reconstituting the wholeness of the past in the present. The history of Ives's Emerson music is likewise one of trying to piece back together the music of the past, in this case an abandoned overture. As his health deteriorated and he grew increasingly unable to maintain the compositional productivity of his earlier days, Ives may have come to idealize this work of his younger, more confident self, regarding the overture as more pure than its subsequent labored reworkings by virtue of its being spontaneous, incomplete, and not ossified in print. The improvisatory quality of his transcription recordings, in striking contrast to the fixed and familiar form of the *Concord* Sonata, reflect his desire to make this old music new again, an indication of what Richard Kramer has recently referred to as the romantic aesthetic of the "unfinished," in which "the act of composition may be said to emulate the spontaneity of improvisation, to capture intuition," whereas "in the fixing of text, intuition is embalmed, masked over" (2008: viii). Ives's continual reworking of the Emerson music over the decades was not a march toward some definitive creative achievement, but rather the work of a wistful yet determined composer seeking to capture a past intuition and bring it back to life.

Notes

Introduction

1. Stuart Feder has made this point as well, interpreting Ives's reverse-chronological ordering as an outgrowth of Ives's fixation on the past: "Ives had in mind a time sequence that would roughly reverse the now all-too-rapid flow of time: the last would come first and the first last (although this scheme was not slavishly pursued)" (1992: 312).

2. Emerson's and Thoreau's concern with this mode of temporal experience is the focus of Guthrie 2001.

3. Broyles made a similar point, less polemically: "Ives's passion for humanity was genuine, although it is idealized and abstracted. . . . Rather than expanding his nineteenth-century local view into a broader one that incorporated all humanity, he instead sought to cram all of humanity into a nineteenth-century town" (1996: 135).

4. Heinrich Koch defined it as "the insertion of unessential melodic ideas between the segments of a phrase"; see 1983: 53.

5. Here, Kramer actually seems to echo Morgan's writing on Ives; Morgan argued that fragmentation in Ives's music is "not designed to lead from one event to another in sequential succession; rather, it produces a multidimensional framework in which relationships can be established simultaneously in both directions" (1977: 150–51).

6. A relatively early, and exemplary, analytical study that characterized Ives's music in a similar way is William Brooks's analysis of the *Fourth Symphony*. As evident from the following passage, Brooks's conception of the music resembles mine in spirit, although his analytical approach is quite different:

> Most of [Ives's technical procedures] are designed to make "fixed" pieces changeable, not necessarily by physically altering their details in successive presentations, but rather by inviting the listener to hear them in substantially different ways each time they are played. . . . In many of Ives's works, diverse materials can be collected and organized in many different ways by attending to different relational dimensions as the piece unfolds. Thus Ives offers musical networks rather than musical arrows. The listener is encouraged to enter into these, to structure them in his own way. . . . By choosing a path through these interrelationships, each individual listener can find his own route to the universal web that ultimately binds all together. (1974: 6)

7. The sexist term "Man" was part of Ives's "social grammar of prejudice," as Judith Tick has called it (1993: 84), and I have elected to incorporate it here in the interest of faithfulness to Ives's language and thought.

8. See, for example, L. Kramer 2008 on the way acoustic horizons suggest timelessness in each of the movements of *A Symphony: New England Holidays*.

9. Ives explained briefly how mental images stimulate artistic intuitions in the Prologue (1961: 7).

10. Burkholder analyzes the movement this way; see 1995: 262–66.

1. God/Man

1. All score references are to Ives 1995.

2. The derivation is even more obvious in Ives's pencil sketch for the piece (f6014–15; see Sinclair 1999: 264). Here, Ives sketched Verse 7 with each choir at the same pitch level as in Verses 2–3, indicating their proper transposition with two marginal notes: "all minor 3rd higher to amen bottom" and "to E♭ trans E♭ to bottom."

3. For a comparative study of Ives and Stravinsky, see Buchman 1996, one of numerous essays that pairs off Ives with another composer—a curious phenomenon that reflects a long-standing anxiety about the security of Ives's position in the canon.

4. The effect is quite similar to the end of Stravinsky's *Symphonies of Wind Instruments* (1920), one of the pieces Cone analyzes in his essay.

2. Community/Individual

1. All score references are to Ives 1990a.

2. For a complete account of the source materials for the *Ragtime Dances* and the piano sonata, see Sinclair 1999: 188–91.

3. All score references are to Ives 1990b, a corrected version of the original 1954 edition edited by Lou Harrison and William Masselos.

4. For an alternative approach that treats the scherzo movements as lying "outside the trajectory of [the other movements]," see L. Kramer 1996: 58.

5. "Happy Day" fits easily into this thematic family as well, as is evident from its refrain:

Happy day, happy day,
When Jesus washed my sins away!
He taught me how to watch and pray
And live rejoicing every day;
Happy day, happy day,
When Jesus washed my sins away!

In their discussions of this hymn alongside "Welcome Voice" and "Bringing in the Sheaves," Marshall and Burkholder privileged musical similarities over textual ones (Marshall 1968: 53 and Burkholder 1995: 80, 213); Marshall went so far as to provide full keyboard arrangements of each hymn without including the texts or even mentioning them in his essay. The musical connections are compelling if not particularly surprising; all three feature the commonplace melodic motion $\hat{2}$–$\hat{1}$–$\hat{3}$–$\hat{2}$–$\hat{1}$. But given the relationship between the words of these hymns and Ives's programmatic commentary on the sonata, he was likely more interested in what the hymns are about than the conventional cadential formula they share.

6. Burkholder took the numerous references to patriotic songs in the quartet as evidence in support of Ives's claim (1995: 348–49).

7. For a convenient summary of the marginalia on Ives's sketch of the quartet, see Tick 2008: 345–47.

8. Ives did continue to castigate Rollo in his marginalia, however. For instance, in mm. 58–66, where the second violin drops from the texture completely, Ives wrote "Too hard to play, *so it just can't* be good music, Rollo!" His mocking continues in the following measures (67–72), where the second violin returns with a mechanical rhythm: "Beat time Rollo."

3. Intuition/Expression

1. This collection was erroneously titled *Eighteen Songs,* a mistake corrected in the revised 1962 edition.
2. The text is taken from Ives 2004, which eliminates several irregularities of capitalization and punctuation from the 1922 edition.
3. Also relevant are Ives's proposal "Concerning a Twentieth Amendment," his related correspondence with William H. Taft, and an unpublished 1920 editorial; see Ives 1961: 204–14.
4. For example: "[Ragtime] is something like wearing a derby hat on the back of the head, a shuffling lilt of a happy soul just let out of a Baptist church in old Alabama. Ragtime has its possibilities. But it does not 'represent the American nation' any more than some fine old senators represent it" (1961: 94).
5. Many have discussed wedge structures in Ives's music; see in particular Winters (1986: 24–126) and Lambert (1997: 53–65).
6. Hitchcock renders the final chord as a dotted whole note and eliminates the fermata; see 2004b: 163.
7. "Hog-heart" seems roughly equivalent to "hog-mind," Ives's term for the self-obsessed Minority; he changed "hog-heart" to "'ole mole" in *Nineteen Songs.*
8. David Hertz has suggested a deeper connection, arguing that Ives was familiar with the Mallarmé poem on which Debussy's tone poem is based (1993: 105–6).
9. For a similar account of this passage's derivation from Debussy's *Prélude,* see Gibbens 1985: 43–51.

4. Elements of Narrative

Much of this chapter was published previously in McDonald 2004.

1. For an overview of narrative studies in musicology from their heyday in the early 1990s through their decline later in the decade and into the early 2000s, as well as a summary and critique of the main theoretical issues confronted during these years, see McDonald 2004: 263–66.
2. For the purposes of this study, the differences between these two versions are not of great consequence; I focus my comments on the original version. Among the differences, most notable is that the Question itself, uniform in its seven appearances in the original version, has a variable last note in the revised version: whereas the original version of the Question always ends on B♭, the ultimate note of the revised version alternates between C and B♮ in successive statements of the Question—the sort of revision that led Elliott Carter to make his famous claim that Ives might have revised his works later in life in order to "jack up the level of dissonance" (Perlis 1974: 138). For a detailed account of *The Unanswered Question*'s compositional history see Hitchcock and Zahler 1988.
3. Ives suggested an alternative scoring in the original version of the piece, apparently indicating that two pianos could be substituted for the flute quartet. He offered further possibilities in an explanatory note that accompanied his revisions in the 1930s:

oboe and clarinet in place of the lower two flutes; and English horn, oboe, or clarinet in place of the trumpet. See Ives 1985: 10.

4. Burkholder suggests that such independent layers show the influence of the organ—an instrument that facilitates the superimposition of sonically distinct material—on Ives's compositional style (2002: 276). Burkholder's thesis is provocative in the case of *The Unanswered Question:* note that Ives scored the piece for strings, flutes, and trumpet, arguably the most idiomatic and common organ stops.

5. In Work-list C, Ives entitled the piece *Largo to Presto: The Unanswered Question (A Cosmic Landscape)* (Ives 1972: 152).

6. As explained by Nina Kolesnikoff, in the story, "Events are linked together according to their temporal sequence and causality," whereas in the discourse (or "plot"), these events "are rearranged, disrupting the chronological order and causal connections" (1993: 632). The distinction between story and discourse is roughly equivalent to the Russian formalists' distinction between *fabula* and *syuzhet* and the German distinction between *erzählte Zeit* and *Erzählzeit.* Seymour Chatman's *Story and Discourse: Narrative Structure in Fiction and Film* (1978) is a standard English-language introduction to these concepts.

7. This facet of Ives's style is featured in Lambert 1997.

8. More simply, as Sarah Kozloff writes, "Because narrative films are narrative, someone must be narrating" (1988: 44).

9. See also Laffay 1964 on the notion of a *grand imagier,* an approximate equivalent to the filmic narrator; Metz invoked the same concept in the quotation above. For a view contrasting these, see Bordwell 1985: 61–62.

10. Even the potential circular returns suggested in Examples 4.5 and 4.6 have analogues in the strings. The string music is itself circular, periodically returning to the same G-major triad with which the piece begins. Furthermore, in the opening progression of mm. 1–14, the outer strings outline a wedge of their own, each traversing the path from G to C to G but in contrary motion, suggesting a pure, diatonic version of the flutes' wedge in Answers 1–3.

11. James Kavanaugh has identified and discussed at length several works that express this Platonic notion, examples of "Transcendental Pythagoreanism," a philosophy he associates with Thoreau and Hawthorne and traces to nineteenth-century German philosophers, Schopenhauer in particular (1978).

12. In other words, the strings and flutes occupy different discursive levels, resulting in what might be experienced as a discursive shift each time the flutes enter and exit the texture. Robert Hatten has written frequently about such implied changes in the level of discourse, particularly in the music of Beethoven. See 1991; 1994: 174–88, 196–202; 2004: 35–52; and Almén and Hatten 2012: 63–66, 69.

13. Abbate, for instance, claims that music cannot "possess *narrativity* without the *distance* engendered by discursive formulation" (1991: 26), a circumstance she regards as unusual but which applies well to *The Unanswered Question.* Likewise, *The Unanswered Question* exemplifies the precondition Karol Berger identifies as essential to diegesis in music, or any other medium: presence "of at least two distinct ontological levels," in which "the narrated world is hierarchically subordinated to the world of the narrator" (2000: 169).

14. Here, my opinion is at odds with Wayne Shirley's: he argues that "Ives's program [does not] particularly suggest Emerson's ideas" (1989: 9).

15. Rather than taking the statement "Thou art the unanswered question" literally, we might understand it to mean "*Thy meaning* is the unanswered question."

16. Although this structural correspondence might not challenge Shirley's statement that "no amount of ingenuity can torture *The Unanswered Question* into a 'tone poem on "The Sphinx"'" (1989: 9), it suggests a much closer connection to the poem than Shirley is willing to recognize.

17. This is Ives's explanation of our apprehension of "substance" (1961: 75).

18. See also Emerson's poem *World-Soul* (also from 1847), very similar in its themes and imagery to *The Sphinx* (1994: 17–20). Here again, Emerson focuses on a "secret" (see stanza 7) whose answer apparently resides in the "World-Soul."

19. Burkholder warns against applying ideas from the *Essays* to compositions other than the *Concord* Sonata and its contemporaries: "The aesthetic program set forth in the *Essays*, intended solely as an explanation or defense of the musical language and expressive aims of the *Concord* Sonata, has been applied indiscriminately to works from all periods of Ives's life. . . . But the *Essays* certainly do not pertain to the whole of Ives's output, for the philosophical position they articulate is Ives's final, hard-won synthesis of the many conflicting views of music he had either held or encountered during his lifetime. Earlier works do not fulfill the artistic program of the *Essays*, for the simple reason that it had not yet been formulated" (1985: 5–6).

20. This interpretation is deep-seated. In an important early commentary on Ives, the critic Lawrence Gilman applies Ives's characterization of Emerson directly to Ives without acknowledgment: he refers to Ives as "a great adventurer in the spiritual world, a poet, a visionary, a sage, and a seer" (1939: 9). If the *Essays* implied a connection between Ives and Emerson, Gilman certainly follows its lead.

21. The opening conceit of a pure, tonal context disrupted by an atonal element is found in other pieces by Ives, sometimes with clearer reference to his personal circumstances as a composer. See, for instance, the piano piece *Song Without (good) Words* (from Ives's *Set of Five Take-Offs*), composed about a year after the first version of *The Unanswered Question*. The first five measures establish the melody and accompaniment texture and tonal idiom (F major) one associates with the Mendelssohnian genre. Then, suddenly, the phrase breaks down, dissolving into dissonant clusters of the sort one finds in thoroughly atonal environments elsewhere in Ives's music. The remainder of the piece plays out the tension between the tonal setting and the atonal irritants established so saliently in the opening measures. The solo-piano piece *Varied Air and Variations* (ca. 1920–22), according to Ives's marginalia, enacts a piano recital in which the various sections represent, alternately, music performed by a pianist and reactions from the audience of "box belles"; the more dissonant stretches of the performance elicit "Protest" from these women, which Ives depicted with quiet pitch clusters (see mm. 1–5, 15–19, and 29–33)—not unlike the flute music of the first three Answers, or the Answerers' "Silent Conference."

22. Ives's recollection of the violinist Franz Milcke's reaction to Ives's Third Violin Sonata (1972: 70).

23. Leonard Bernstein, in his famous lectures at Harvard, offered a related interpretation of *The Unanswered Question*. Rather than solely a personal statement by Ives, the piece may be understood as a broad commentary on the future of music and its harmonic language. Bernstein interprets Ives's Question as "not a metaphysical one so much as a strictly musical question: Whither music in our century?" (1976: 269). For Bernstein, the piece expresses "the dilemma of the new century": "On the one hand, tonality and syntactic clarity; on the other, atonality and syntactic confusion" (269). He reaches a similar conclusion to mine regarding the ending: "Is that luminous final triad the an-

swer? Is tonality eternal, immortal? Many have thought so, and some still do. And yet that trumpet's question hangs in the air, unresolved, troubling our calm" (269).

5. Ives and the Now

A similar version of this chapter was published previously as McDonald 2012.

1. My informal use of "slide" should not be confused with the neo-Riemannian "slide relation," which pertains to a major and minor triad with a common third (C major and C♯ minor, for example).

2. Ives's use of *ascending* semitonal shifts to represent the onset of memory suggests an understanding of memory and dreaming as heightened states of consciousness. An opposite (and more intuitive) strategy in the music of Debussy is outlined in Rings 2008 (203).

3. Throughout this chapter, I use the designation "m. 4.2" (for example) to refer to m. 4, beat 2.

4. The progression A^7–D^7 suggested in Example 5.4 is particularly meaningful in light of a correspondence noted by Robert P. Morgan between the "Summer evenings" measure and a passage from Wagner's Prelude to *Tristan und Isolde* (1997: 14). Morgan observes that the upper melody of the piano in the first half of Ives's m. 10 is a rhythmically altered version of the melody from the *Tristan* Prelude, mm. 16–17 (the dramatic deceptive motion), transposed down a major second. Probing further, we can see that Wagner's deceptive progression B^7–E^7–F (mm. 13–17), transposed down a major second, becomes A^7–D^7–E♭. The latter progression comprises Ives's constellation of chordal roots discussed above, and it is realized in mm. 10, 15, and 21–22 of Ives's song, with A^7 of m. 10 proceeding to the D^7 of m. 15 as suggested in Example 5.4, and the final D♯ harmony of mm. 21–22 thwarting D^7's resolution onto G.

5. Freud writes: "A humiliation that was experienced thirty years ago acts exactly like a fresh one throughout the thirty years. . . . As soon as the memory of it is touched, it springs into life again and shows itself cathected with excitation" (1955b: 578). Similarly, the sudden rush of memories that overtakes Ives's persona correlates with Freud's notion of *Nachträglichkeit* (or "deferred action"), which, like Ives's song, is founded upon the idea of communion between past and present.

6. The Proust-Ives connection is often alluded to but rarely explored in depth. See, for instance, Hepokoski 1994 and Block 1997, whose titles make unmistakable references to *Remembrance,* but neither of which ever refers to Proust or his novel by name.

7. Rings invoked Proust and the *"moment bienheureux"* in a related musical context, a parenthetical passage in Debussy's piano prelude *Des pas sur la neige* (2008: 203–5).

8. Kern weaves into his account Ives's representation of clashing marching bands in the "Putnam's Camp" movement of *Three Places in New England* (2003: 75).

9. *Psalm 14* offers a straightforward musical analogue of parallel editing: Verse 7 cross-cuts the music of Verses 2 and 3 and unites the endings of each verse with the final bitonal cadence.

10. Stuart Feder speculates that Ives became increasingly fixated on his own mortality around 1918, due to his health problems and his tendency to measure his own life against that of his father's (George Ives died at forty-nine; Charles would turn forty-nine in 1923) (1990: 284–91).

11. This connotation is not merely metaphoric; rather, it was part of the way early filmgoers grappled with the new conventions of narrative film. Anecdotal evidence is provided by my son Leo, who as a two-year-old was just beginning to come to terms with

these conventions himself. While watching *The Muppet Movie,* during a scene in which Kermit and Miss Piggy take leave of their Muppet companions to enjoy a romantic dinner together, he suddenly began to sob: "What happened to Fozzie??"

6. Cumulative Composition

1. I use the expression "Emerson music" in a somewhat limited sense to refer to Ives's music that derives from his *Emerson Overture;* many other pieces of Ives's—*The Unanswered Question,* for example—seem to have been inspired by and/or emulate the writings and lectures of Emerson.

2. As elsewhere in the book, all dates are based on the most recent research of Gayle Sherwood Magee and James Sinclair, as it appears in Grove Music Online and Sinclair's *Catalogue.*

3. Ives recalled that he worked on the piece specifically during the years 1910–11 (Ives 1972: 200).

4. Ives's daughter, Edith, referred to these pages in a 1935 letter to John Kirkpatrick, when the pianist was contemplating performing the sonata: "Under separate cover the remains of the old overture, which you asked Father for, are being sent. About half a dozen pages are all that are found. These are quite indistinct in places and difficult to make out. Father thinks they won't be of much help, and doubts if they are worth spending much time over" (Ives 1972: 203).

5. Porter's reconstruction and his accompanying commentary—both unpublished— have been crucial resources informing my analysis of the overture and its relationship to subsequent works. The score is available for rent from Associated Music Publishers (Ives 1998).

6. A small, modified portion of the sketches for Study no. 1 is incorporated in *Scherzo: Over the Pavements* (c. 1910), a work for chamber ensemble (see mm. 68–72), but the remainder of the *Scherzo* has little to do with the constellation of pieces under consideration here. Studies nos. 11 and 23 also incorporate passages from the overture, but no music from its opening section.

7. Ives claimed to have completed the "Emerson" movement in 1912 (Ives 1972: 202), but the earliest sketches seem to date no earlier than 1915 (Sinclair 1999); these include various patches and revisions. Ives completed a revised ink score c. 1919 (Sinclair 1999) and published the entire sonata in 1920.

8. For a detailed comparison of the two editions, see Block 1997.

9. In 1943, Ives recorded excerpts from the "Emerson" movement (Ives 1999: tracks 32–34), but these do not involve the portion of the movement under consideration here.

10. Ives claimed to have composed the first movement between 1915 and 1918 (Ives 1972: 202).

11. Many of the tracks on this disc have been available since 1974 on LP as part of the collection *Charles Ives: The 100th Anniversary.*

12. Sandra Rae Clark's dissertation on the *Concord* Sonata and its "choices and variants" sets the standard here; see Clark 1972.

13. Here, as elsewhere in these sketches, Ives used a sign as a continuity indicator—in this case a circled triangle with a dot at its center.

14. F2225–26, f4784, and f2221–22 contain the sketches corresponding to Cadenza 4; f2225 includes a patch labeled "see from Cadenza #4 Piano Concerto Emerson."

15. Here is a rare instance in which Porter's solution to a problem in the sketches is not convincing. Musically, the transition to and from the crossed-out measure is jar-

ring in a way that seems incongruous with the style of the overture. Furthermore, Porter's solution results in the last measure of the patch occurring twice, in different musical contexts, first at 0:39–0:41 and then again at 1:47–1:50 (the latter incarnation is found on the penultimate measure of p. 3 of Ives's sketches). Yet Ives did not repeat this measure within any other piece, sketch, or recording. A much more likely scenario is that Ives's patch reflects his evolving treatment of the overture material as manifested in the first transcription. The entire patch corresponds to mm. 6–10 of the transcription, and Ives might well have intended for the patch to be followed by the ultimate measure on p. 3 of the sketches (the equivalent of m. 11 of the transcription). In this scenario, the patch would have been a means of skipping over Cadenza 2.

16. Ives's sketch includes a small amount of music, the equivalent of the first quarter-note beat of p. 1/2 of the *Concord* movement, that is not present in *The Anti-Abolitionist Riots*. In the overture, as in the *Concord* movement, this music supplies the third of three E octaves that initiate a statement of the Beethoven's Fifth motive, E–E–E–C♯ (this motive is missing from the opening of *The Anti-Abolitionist Riots*). If the deleted measure on p. 2 of the sketches is omitted as I have suggested, the concluding C♯ initiates another statement of the motive, C♯–C♯–C♯–A (0:42–0:51).

17. See, for instance, p. 6 of Ives's sketch, where one note refers to the upcoming "3rd Cadenza" (see the third system), while another refers to the same cadenza as "Cadenza #4" (see the lower right corner) (Porter 1998).

18. This backtracking can be heard between tracks 5 and 6, where the cause is apparently technical, and at 0:20 of track 12, where the cause is not apparent. In both of the later 1930s recordings, Ives modifies the music derived from the end of Cadenza 2, as heard in the 1933 recording, using the first transcription as a model. Compare track 1, 1:17–1:43, with track 5, 0:58–1:14, and track 11, 0:57–1:13: the first derives from *The Anti-Abolitionist Riots* (from the end of p. 3/5 through the end p. 4/1), whereas the latter two both derive from the slightly truncated version of this passage in the first transcription, mm. 7–10. (Note that in *The Anti-Abolitionist Riots,* the first transcription, and all three recordings, the passage in question is followed directly by section F.) Unlike Ives's 1933 recording, the later 1930s recordings essentially revert to the truncated version of Cadenza 3, as it appeared in the *Concord* movement and first transcription: compare track 1, 2:41–3:29, with track 6, 0:36–1:08, and track 11, 2:21–2:56 (Ives took a second pass at the latter version, as can be heard on track 12, 0:24–0:52). The first of Ives's later 1930s recordings ends about midway through the fourth cadenza, for no apparent reason. He may simply have been exhausted, as suggested by his moan near the end of the recording, at 2:08 of track 6. The second of these recordings omits only a short portion of the end of the cadenza, the equivalent of the final few seconds of the 1933 recording (1:15–1:29 of track 2).

19. In addition to these two systems, most of p. 1/3 from "Emerson" is preserved in the transcription as well, but Ives copied out this music by hand. Even though there seems to be no meaningful musical division between the end of p. 1/3 and the beginning of p. 1/4, Ives inserted an interpolation at precisely the equivalent spot in the overture, as discussed above; refer to Figure 6.2, where the gap shown in section G for both the "Emerson" movement and first transcription corresponds to the interpolation.

20. Block has made a similar argument about the second edition of the *Concord:* "Ives's principal *Concord Sonata* revisions were largely motivated by a wish to *restore* ideas from an earlier work, the *Emerson Overture*" (1997: 29). But Block had little to say about why Ives wanted to restore these ideas, nor about why the revised *Concord* Sonata

should be regarded as the privileged site in which this restoration occurred; his essay seems to take the latter as self-evident.

21. Block does suggest the presence of artistic motivations, but his essay is more concerned with making a negative argument—that Elliott Carter was incorrect in his charge that Ives revised his works in order to "jack up" the dissonance.

22. Burkholder did not explore the possibility of multi-movement cumulative settings along the lines of what I describe here. He perhaps hinted at the possibility of such a setting in a brief discussion of Ives's First Piano Sonata (1995: 243–44), but otherwise all his examples of cumulative settings are confined to single movements. In his analysis of the *Concord* Sonata, he understood the human-faith-melody as the product of a cumulative setting within the confines of "The Alcotts" movement (1995: 195–200), although he did acknowledge the presence of related material in each of the other movements. Nonetheless, the essential elements of the form are clearly present in Ives's treatment of the melody in the *Concord* as a whole.

23. Burkholder cites a number of studies that locate the human-faith-melody at the end of "The Alcotts" (1995: 199–200 and 459–60, notes 78 and 79). There has been some disagreement, however, as to whether to include the portion of the melody that I have labeled part B. I agree with Burkholder that the entire melody, as represented in Examples 6.5 and 6.6, should be heard as a unit, based on musical evidence as well as Ives's association of the melody with Beethoven in his "Alcotts" essay in the quotation cited above. This interpretation has become standard: Block's handbook on the *Concord* simply takes for granted that "human-faith-melody" refers to the entire melody of the last two systems of "The Alcotts" (1996: 32–33).

24. For extended accounts of the melody's apparent derivation from these borrowed sources, see Burkholder 1995: 195, 198; and Block 1996: 32–37.

25. Block allowed that the correspondence with Schubert's melody may have arisen "by accident" and thus concluded that "the question of whether Ives intentionally borrowed Schubert's famous opening must remain unanswered" (1996: 58, 60). Yet he devoted several paragraphs to the possible origins and significance of the connection, and seems to have lamented how "one looks in vain for another note or two of Schubert's theme or a literary clue in the form of a 'memo' that would provide a more positive identification" (60).

Bibliography

Scores and Recordings

Ives, Charles E. 1920. Sonata no. 2 for Piano: *Concord, Mass., 1840–60*. Redding, CT: published by the author. Reprint. New York: Edwin F. Kalmus, 1968.

———. 1922. *114 Songs*. Redding, CT: published by the author. Reprint. New York: Associated Music Publishers, Peer International Corporation, and Theodore Presser Company, 1975.

———. 1947. Sonata no. 2 for Piano: *Concord, Mass., 1840–60*. 2nd ed. New York: Arrow Music Press.

———. 1949. *The Anti-Abolitionist Riots in the 1830's and 1840's*. Edited by Henry Cowell. New York: Mercury Music.

———. 1954. String Quartet no. 2. New York: Peer International.

———. 1983. *I Come to Thee*. Ives Society Critical Edition, edited by John Kirkpatrick. New York: Associated Music.

———. 1985. *The Unanswered Question for Trumpet, Flute Quartet, and Strings*. Ives Society Critical Edition, edited by Paul C. Echols and Noel Zahler. New York: Peer International.

———. 1990a. *Ragtime Dances: Set of Four Ragtime Dances for Theater Orchestra*. Ives Society Critical Edition, edited by James B. Sinclair. New York: Peer International.

———. 1990b [1954]. Sonata no. 1 for Piano. Edited by Paul C. Echols with additional corrections by John A. Buchanan and Jerry E. Bramblett. New York: Peer International.

———. 1995. *Psalm 14*. Ives Society Critical Edition, edited by John Kirkpatrick and Gregg Smith. Bryn Mawr: Merion Music.

———. 1998. *Emerson Concerto*. Reconstruction by David G. Porter. Associated Music Publishers, Inc.

———. 1999. *Ives Plays Ives: The Composer at the Piano in Four Recording Sessions, 1933–1943*. Charles Ives, piano and voice. Liner notes by James B. Sinclair, Vivian Perlis, Richard Warren Jr., and David Gray Porter. Composers Recordings, Inc. CRI CD *810*.

———. 2002a. *Four Transcriptions from "Emerson"* for Piano Solo. Ives Society Critical Edition, edited by Thomas M. Brodhead. New York: Associated Music Publishers, Inc.

———. 2002b. *Orchestral Set no. 2*. Ives Society Critical Edition, edited by James B. Sinclair. New York: Peer International.

———. 2003. *Emerson Concerto*. National Symphony Orchestra of Ireland, James B. Sinclair, conductor; Allen Feinberg, piano. Naxos 8.559175. CD.

———. 2004. *129 Songs*. Ives Society Critical Edition, edited by H. Wiley Hitchcock. Music of the United States of America, vol. 12. Middletown, WI: A-R Editions.

Articles, Books, Catalogues, and Unpublished Commentaries

Abbate, Carolyn. 1991. *Unsung Voices: Opera and Musical Narrative in the Nineteenth Century*. Princeton, NJ: Princeton University Press.

Almén, Byron. 2008. *A Theory of Musical Narrative*. Bloomington: Indiana University Press.

Almén, Byron, and Robert Hatten. 2012. "Narrative Engagement with Twentieth-Century Music: Possibilities and Limits." In *Music and Narrative since 1900*, edited by Michael Klein and Nicholas Reyland, 59–85. Bloomington: Indiana University Press.

Austin, Larry. 1997. "The Realization and First Complete Performances of Ives's *Universe Symphony*." In *Ives Studies*, edited by Philip Lambert, 179–232. Cambridge: Cambridge University Press.

Ballantine, Christopher. 1979. "Charles Ives and the Meaning of Quotation in Music." *Musical Quarterly* 65/2: 167–84.

Barthes, Roland. 1977. *Image-Music-Text*. Translated by Stephen Heath. New York: Hill and Wang.

Berger, Karol. 1992. "Toward a History of Hearing: The Classic Concerto, A Sample Case." In *Convention in Eighteenth- and Nineteenth-Century Music: Essays in Honor of Leonard G. Ratner*, edited by Wye J. Allanbrook, Janet M. Levey, and William P. Mahrt, 405–29. Stuyvesant, NY: Pendragon Press.

———. 2000. *A Theory of Art*. New York: Oxford University Press.

———. 2007. *Bach's Cycle, Mozart's Arrow: An Essay on the Origins of Musical Modernity*. Berkeley: University of California Press.

Bergson, Henri. 1910. *Time and Free Will: An Essay on the Immediate Data of Consciousness*. Translated by F. L. Pogson. London: Allen and Unwin.

Bernstein, Leonard. 1976. *The Unanswered Question: Six Talks at Harvard*. Cambridge, MA: Harvard University Press.

Block, Geoffrey. 1996. *Ives: Concord Sonata*. Cambridge Music Handbooks. Cambridge: Cambridge University Press.

———. 1997. "Remembrance of Dissonances Past: The Two Published Editions of Ives's *Concord Sonata*." In *Ives Studies*, edited by Philip Lambert, 27–50. Cambridge: Cambridge University Press.

Booth, Wayne. 1983. *The Rhetoric of Fiction*. 2nd ed. Chicago: University of Chicago Press.

Bordwell, David. 1985. *Narration in the Fiction Film*. Madison: University of Wisconsin Press.

Botstein, Leon. 1996. "Innovation and Nostalgia: Ives, Mahler, and the Origins of Twentieth-Century Modernism." In *Charles Ives and His World*, edited by J. Peter Burkholder, 35–74. Princeton, NJ: Princeton University Press.

Brodhead, Thomas M. 1994. "Ives's *Celestial Railroad* and His Fourth Symphony." *American Music* 12/4: 389–424.

Brooks, William. 1974. "Unity and Diversity in Charles Ives's Fourth Symphony." *Anuario Interamericano de Investigacion Musical* 10: 5–49.

Brown, Marshall. 1992. "Origins of Modernism: Musical Structures and Narrative Forms." In *Music and Text: Critical Inquiries*, edited by Steven Paul Scher, 75–92. Cambridge: Cambridge University Press.

Broyles, Michael. 1996. "Charles Ives and the American Democratic Tradition." In *Charles Ives and His World,* edited by J. Peter Burkholder, 118–60. Princeton, NJ: Princeton University Press.

Buchman, Andrew. 1996. "Ives and Stravinsky: Two Angles on 'the German Stem.'" In *Charles Ives and the Classical Tradition,* edited by Geoffrey Block and J. Peter Burkholder, 131–49. New Haven, CT: Yale University Press.

Bullough, Edward. 1957. *Aesthetics: Lectures and Essays.* Edited by Elizabeth M. Wilkinson. Stanford, CA: Stanford University Press.

Burke, Richard N. 1999. "Film, Narrative, and Shostakovich's Last Quartet." *Musical Quarterly* 83/3: 413–29.

Burkholder, J. Peter. 1985. *Charles Ives: The Ideas Behind the Music.* New Haven, CT: Yale University Press.

———. 1995. *All Made of Tunes: Charles Ives and the Uses of Musical Borrowing.* New Haven, CT: Yale University Press.

———, ed. 1996. *Charles Ives and His World.* Princeton, NJ: Princeton University Press.

———. 2002. "The Organist in Ives." *Journal of the American Musicological Society* 55/2: 255–310.

Burkholder, J. Peter, Gayle Sherwood, and James B. Sinclair. "Charles Ives: Works." In *Grove Music Online,* edited by Laura Macy, www.grovemusic.com. Accessed December 29, 2012.

Chatman, Seymour. 1978. *Story and Discourse: Narrative Structure in Fiction and Film.* Ithaca, NY: Cornell University Press.

———. 1990. *Coming to Terms: The Rhetoric of Narrative in Fiction and Film.* Ithaca, NY: Cornell University Press.

Clark, Sondra Rae. 1972. "The Evolving *Concord Sonata:* A Study of Choices and Variants in the Music of Charles Ives." Ph.D. diss., Stanford University.

———. 1974. "The Element of Choice in Ives's *Concord Sonata.*" *Musical Quarterly* 60/2: 167–86.

Clüver, Claus. 1991. "Musical Trainrides in the Classroom." *Indiana Theory Review* 12: 163–85.

Cone, Edward T. 1962. "Stravinsky: The Progress of a Method." In *Perspectives of New Music* 1/1: 18–26.

———. 1982. "Schubert's Promissory Note: An Exercise in Musical Hermeneutics." *19th-Century Music* 5/3: 233–41.

———. 1995. "Attacking a Brahms Puzzle." *Musical Times* 136/1824: 72–77.

Cowell, Henry, and Sidney Cowell. 1969 [1955]. *Charles Ives and His Music.* New York: Oxford University Press.

Doane, Mary Ann. 2002. *The Emergence of Cinematic Time: Modernity, Contingency, The Archive.* Cambridge, MA: Harvard University Press.

Emerson, Ralph Waldo. 1902. *The Works of Ralph Waldo Emerson.* London: Macmillan.

———. 1990. *The Oxford Authors: Ralph Waldo Emerson.* Edited by Richard Poirier. New York: Oxford University Press.

———. 1994. *Collected Poems and Translations.* Compiled by Harold Bloom and Paul Kane. New York: Penguin Books.

Feder, Stuart. 1990. "The Nostalgia of Charles Ives: An Essay in Affects and Music." In *Psychoanalytic Explorations in Music,* edited by Stuart Feder, Richard L. Karmel, and George H. Pollock, 233–66. Madison, CT: International Universities Press, Inc.

———. 1992. *Charles Ives, "My Father's Song": A Psychoanalytic Biography*. New Haven: Yale University Press.

———. 1999. *The Life of Charles Ives*. Cambridge: Cambridge University Press.

Freud, Sigmund. 1955a [1900]. *The Interpretation of Dreams*. In *The Standard Edition of the Complete Psychological Works of Sigmund Freud*, translated and edited by James Strachey, vols. 4–5. London: Hogarth Press.

———. 1955b [1915]. "The Unconscious." In *The Standard Edition of the Complete Psychological Works of Sigmund Freud*, translated and edited by James Strachey, vol. 14: 166–204. London: Hogarth Press.

Gaudreault, André. 1988. *Du littéraire au filmique: système du récit*. Paris: Méridiens Klincksieck.

———. 2009. *From Plato to Lumière: Narration and Monstration in Literature and Cinema*. Translated by Timothy Barnard. Toronto: University of Toronto Press.

Genette, Gérard. 1980. *Narrative Discourse: An Essay in Method*. Translated by Jane E. Lewin. Ithaca, NY: Cornell University Press.

Gibbens, John Jeffrey. 1985. "Debussy's Impact on Ives: An Assessment." D.M.A. diss., University of Illinois, Urbana-Champaign.

Gilman, Lawrence. 1939. "Music: A Masterpiece of American Music Heard Here for the First Time." *New York Herald Tribune* (January 21, 1939): 9.

Grey, Thomas. 1992. "Metaphorical Modes in Nineteenth-Century Music Criticism: Image, Narrative, and Idea." In *Music and Text: Critical Inquiries*, edited by Steven Paul Scher, 93–117. Cambridge: Cambridge University Press.

Gunning, Tom. 1990. "The Cinema of Attractions: Early Film, Its Spectator and the Avant-Garde." In *Early Cinema: Space, Frame, Narrative*, edited by Thomas Elsaesser and Adam Barker, 56–62. London: British Film Institute.

———. 1991. *D. W. Griffith and the Origins of American Narrative Film*. Urbana: University of Illinois Press.

Guthrie, James R. 2001. *Above Time: Emerson's and Thoreau's Temporal Revolutions*. Columbia: University of Missouri Press.

Hatten, Robert. 1991. "On Narrativity in Music: Expressive Genres and Levels of Discourse in Beethoven." *Indiana Theory Review* 12: 75–98.

———. 1994. *Musical Meaning in Beethoven: Markedness, Correlation, and Interpretation*. Bloomington: Indiana University Press.

———. 2004. *Interpreting Musical Gestures, Topics, and Tropes: Mozart, Beethoven, Schubert*. Bloomington: Indiana University Press.

———. 2006. "The Troping of Temporality in Music." In *Approaches to Meaning in Music*, edited by Byron Almén and Edward Pearsall, 62–75. Bloomington: Indiana University Press.

Hepokoski, James. 1994. "Temps Perdu." *Musical Times* 135/1822: 746–51.

———. 1998. Review of Walter Werbeck, *Die Tondichtungen von Richard Strauss*. *Journal of the American Musicological Society* 51/3: 603–25.

Hertz, David Michael. 1993. *Angels of Reality: Emersonian Unfoldings in Wright, Stevens, and Ives*. Carbondale: Southern Illinois University Press.

Hitchcock, H. Wiley. 2004a. "Ives as Songwriter and Lyricist." In *129 Songs*, edited by H. Wiley Hitchcock, Music of the United States of America, 12: xvii–lxxi. Middletown, WI: A-R Editions.

———, ed. 2004b. *Critical Commentaries for Charles Ives, 129 Songs*. www.charlesives.org/critical_commentary/Ives%20129%20Songs.pdf. Accessed October 31, 2012.

Hitchcock, H. Wiley, and Noel Zahler. 1988. "Just What Is Ives's Unanswered Question?" *Notes* 44/3: 437–43.

Ireland, Ken. 2001. *The Sequential Dynamics of Narrative: Energies at the Margins of Fiction*. London: Associated University Press.

Ives, Charles E. 1961. *Essays Before a Sonata, The Majority, and Other Writings*. Edited by Howard Boatwright. New York: W. W. Norton & Company.

———. 1972. *Memos*. Edited by John Kirkpatrick. New York: W. W. Norton & Company.

Karl, Gregory. 1997. "Structuralism and Musical Plot." *Music Theory Spectrum* 19: 13–34.

Kavanaugh, James. 1978. "Music and American Transcendentalism: A Study of Transcendental Pythagoreanism in the Works of Henry David Thoreau, Nathaniel Hawthorne, and Charles Ives." Ph.D. diss., Yale University.

Kern, Stephen. 2003 [1983]. *The Culture of Time and Space: 1880–1918*. Cambridge, MA: Harvard University Press.

Kinderman, William. 1988. "Thematic Contrast and Parenthetical Enclosure in the Piano Sonatas, Op. 109 and 111." In *Zu Beethoven: Aufsätze und Dokumente*, edited by Harry Goldschmidt, 43–59. Berlin: Verlag Neue Musik.

Kirkpatrick, John. 1960. *A Temporary Mimeographed Catalogue of the Music Manuscripts and Related Materials of Charles Edward Ives, 1874–1954*. New Haven, CT: Yale University Music Library.

———. 1983. "Commentary." In Charles Ives, *I Come to Thee: SATB with Organ*, edited by John Kirkpatrick. New York: Associated Music Publishers.

Klein, Michael, and Nicholas Reyland, eds. 2012. *Music and Narrative since 1900*. Bloomington: Indiana University Press.

Koch, Heinrich. 1983. *Introductory Essay on Composition: The Mechanical Rules of Melody, Sections 3 and 4*. Translated by Nancy Kovaleff Baker. New Haven, CT: Yale University Press.

Kolesnikoff, Nina. 1993. "Story/plot." In *Encyclopedia of Contemporary Literary Theory: Approaches, Scholars, Terms*, edited by Irena R. Makaryk, 631–32. Toronto: University of Toronto Press.

Kozloff, Sarah. 1988. *Invisible Storytellers: Voice-over Narration in American Fiction Film*. Berkeley: University of California Press.

Kracauer, Siegfried. 1993. "Photography." Translated by Thomas Y. Levin. *Critical Inquiry* 19/3: 421–36.

Kramer, Jonathan. 1973. "Multiple and Non-Linear Time in Beethoven's Opus 135." *Perspectives of New Music* 11/2: 122–45.

———. 1988. *The Time of Music*. New York: Schirmer Books.

Kramer, Lawrence. 1991. "Musical Narratology: A Theoretical Outline." *Indiana Theory Review* 12: 141–62.

———. 1995. *Classical Music and Postmodern Knowledge*. Berkeley: University of California Press.

———. 1996. "Powers of Blackness: Africanist Discourse in Modern Concert Music." *Black Music Research Journal* 16/1: 53–70.

———. 2008. "Music and the Politics of Memory: Charles Ives's *A Symphony: New England Holidays*." *Journal of the Society for American Music* 2/4: 459–75.

Kramer, Richard. 2008. *Unfinished Music*. Oxford: Oxford University Press.

Laffay, Albert. 1964. *Logique du cinéma: création et spectacle*. Paris: Masson.

Lambert, Philip. 1997. *The Music of Charles Ives*. New Haven, CT: Yale University Press.

Leydon, Rebecca. 2001. "Debussy's Late Style and the Devices of the Early Silent Cinema." *Music Theory Spectrum* 23/2: 217–41.

Lothe, Jakob. 2000. *Narrative in Fiction and Film.* Oxford: Oxford University Press, 2000.

Magee, Gayle Sherwood. 2008. *Charles Ives Reconsidered.* Urbana: University of Illinois Press.

Marcotte, Gilles. 1997. "Des Musiques Qui Parlent." *Liberté* 39/3 (231): 180–86.

Marshall, Dennis. 1968. "Charles Ives's Quotations: Manner or Substance?" *Perspectives of New Music* 6/2: 45–56.

Masselos, William. 1990 [1954]. "Preface (1979)." In Charles E. Ives, Sonata no. 1 for Piano, edited by Paul C. Echols with additional corrections by John A. Buchanan and Jerry E. Bramblett: iv. New York: Peer International.

Maus, Fred Everett. 1991. "Music as Narrative." *Indiana Theory Review* 12: 1–34.

McCreless, Patrick. 1991. "The Hermeneutic Sentence and Other Models for Tonal Closure." *Indiana Theory Review* 12: 35–73.

McDonald, Matthew. 2004. "Silent Narration? Elements of Narrative in Ives's *The Unanswered Question.*" *19th-Century Music* 27/3: 263–86.

———. 2012. "Ives and the Now." In *Music and Narrative since 1900,* edited by Michael L. Klein and Nicholas Reyland, 285–307. Bloomington: Indiana University Press.

Meelberg, Vincent. 2006. *New Sounds, New Stories: Narrativity in Contemporary Music.* Amsterdam: Leiden University Press.

Mellers, Wilfrid. 1987 [1964]. *Music in a New Found Land: Themes and Developments in the History of American Music.* New York: Oxford University Press.

Metz, Christian. 1974. *Film Language: A Semiotics of the Cinema.* Translated by Michael Taylor. New York: Oxford University Press.

Metzer, David. 2003. *Quotation and Cultural Meaning in Twentieth-Century Music.* Cambridge: Cambridge University Press.

Monelle, Raymond. 2000. *The Sense of Music: Semiotic Essays.* Princeton, NJ: Princeton University Press.

Morgan, Robert P. 1977. "Spatial Form in Ives." In *An Ives Celebration: Papers and Panels of the Charles Ives Centennial Festival-Conference,* edited by H. Wiley Hitchcock and Vivian Perlis, 145–58. Urbana: University of Illinois Press.

———. 1997. "'The Things Our Fathers Loved': Charles Ives and the European Tradition." In *Ives Studies,* edited by Philip Lambert, 3–26. Cambridge: Cambridge University Press.

Nattiez, Jean-Jacques. 1990. "Can One Speak of Narrativity in Music?" Translated by Katharine Ellis. *Journal of the Royal Musical Association* 115/2: 240–57.

Newcomb, Anthony. 1984. "Once More 'Between Absolute and Program Music': Schumann's Second Symphony." *19th-Century Music* 7/3: 233–50.

———. 1987. "Schumann and Late Eighteenth-Century Narrative Strategies." *19th-Century Music* 11/2: 164–74.

———. 1992. "Narrative Archetypes and Mahler's Ninth Symphony." In *Music and Text: Critical Inquiries,* edited by Steven Paul Scher, 188–236. Cambridge: Cambridge University Press.

Owens, Tom C., ed. 2007. *Selected Correspondence of Charles Ives.* Berkeley: University of California Press.

Perlis, Vivian. 1974. *Charles Ives Remembered: An Oral History.* Urbana: University of Illinois Press.

Porter, David G. c. 1998. "On the Reconstruction of Charles Ives's 'Emerson' Piano Concerto." Unpublished commentary.

Proust, Marcel. 2006 [1913]. *Remembrance of Things Past.* Volume 1. Translated by C. K. Scott Moncrieff. Hertfordshire, U.K.: Wordsworth Editions.

Ratner, Leonard. 1980. *Classic Music: Expression, Form, and Style.* New York: Schirmer.

Rings, Steven. 2008. "*Mystères limpides:* Time and Transformation in Debussy's *Des pas sur la neige.*" *19th-Century Music* 32/2: 178–208.

Rossiter, Frank R. 1975. *Charles Ives and His America.* New York: Liveright.

Sherwood, Gayle. 2001. "Charles Ives and 'Our National Malady.'" *Journal of the American Musicological Society* 54/3: 555–84.

———. *See also* Magee, Gayle Sherwood.

Shirley, Wayne. 1989. "Once More through *The Unanswered Question.*" *Institute for Studies in American Music Newsletter* 18/2: 8–9, 13.

Sinclair, James. 1999. *A Descriptive Catalogue of the Music of Charles Ives.* New Haven, CT: Yale University Press. Available at drs.library.yale.edu. Revised 2012. Accessed December 31, 2012.

Starr, Larry. 1992. *A Union of Diversities: Style in the Music of Charles Ives.* New York: Schirmer.

Swafford, Jan. 1998. "Charles Edward Ives." Peermusic, Ltd. www.charlesives.org/02bio .htm. Accessed December 28, 2012.

Tarasti, Eero. 1991. "Beethoven's 'Waldstein' and the Generative Course." *Indiana Theory Review* 12: 99–140.

Thoreau, Henry D. 2004. *Walden: A Fully Annotated Edition.* Edited by Jeffrey S. Cramer. New Haven, CT: Yale University Press.

Tick, Judith. 1993. "Charles Ives and Gender Ideology." In *Musicology and Difference: Gender and Sexuality in Music Scholarship,* edited by Ruth A. Solie, 83–106. Berkeley: University of California Press.

———. 1997. "Charles Ives and the Politics of Direct Democracy." In *Ives Studies,* edited by Philip Lambert, 133–60. Cambridge: Cambridge University Press.

———, ed. 2008. *Music in the USA: A Documentary Companion.* Oxford: Oxford University Press.

Treitler, Leo. 1989. *Music and the Historical Imagination.* Cambridge, MA: Harvard University Press.

Webster, James. 1991. *Haydn's "Farewell" Symphony and the Idea of Classical Style.* Cambridge: Cambridge University Press.

White, Hayden. 1992. "Form, Reference, and Ideology in Musical Discourse." In *Music and Text: Critical Inquiries,* edited by Steven Paul Scher, 288–319. Cambridge: Cambridge University Press.

Winters, Thomas Dyer. 1986. "Additive and Repetitive Techniques in the Experimental Works of Charles Ives." Ph.D. diss., University of Pennsylvania.

Index

123; elements of narration, 114–20; elements of narrative structure, 104, 106–107, 110–14, 138–39; Emerson as Silences surrogate, 125; Emerson's *The Sphinx* and, 104, 106–107, 121–24, 173nn16–18; God/Man subduality in, 17; harmonic relationships, 117, *117*; Invisible Answer, 118, 119, 124–25; Ives's symbolic presence in, 125–26; melodic relationships, *118*; narrator as represented in strings, 120, 125–26; organ's possible influence on, 172n4; program note for, 104, 123, 124; "Question" music, 107, *107*, 110, 116–17; versions, 171n2 (chap4); viewed as veiled autobiography, 126
Universe Symphony (Ives), 23, 57
utopianism, Ives and, 8

Varied Air and Variations (Ives), 173n21

Wagner, Richard: Ives's views on, 16, 25, 90–91; Prelude to *Tristan and Isolde,* 25, *89,* 90–91, 92, 145, 156, 174n4; *Schreckensfanjare* notion, 66–67
Werbeck, Walter, 54
Westminster Chimes melody, 65, 66
"What a Friend We Have in Jesus" (hymn), 52
"Where Is My Wandering Boy?" (hymn), 43, 51, 53
Whitman, Walt: "O Captain! My Captain!," 72, 79–80, 84
Wilson, Woodrow, 70
World War I, 76, 83–84, 141

MATTHEW McDONALD is Assistant Professor of Music at Northeastern University in Boston, Massachusetts, where he teaches courses in music theory, music history, and film music. His writing focuses on early modernist music and music in film. In 2010, he received a fellowship from the American Council of Learned Societies to support his research on Charles Ives.

www.ingramcontent.com/pod-product-compliance
Lightning Source LLC
Chambersburg PA
CBHW070411100426
42812CB00005B/1709